The Surprise
of Cremona

THE SURPRISE OF CREMONA

Edith Templeton

One Woman's Adventures in
Cremona, Parma, Mantua,
Ravenna, Urbino and Arezzo

METHUEN

A METHUEN PAPERBACK

First published in Great Britain 1954
by Eyre & Spottiswoode Ltd
This paperback edition first published 1985
by Methuen London Ltd
11 New Fetter Lane, London EC4P 4EE
Reproduced, printed and bound in Great Britain by
Hazell Watson & Viney Limited,
Member of the BPCC Group,
Aylesbury, Bucks

ISBN 0 413 55360 4

FOR AUNT ALICE

CONTENTS

CREMONA

I have always wondered what cherubs look like when they grow up, and now I know. As I enter the train in Calais, I find the lady who will share my compartment for the night already established on the settee. Everything that goes to make a cherub is still there – the tilted nose, the round blue eyes, the bright curls, the pink flesh – but enlarged to a gigantic scale and buried in fat. At the faintest smile her pretty pig's face breaks into dimples. I imagine she has dimples on her elbows, too, and on her knees.

At once we start to talk. Her English is very good. She tells me she is Swedish. I suppose she is a Civil Servant, or a lecturer at a university.

Although she is so pleasant and smiles so readily, there is a sadness about her. Naturally, I think. She is obviously a descendant of the Valkyries, those giant virgins of the Nordic sagas who had to pick up the fallen warriors on the battle-fields and convey them to Valhalla. Valhalla must have been a sort of celestial beer-garden for the military and their hounds only: civilians and dogs need not apply.

But what place is there to-day for a Valkyrie, built for power and the lugging of heavy weights, when there exists no shield which would cover those bulging arms, no armour which would encase that mountainous bosom? No wonder she is sad.

We go together to the dining-car and share a bottle of claret. Each of us could easily have drunk the double of what we have allowed ourselves, and we tell each other that nowadays travelling money is so limited that one is forced to curb one's desires.

Upon our return, we find the beds made and we test all the gadgets. As always, I am delighted by that medallion inset into the panelling above each bed, lined with stamped velvet and surmounted by a hook, which is provided for the night rest of men's pocket watches.

The Valkyrie stands about, ill at ease, pondering.

"Are you going to bed yet?"

"Yes, I think I will," I say; "sleeping-cars are made for sleeping. And there is such a lot of sleep to get through before to-morrow morning."

Again she ponders. "But, do you think it is all right that we should undress already? Because of the men, you know."

"What men?" I ask.

"The passport control. And the foreign-currency control. And the customs inspection."

I reassure her. "They'll come and go during the night. We shall never know they have been."

And still she is musing, mournfully. "Ah, no, how can it be so? We have not yet shown our passports to anybody. And how can they look at our passports if they are in our hand-bags? How could they find them?"

I undress and climb up into my berth.

She undresses, too. She puts on an elaborate nightgown of black silk, edged with frills of pink lace. She brushes her curls and ties them round with a strip of pink satin. Then, to my surprise, instead of washing off her make-up, she powders her face and puts rouge on her lips. She gets into a dressing-gown of black satin sprigged with pink flowers, buttons it up carefully, fastens the pink silk cord round her waist and reclines on the bed.

"I shall not go to bed yet," she tells me; "it would not be proper for the men to see me in bed."

"The attendant will come round in a while to collect the passports," I say, "and that will be all. There will be no one else. And in any case, don't worry about him. He is used to sorrow."

She listens, but it is obvious that she does not believe me. She presses her lips together and shakes her head. I hate seeing her thus, unhappy and bewildered. In days past she might have shaken her head like this while hovering in the clouds above a battlefield: "One, two, three; now, where is the fourth immortal hero? I could have sworn there were four of them. Now, where did I put him?"

After a short while there is a knock at the door and the sleeping-car conductor puts his head inside.

"Ladies, your passports, if you please."

After we have handed him the passports he says: "And now I wish you a good night. You shall not be disturbed any more. I'll call you in good time to-morrow morning; we shall arrive in Milan at eight-thirty."

As soon as he is gone the Valkyrie rears up in bed. She seems very excited.

"I shall now take off my dressing-gown," she informs me; "I must get some sleep; you agree, don't you?"

"Oh, yes, quite."

"And when the men come," she says, "they will see me in my nightdress. It cannot be helped, can it?"

"They will not come," I say, hoping to soothe her excitement, which I ascribe to excessive prudishness.

Once more she rears, her dimples quivering. "What? They will not come? The men?"

"No, of course not," I reply; "that is the beauty of travelling by sleeper. The conductor will deal with them outside, when we touch the frontiers."

"What? Outside? They will not come in?"

"No, of course not."

"And they will not look at my luggage and ask if I have anything to declare?"

I shake my head.

She looks up at me with a face crumpled with disappointment. "It is not right. How can they do their duty if they do not come in here?" Now I understand. The elaborate dressing for the night and making up. The plan to reveal herself to the first 'men' in her dressing-gown, to the following 'men' in her night-dress. And now – nothing. No men will see her in bed. Poor Valkyrie, where are the Nordic warriors who should have slumbered in your arms?

"Good night," I say sadly; "I hope you sleep well."

On the following morning we start the inevitable conversation.

"I say, how much are you going to tip him?"

"That is just what I wanted to ask you."

Slowly we circle nearer and nearer to what is in both our minds.

"After all, he gets paid for his job."

"And he's bound to get some exorbitant tips from rich people always."

"And the money allowance is so tight these days."

"Exactly. And if one were to tip every person who expects it, one could never take a holiday at all."

We both agree that it isn't as though we were mean. We are only prudent and provident. We are models of what Mrs. Gaskell used to call 'elegant economy'. We do not pamper ourselves either, do we? Did we not share a bottle of wine last night? It cuts into our own flesh, too, does it not? After all, no one is living the way one used to live before the war.

As I alight on the platform in Milan I think: "No one in the world can make you feel as low as a sleeping-car conductor whom you did not tip."

I take the train to Cremona. The countryside we are traversing is part of the Lombardic plain, and I do not think much of it. Meadows of thin, watered-down green and fields are crossed and bordered by canals of water and narrow rivulets which come and go without linking anything in particular, or holding anything together. It is a messy landscape, all in bits and pieces, untidy, like an unmade bed.

I imagine the angel who fashioned it came running up to God every five minutes and whined: "What shall I put in now?"

And God yawned and said: "Oh, another field."

"And then?"

"Oh, another meadow. Just carry on, will you? It doesn't much matter, just keep it flat, will you?"

And out of this soggy soil there grow masses of reeds and trees which also look reedy, as though they had grown too fast and were sorry for themselves. In patches there are quite a lot of trees, and they stand there, looking at each other, saying: "Well, what do you think, shall we get together and make up a wood?" And then they say: "Oh, never mind. It's too much trouble," and they straggle for a while and peter out in the end.

Later on it gets a bit more orderly. The fields and water-courses are lined with elms and willows, all with their crowns lopped off and sprouting thin, straight branches. It is sad to look at all those mutilated trees.

I ask a girl on the seat opposite the reason for this universal pollarding.

"It must be done," she says, "every three years. It strengthens the trees, otherwise they would grow weak and die. It is done for their own good."

I don't believe a word of it. I had so much done to me in my youth 'for my own good' that I have become suspicious of the phrase.

"Besides," she adds, "natural willow branches are no good to anybody, but the boughs from poll willows are very useful for osier work."

Ah, well, now she is talking.

In Cremona station I tell the porter that I want to take a carriage, and I am snubbed immediately.

"Here we have no *carozzas*. They are old-fashioned. Horses are old-fashioned. Here we are modern, we have only taxis."

I dare not tell him that there are towns in Italy which are so truly modern that they provide horse-drawn carriages for those who have a liking for them.

I drive to the Albergo Bristol. I have looked it up in my guidebook. It is the largest hotel in the town, and is classed as second category.

To the ordinary traveller like me, with limited means and yet not so poor as to be able to flaunt that poverty with pride, it is a wonderful relief to come to a town where there is no first-class hotel. On such occasions one can allow oneself the luxury of looking straight

into the eyes of him who asks: "And where are you staying?" And
to reply: "At the so-and-so. It's not – well – but it is clean. Not bad
really. Anyway, there is no better place, so I must not complain."

Meanwhile the taxi, fully conscious of its modernity, knocks and
leaps through badly cobbled streets, determined to give all that a
taxi is capable of giving.

Did I know that it has a klaxon? In case I didn't, let it be sounded
long and full. True, there is no one in the way to be warned of our
approach just now, but the tooting is impressive, and it will make
those people in the café on the pavement look up and take notice.

The steering is in perfect order, too. This vehicle in front of us is
only a bicycle, there is really no need to go to one side in order to
avoid it, but let us swerve madly, just to show that we can. This
swerve was in the grand manner. Did the *signora* think we would
hit the lamp-post? Well, we might have done, but we have brakes,
good, strong, screeching brakes. Yes, truly, they work very well.

Did this sudden jerk knock the *signora's* head against the roof of
the car? Still, it was nothing. Better than being rammed against the
lamp-post. And here we are, right in front of the hotel. Quick,
wasn't it? That's the worst of a small town like Cremona; before
you can work up a good speed and enjoy yourself, the run comes to
an end.

The Albergo Bristol lies in a quiet, dark street. It is an old, spacious
house, the façade ochre and pleasantly dilapidated. The inside is
spacious, too, leisurely, cool and dim, with palms in majolica tubs
casting feathery shadows on the cracked mosaic floor.

Approaching the reception desk I walk straight into a family row,
obviously between the owner and his wife. She is a beautiful, tall,
dark, full-limbed woman, he small, bald, and sandy.

She is flaying the leaves of a book – account-book or ledger of
some sort – and in between she flings up her arms as though invok-
ing the gods to be her witness in a tragic deed. Her speech is fast
and tormented, as though whipped by the Furies.

I cannot understand a word, but I believe it must be something like: "Yes, I have killed the children. Both the children. Do you not believe me? Here they are, swimming in their blood."

In face of this Medea he does not cut a good figure. He keeps raising and lowering his shoulders, and muttering: "Ah, women, women."

There are two waiters in front of the door leading to the dining-room, and they are listening, it seems, more out of politeness than out of interest.

As soon as Medea sees me, she closes the book and turns to me with a deep, lovely smile, while he steps aside, sulking. Has my arrival put an end to it? I wonder. No, because the two waiters are still there, waiting for more to come. And they should know.

As I trail up the stairs behind the boy who carries my cases I ask: "What was it all about?"

"Nothing. A long-distance call she didn't put on a bill."

"Is it dreadful? Was it a very expensive call?" I ask.

"No. Only to Brescia."

"So, it's not a very heavy loss, is it?"

"It's no loss at all," says the luggage-boy, "because the guest in question – he's a director – he comes here every week. They'll charge him for it next time."

"So it's really nothing?"

"Of course it's nothing. It only means a salad in the book-keeping."

I sigh with relief. "I see," I say; "I am so glad."

Now the bald, sandy owner will not have to marry an insipid foreign princess to improve his standing, and Medea will not have to embroider a poisoned gown and send it to them as a wedding present and kill them both, and she will not have to flee the country in a chariot drawn by fiery dragons.

"Really, I am so glad," I say.

The boy looks at me. He says "*Per carità*," which means something like "for Heaven's sake."

I know that he is thinking that all foreigners are mad, and that

I, being a foreigner, am mad too, and have I not proved it just now by taking such an interest in the intricacies of hotel book-keeping? And with an expression of resignation and wisdom he now remarks: "I suppose you'll want to see the cathedral?"

"Yes, of course," I say.

He nods, fully satisfied. He was right. I am mad, like all the others. Still, even so, I have to be provided with a room. And, oozing superior graciousness, he opens a door for me.

Quite near the hotel, the dark, quiet street opens into a wider one which borders on to the public gardens. They are a sorry sight, with meagre plants greyed with dust and a filthy little pond surmounted, on one side, by an arrangement of artificial rocks, and enlivened by a couple of wild ducks who are gliding beneath the trailing branches of a weeping willow and trying to look Chinese. This is the exotic corner. It is as necessary to a public garden as palms are to the Ritz.

Near the entrance, by a booth, there is a donkey got up in scarlet-lined reins studded with brass nails. He is one of those donkeys from Sardinia, the Peter Pans among donkeys; that is to say, he is only half the size of ordinary donkeys. Like all donkeys, he has a self-sufficient and humorous look, as though he were enjoying a private joke of his own. He is harnessed to a little carriage.

His keeper tells me that the donkey is hired out to children for a trot round the garden at thirty lire a run. Donkeys for the delectation of children are a common sight in Italy, and every time I come across one I contemplate him with an aching heart. Why is it taken for granted that only children enjoy donkey rides? I am certain that many grown-ups would appreciate them, too. This is one of life's injustices. I content myself with stroking the donkey, and engage in a talk with the keeper. He is an old man, seething with indignation. It seems that the donkey earns a lot of money, but the donkey's owner pockets it all and does not give the animal enough to eat. Last year they had a goat for the carriage but the goat got tired.

I am expected to make a comment, and so I say: "It is a good thing, really. Goats aren't half as nice as donkeys."

"How do you know?" growls the keeper; "have you ever had a goat?"

"No."

"Then, how can you make such a statement?"

"I just imagined it, you know."

"That's not good enough. If you don't know goats, you shouldn't have opinions about them."

He talks nonsense, of course. I don't have to keep a goat in order to find out my feelings about them. I know I dislike them. And if I had a goat, my dislike would probably grow into hatred. Before we part he has made me promise to be fairer to goats in future.

I think I will go now and have a look at the cathedral. I am in no mood to be fair to the cathedral, but it will not talk back. I traverse a little street leading to the cathedral square. It is already pervaded by that sleepiness which surrounds so many churches.

I come out into the full sunlight and there it is, the famous cathedral, festooned with pigeons, beggars, and flower-sellers, striped pink and yellow, and glinting with many rows of delicate, white, colonnaded galleries, which seem to keep it from bulging out, like the laces of a corset. I walk slowly round it.

At the back there is not so much dressing up, the walls are plain brick and have been patched with grey stone in many places. Also, the galleries have given out, there is only one row of those little white columns and arches, and here, sure enough, with nothing to hem it in, the cathedral has spread out into massive rounded bulges. These apses look strong and aggressive. Here is the true cathedral, the fortress of God.

I go back once more to the front, and am dazzled by the coquettish display of those slender white galleries and the pretty white saints and those two graceful white pediments, curved like swans' breasts, which gleam above the portal. Clearly stuck on during the Baroque, as an afterthought.

The Baroque was a restless, self-assertive time. They could never leave anything well alone. Do I like those swans' breasts? I don't know. I only know that I want a coffee.

I sit down in the café on the opposite side of the square and try to sort it out.

The cathedral is overwhelming and all wrong. It started as honest striped brick, pink and yellow, and later on it got ideas and put on all those white trimmings which are far too subtle. It makes one uncomfortable.

The longer I look at it I see the cathedral as a country woman who wanted to smarten herself up before going to the town. She put a white camellia on the lapel of her rough, heathery tweed coat and thought she would become presentable.

The coffee arrives.

First the waiter brings another chair and places my hand-bag on it. Then he opens the little sealed envelope of waxed paper in which the sugar is contained and empties it into my cup, anxious to make sure that I do not have to exert myself in any way.

I am always touched anew by the manners of the Italian waiter, by his forethought and helpfulness. He has the gift of making each man or woman he serves into a duke or a duchess, for the span of time it takes to sip a coffee.

Nobody else has the trick of lighting your cigarette for you in breezy weather: he brings an empty tumbler and turns it upside down on his palm, while the match is briskly struck and placed inside the glassy shelter, burning steadily while you take its light at leisure.

Nobody else can dress a salad as well as he: he sprinkles salt and vinegar into a large spoon and stirs with a fork, holding it above the bowl so that nothing shall be wasted. With this mixture he drenches the salad. Afterwards he adds the oil, pouring it in slow circular movements which hold the fascination of a ritual act. At last the salad is dressed, not by a heartless and thoughtless whirling about, but the green leaves are lifted with two spoons and allowed to sink gently back into the bowl. And here is your salad, glistening with the smooth Italian oil, which, when swallowed, runs down your throat like a ribbon of silver satin.

The Italian waiter restores to you that rarest of all human qualities, the feeling of dignity. He will always give you a table to yourself. He will never expect you to cram in with other guests. He would never dare to bring your bill if you have not asked for it. If you feel like it, you can sit in a café till late at night, while the tables around you will be stacked with chairs and the cloths be folded up and carried inside. But you will not be asked to leave.

Of course, this is not done for nothing; the waiter will want to be paid. But whereas the Swiss, for instance, regards you as an automaton which first gulps coffee and then emits money, the Italian treats you as a human being who enjoys a coffee and pays for it afterwards.

I once talked to some Italians who complained about the lack of education in their country. "The people have no culture," they said; "you wouldn't believe it, how many people still do not know how to read and write."

"I quite believe it," I said, "but when you eat at the tiniest inn your table is laid with a white linen cloth and you are given a large, white, heavy linen napkin. And when you order fruit the cherries and apricots are not brought on a plate, a mere handful, but generously piled in a dish and floating in iced water. To me, this is real culture and real education."

I order another coffee, and while I wait for it a man approaches with a sheaf of leaflets and gives me one of them.

On the cover there is a coloured picture of a bride and groom emerging from church. Around them are the wedding guests, family, and onlookers, and they all show signs of great astonishment and distress, caused by the sight of a young woman in poor clothes who confronts the bridal couple. She is holding two small children in her arms. The bride is open-mouthed, the groom nearly swooning. I am afraid those children are his.

It must be an advertisement, I think, but for what? All that comes to my mind is a preparation against body odour. "Do you keep yourself as fresh and dainty as you should? Look at this poor woman, with two children and yet unmarried. Whereas the young bride has used our preparation and has succeeded in finding the bliss of matrimony."

On further thought I think that I must be wrong. If that poor woman really does have B.O., she wouldn't have got to the stage of having two brats. On the other hand, why not? I could think of something like: "She was good enough for casual dalliance. But when it came to choosing a mate for life he knew he could only elect a girl whose body was sweet and fresh, unsullied by the taint of stale perspiration. Do not cast this leaflet aside. Although you may not have two fatherless children, fundamentally your trouble may be the same. There are things which even your best friends never tell you."

I have often read this last sentence in B.O. advertisements, and have thought that it shows an ignorance of the meaning of friendship. I always find it amazing what one's best friends do tell one. But enough of these idle speculations. I must know what it is about. I turn the first page. I read: "The sunlight slanted into the room, poorly but neatly furnished, and shone on to the cradle where two children slept the sleep of the innocent. Whereas –" It is a chapter of a novel, published by Mondadori in Milan, at the very reasonable price of eight hundred lire. The publishers express their conviction that once you have sampled the first chapter you will feel compelled to buy the book.

At once I am filled with indignation. Why couldn't my publishers do the same for me and, say, send their office-boy to the Café Royal with samples of my latest novel?

The waiter comes with the coffee and I show him the leaflet and ask his opinion. He looks at the picture and reads some of the text.

He is not favourably impressed. "It is not a good book," he says. I am as convinced of it as he is, but I am curious to know how he arrived at his judgment.

I say: "What makes you think it is bad?"

"Because it is stupid. The stupidity stands out a mile. Look at it. She coming to the wedding. What good will that do her? Couldn't the writer have thought of something more intelligent?"

"Still, he got a story out of it," I say; "it is very hard getting a story out of anything, even if it is a silly one."

"That could well be," says the waiter. "I have never thought about it before, but I see what you mean. My friend Sandro got a girl into trouble too, but you couldn't make a story out of it."

"I'm sure you couldn't," I say, "because there was probably nothing more to it."

"Well, I wouldn't say that," remarks the waiter; "there was quite a lot to it. Sometimes I almost think it could be made into a story – anyway – half of it – because it gave us so many surprises. To begin with, we none of us thought that Sandro would ever change his way of life. He was a bachelor, at the time it happened he was already forty, and he lived in the house of two old maids who looked after him very well. They even darned his socks. And he never wanted to get married at all. He got all the women he wanted, as it was.

"Then he had this love-affair and he got the girl into trouble, and when the child was well on the way he said suddenly that he would stand by her and that he was going to marry her. I said to him, and all the others said to him: 'Look here, you are too settled in your ways, you don't know what it is like getting married at your time of life. Don't force yourself into it if you don't feel like it.' But Sandro swore he was fond of her and he had made up his mind and was going to marry her. So, that was a bit of a surprise, wasn't it? Almost good enough for a story."

"Well," I say, "Sandro sounds a decent man. But in a story you cannot have things as straightforward as that and as pleasant, you know. You must get a hitch somewhere. Now, in a novel, Sandro would have turned a deaf ear to the girl's entreaties and – "

"But, I am telling you," says the waiter, "it was very odd in its own life-like way. Sandro said he'd marry her and the girl was happy and he was happy, do you see."

"Yes, I see," I say, "but that's not odd enough for a story. If you do not get a complication you have nothing to write about. Now, if they were both happy, what would there be to write about?"

"But there was a complication. A dreadful, mysterious one," says the waiter. "As soon as Sandro made his decision he began to feel ill. He could not eat and he could not sleep, and he grew pale and lost weight. He went to see his doctor and the doctor examined him and could not find anything wrong. And yet, Sandro was in a terrible way. We all saw it, and we said to him: 'Look here, this marriage is simply preying on your mind. You are not cut out for marriage. Give the girl some money and be nice to her, but leave her alone.' The doctor, too, said the same. But Sandro wouldn't listen to our advice and he got worse and worse. The doctor told him to take a holiday, and Sandro went to Montecatini for a month, and when he came back he was a changed man, wonderfully well and happy.

"So we all said to him: 'There you are, you had a good time and you didn't think of the girl and you recovered. So, for Heaven's sake, give it up, we all know you are decent at heart but it was just not meant to be, and your very being revolts against the idea.' He would not listen to us and, sure enough, he went into a decline once more and simply wasted away before our eyes and had to postpone the wedding because he was in a dreadful state.

"He went to the doctor again and again; the doctor couldn't find anything wrong with him, and told him it was all due to worry and that he should give up the girl."

"That's terribly interesting," I say. "And, you know, this really could have been in a novel because it's all psychological, and it would make a lovely story to show that one shouldn't force oneself to be decent. One could make a point about the laws of conventional decency and about the laws of inner decency, peculiar to each man, and how the two decencies get into conflict and – "

"It wasn't like this at all," says the waiter. "I know Sandro, and

I know he is a nice man through and through, and there was no inner decency in him peculiar to himself, and so I said to him: 'Go to the doctor again, and tell him if he cannot find anything the matter with you, you won't pay his bill, and you'll go to the competition.' And Sandro went again, and the doctor did some thinking, and then he cut off a strand of Sandro's hair and took some clippings off Sandro's nails."

The waiter pauses, and I remain silent. My head is in a whirl. What is this, now? I suppose the doctor was going to do some black-magic ritual with hair and nails and livers of frogs killed at midnight. I am sure the doctor diagnosed Sandro as a heavy hysteric, and was going to try some suggestion, by magic, to cure him. Terribly clever, of course. So well calculated to impress the mind of a simple man.

And once more the waiter's tale takes a completely unexpected turn.

"The doctor put those clippings in an envelope and sent them by registered mail to Milan, to the Institute of Pathology, and the report came back that they had found large quantities of arsenic in them.

"So, first of all the doctor told Sandro to eat all his meals out and not to say a word to anybody, and he got in touch with the police. It was all as clear as could be. The two old ladies had cherished Sandro and they had not wanted to lose him, and they preferred to see him dead rather than alive and married. And this was proved by the fact that Sandro had recovered at once when he was away in Montecatini, and had got sick again at once as soon as he was back home."

"Ghastly," I say, "and I suppose, to look at them, they were dear, gentle old souls who crocheted lace mats and had all their vases filled with flowers?"

"You are right," says the waiter, "to look at them they are dear old souls. Would you like to see them?"

"No, thank you," I say, "I don't particularly want to travel to Rome just to visit the criminal loony bin."

"But you are wrong," remarks the waiter. "They are here, in Cremona, in their own house."

"Really? You said the doctor called the police at once."

"So he did. The police came straight away, within an hour, with a search-warrant. The two old ladies opened the door to the police very sweetly, and offered to make them a cup of coffee, but the police excused themselves with a shudder, saying that they had no time for coffee. They searched the house and the grounds the way the police do, you know, floorboards and mattresses and the hems of curtains and the lavatory cistern. There was not a grain of arsenic in the place. They took with them samples of the spaghetti and the sugar and other provisions in the house and had it all analysed, and there was nothing that could be determined, except just spaghetti and sugar and so on and perhaps a dead fly or two. And they made inquiries at drug-stores and chemists and traced the old ladies' movements and searched everywhere where they might have obtained arsenic in some form, but they couldn't find anything in the least suspicious.

"Sandro moved to his girl's place and married her and has been well and happy ever since. And the two old ladies are well and happy too, only they haven't got another boarder. Nobody would dare. You know what people are like – they talk. And yet – it's a mystery. Nothing was ever explained. That is why it would never do for a story."

What is there for me to say? The waiter in all his humility has given me the skeleton of a story worthy of Maupassant, with the brutality, the absence of moral judgment, the utterly compelling truth which only the master can produce. But I cannot tell him so, he has never heard of the master.

"Still, it has a happy ending," I remark, fully aware how trite this is.

"Yes, it has a happy ending," says the waiter, "because nobody was interfered with and they were all allowed to go on with this thing which we call life."

After such good entertainment I do not feel like looking at the inside of the cathedral. I do not want to look at any other monument either. I want talk and more talk. As I have no introductions to anyone in Cremona I think it would be a good idea if I went to see somebody on the staff of the local paper. I feel sure that they will be helpful.

I ask my way to the offices of what is called something like *The Lombard Mail*. I have to traverse a vast unpaved square filled with heaps of rubble, and from there I turn into a desolate narrow street which looks as though it led nowhere. It is a cul-de-sac in the real and symbolic meaning of the word.

Outside a tumble-down building I can hear already the clanking of the presses, but once inside there is none of the bustle which I had expected to find. The machines seem to be running themselves. It is an inferno devoid of devils.

I follow the direction of an arrow and climb to the first floor, walk along a slatternly railed-in gallery which overlooks a filthy court-yard, and arrive at a labelled door.

I knock, and enter an office with two desks. It is a place of lassitude and sad abandon. There are two dark young men, each lounging on top of his desk. One is picking his teeth, the other staring into space. Both are silent, and both look as though they had been silent and idle for an eternity. I imagine they are assistant editors.

I give one of them, who is nearer the door, my letter of introduc-tion, which is a masterpiece of ambiguity addressed to no one in par-ticular, and was given me by the Italian Institute in London.

He reads it and hands it to the other young man, who, before tak-ing it, descends from his desk and seats himself in a chair. During this not a word is spoken.

Afterwards they stare at each other for a time, smiling sadly and still speechless, till the toothpicker, perhaps after having prayed for and received guidance, tells me that I had better see the Editor-in-Chief.

He motions me to follow him and we all three go into the adjoin-ing room, where a man of about forty is sitting behind a table. He has black hair and deep-set eyes which are black and dull like small lumps of coal that have once been put on a fire but never burned properly, and so remained among the cinders, half consumed, useless, and lifeless.

He, too, stares into space, and looks as though he had been sitting and staring thus for an eternity. Perhaps he is carried downstairs in that chair every night, covered with sheets, dusted in the morning, and brought upstairs again.

I imagine the young men will be exactly like him in twenty years' time, and by then, as a concession to their more advanced age, they, too, will sit at their desks instead of on top of them. And the toothpicker will use a gold toothpick by then, instead of a wooden one.

The Chief gives me a desolate look and, still wordless, invites me by a gesture to sit down. The two young men take up positions behind his chair. And still no one speaks.

I begin to realize that, although this office is situated on the first floor, it is really the underworld I have entered. The two young men are acting as a sort of twin Cerberus, the three-headed hell-hound who guards the approach to Hades and, just as Cerberus allowed entry only to the shades of dead men, so they will allow only stale news to pass into this room. And the Chief is the king of this realm of dead news, dead hope, and deathly silence.

They are still looking at me with the hopeless sadness of those whose past is dead and who expect nothing from the future, when I decide that I must say something. If I sit here like this much longer I, too, shall sink into despondency.

I ask the king whether he could give me some advice about points of interest in Cremona.

"There is nothing interesting in Cremona," he replies; "nothing, nothing, nothing."

I think this a bad attitude to take for the editor of a newspaper. How does he fill his pages? Does he come out with headlines like: "Nothing happened again"?

"Can you tell me something about the local history?" I ask.

"There is no local history in Cremona, because nothing ever happened here," he says.

One of the hell-hounds has started to pick his teeth again.

"But I'll give you an introduction," says the king, "to Professor Gualazzini. He is a lecturer of history at the University of Pavia, but he lives here. He will tell you that there is no history of Cremona."

I express my gratitude. I suppose even if there is nothing to be told it is better to have it told by an expert.

There is no typewriter on the king's table. He writes a letter in an abominable hand, like a cock scratching in a manure heap. While he labours no telephone rings, no secretary carries letters to be signed, no office-boy rushes in bearing proofs to be corrected.

"This is the address. You can go and see him now." He gives me a hopeless stare. "That is, if you want to."

And I get another hopeless stare from him and from the two hell-hounds.

"If you want more information come and see me again," says the king without irony.

I leave.

In the outside office the two young men take up their crouching positions on top of their desks. I suppose it is part of their duty to sit as uncomfortably as possible and in the limpest possible attitude. I feel their desolate glances on the nape of my neck as I walk out.

I go to eat and afterwards I go back to my hotel, unpack my clothes and, as it has started to drizzle, I go to bed and sleep till late afternoon. Afterwards, coming out into the street, I stop in front of a newsvendor's kiosk. I see the evening edition of the *Lombard Mail*, and, full of curiosity, I glance at the front page. The head-line of the local news reads like this: "The rain has arrived just in time." I do not understand crops and harvests, but I am glad for the sake of the king in his realm of dead news and dead hopes. The rain has arrived just in time for him.

When I said that I went to eat, it sounded simple. But it was not simple. In Cremona, as in many small Italian towns, it is difficult to find a restaurant. Restaurants are never in the main streets. There is always, in the main streets, an abundance of bars and cafés, but no eating-places, and one gets the impression that the Italians live on black coffee and vermouth.

As one gets hungrier and hungrier one quickens one's pace and walks from one end of the town to the other. One passes disagreeable sights like dentists' surgeries, and comforting sights like shops where one can have antiques mended, and sights which do not affect one at all, like printers' windows with samples of wedding-invitation cards. If one is not quite ravenous yet one can stop and savour to the full the macabre wording on a physician's brass plate:

EMILIO ROSSI, M.U.Dr.
Specialist for all chronic diseases.

How very clever of him, one thinks. If he takes on only patients with chronic diseases, then it is understood that he need never cure them, chronic diseases being what they are. Also, he will keep his patients for ever. This may be amusing but the amusement does not go as far as one's stomach. And still, there is not a restaurant in sight.

Here is my recipe for finding a restaurant in a strange provincial town in Italy: think of the town as a tree, with the Corso as trunk and the inevitable Via Roma and Via Vittorio Veneto as the big branches. Turn from one side street into a yet smaller back street, branch off into an alley and walk, if possible, through a passage connecting two courtyards, and you will find the restaurants hidden like birds' nests in the thinnest boughs.

Now, on my first day in Cremona I had not yet evolved this recipe; like all good things, it took time and sore feet and unshed tears of exasperation to bring it into being. And so, finding myself for the fifth time in the cathedral square I thought I would seek out the waiter and ask his advice. But the café was empty, and the waiter was nowhere to be seen. There was a group of men standing in front of the café and they probably saw that I had reached a stage when I did not distinguish any more between dentists and antique shops and printers and specialists for chronic diseases, and they asked if they could help me.

After I had told them what I was looking for there was a moment of embarrassed silence. Then, two of the men began to talk at once: "There are two good places in the town. The Trattoria Padovana and the Centrale."

"Which is better?" I asked.

"Difficult to say. They are about the same."

Names mean a lot to me. I am immediately against the Centrale. For me it has tubular lights, seats of red imitation leather, and music from a radiogram. Whereas the Padovana sounds broad beamed, old, and shadowy, restful like a brooding hen, with cream soups and wine gravies simmering on the soot-blackened range.

"Which is the way to the Padovana?" I say.

"Take the street over there, follow it till you come to an arch-way – " One of the men stretched out his arm and, distastefully, as though picking a worm from a box full of wriggling worms, he raised a boy by the scruff of his neck from a shrieking, scuffling entanglement of children and told him: "You go with the lady and show her." I was very grateful that he took my stupidity for granted. I hate it when people rely on my wits and tell me "You can't miss it." The Padovana lay brooding in the backyard of an untidy old house and it was most pleasant to enter the large room with its walls painted a yellowish green, against which the white-clad tables shone with a brilliance of new-laid eggs on a bed of last year's faded moss. There were no pictures, no flowers, nor any other attempt at decoration, but on the table in the centre there was a lobster, there were baskets with the yellow apples from Tyrol and bowls with lettuce leaves and bowls with those smooth, plain dark green leaves which are also a salad, and a long, narrow, smoky blue fish in jelly.

First of all I asked for red wine, and while I was waiting to be shown the menu I saw a man entering from a door at the back of the dining-room. He was tall and portly, dressed impeccably, like a man of importance, in striped trousers, a pale grey waistcoat, and a morning coat, and I watched him as he went from table to table, bowing, putting a word here and a smile there, moving on. The *padrone*.

As soon as he came up to me I recognized him. He was one of the men who had stood in front of the café on the cathedral square. But he had kept out of the talk.

"I am so pleased to see you here, madame," he said. "I hope you will be satisfied."

"I am sure I will; it looks very good to me."

He made one of those typically Italian gestures of deprecation. "Yes, my place is supposed to be good. But you will understand, madame, that I could not tell you to come here when I saw you and you were asking for a restaurant. One must leave things to chance."

"I would have come here if you had told me," I say.

"I dare say you would, madame. But would you have thought of me as a man of good taste?"

We smile at each other. He bows and moves on.

I tell the waiter that I do not want *pasta*, in any shape or disguise, and he takes the blow without flinching. He offers me *coppa* instead. What is *coppa*? I want to see for myself. I see him enter a pantry and open an ice-box, one of those huge old-fashioned monuments to coolness with four separate doors and nickel hinges and panels pierced with holes arranged like stars. We had one like this at home, when I was very small, in the days when we pickled our own cucumbers and dried our own mushrooms.

He brings me on a board the lesser half of a charming-looking sausage with a leathery outside and a face the size of a saucer. A minute later he serves it, carved in thin rounds, almost transparent, deep crimson, marbled with glossy white lard. It tastes rather like raw cured ham, but it has a more robust flavour. He tells me that the *coppa* is made in only two places in Italy, here in Cremona and in Parma. The Parmesan *coppa* is sweeter, the Cremonese racier, he thinks.

When he brings me the bread basket I see that the rolls are twisted and baked into adventurous shapes. They are all faintly and disarmingly zoological in their outlines. I chose one which is coiled like a snail with two horns sticking out. But I could also take one shaped like a sea cucumber or one which is a fanciful rendering of a scorpion in its death pangs.

The body of the bread is yielding like clay, and tastes of mould. The crust is thin, brittle, and yellow, flaking at the merest touch. Bad dough badly baked.

The aptest thing one can say about the Cremonese rolls is that they are intriguing. This in itself is already a condemnation, because the job of the roll is to play second fiddle to other more important dishes. The roll should be to the meat what the secretary is to the executive: soothing, aiding, absorbing, and never domineering. Rolls, therefore, should look self-effacing, and when I come across rolls which rivet my attention by their very appearance I am seized at once with grave misgivings.

The rolls of Cremona should not be classed under food but under arts and decorations, and treated accordingly. The wise traveller will no more attempt to partake of them than he would break off and nibble the scroll of a façade.

In the evening I go to call on Professor Gualazzini. He lives in the Via Bertesi, which is in a quarter lying in the opposite direction to the cathedral.

Here are narrow streets with tall houses, all old, dignified, and well kept. I find the turning where the Via Bertesi begins, and as I walk down the street I feel like in a dream. I walk and walk and yet, somehow, I do not seem to make any progress. What is the matter? I stop, and realize that I keep passing the same window, and the same wall made of large, oblong rough stones, over and over again. This reminds me of one of my mother's stories, which has nothing to do with Cremona.

When my mother was a young girl she came to London for a few weeks and one day, while travelling on the Underground, she glanced idly about her in the way people do when they are bored.

Looking straight ahead of her she saw a pair of feet belonging to the woman on the seat opposite, and the longer my mother looked at those feet the more she felt that they were quite outstandingly lovely and that she had never seen such beautiful feet before in all her life. She looked up to see to whom those feet belonged. It was Pavlova.

I have a similar experience just now. I halt and step back, to the other side of the pavement, to see where all those windows belong and only now I find that I have been passing a palace as large and high as Selfridges and yet, if it were put next to Selfridges, Selfridges would look tinny and papery beside it. The palace forms a whole half of this street, and on the opposite side there is another palace of equal dimensions, but the buildings are so discreet in their grandeur that one does not notice them at once. They are built of dark brown stone with a rugged surface, unobtrusive and serviceable, like brown packing-paper.

This is my first taste of the real Cremona. During the next few days I find more streets of this kind, entirely formed of palaces, which are, though not English in style, exceedingly English in feeling: they are monuments of understatement and under-acting. They speak of money and power of such long standing that it has been taken for granted.

They are not aggressive, like, say, the Castel Vecchio in Verona, with its keep and tower and crenellations. Nor are they on the defensive against the murderous mob and their gangsterous equals, like, for instance, the Palazzo Strozzi in Florence, with its formidable iron grilles guarding the windows. Nor do they try to delight, like the Venetian palaces, with fretwork and rosettes. Nor do they try to amuse, like the Palazzo Schia in Vicenza, set with sculptured portraits of the mighty and the raffish.

The entrance of a Cremonese palace is not advertised by an assembly of caryatids: take your time and, in the long run, you will find the door. Their walls are not plastered with heraldic animals and hatchments: why should they be? Let him who cares find out who

is the master and from what family he springs. There is nothing to
be ashamed of, but there is also nothing to be exalted. Let us be quiet,
shall we?

"As you wish," I say, "let's be quiet," and I pass on my way.

I find the professor's house and a door bearing his name. I ring.
There is no answer. I step into the courtyard to find a caretaker and
I see another door, also with the professor's name, but with a different Christian name this time. Probably his brother. A little old man
opens the door. He looks at me above his glasses, neither friendly nor
hostile, but in a manner as though to say: "Say what you have to say
but make it good. If it's nonsense I'll give you a bad mark, and you'll
be annoyed with me and I'll be annoyed with you, and you will
have to come again and try to do better next time."

I quail before this old schoolteacher.

"Could I see Professor Gualazzini?"

"He's not in," he snaps, "he's never in."

"When do you think could I see him?"

"God knows. He comes and goes, he never tells me where he is
and what he is doing. And why should he? I am nobody, of course.
I am only his father."

It sounds very familiar to me.

The father writes down my name and address and tells me that
his son will ring me up.

On the following morning the professor rings up to say he is ill
with 'flu. At midday he rings to say that he still has got 'flu. After
lunch he rings to say that he still has got 'flu but he will see me.
Would I care to come to the museum library some time in the afternoon? About five?

I glance at Medea, who has stood by, listening with a mixture of
interest and approval.

"Don't be there at five," she says, "be late. Waiting for someone
who does not turn up is worse than dying."

It is, of course, just like Medea, to bring death into every sentence.

I go out and wander through the town at random. There are

several churches of various ages, most of them very old – eleventh-
and twelfth-century – simple and irregularly built, but they have
had their faces lifted with Baroque façades stuck on, all equal in their
insipid elegance.

It is a strange thing: I wonder why it is. I never get tired of medi-
ocre romanesque churches or of palaces built in the provincial Venetian Gothic style. But when it comes to Baroque it is a case like the
little girl with the little curl on her forehead; when she was good
she was very, very good, but when she was not she was horrid. Soon
I feel dead tired and disgruntled and I think I have got the recipe by
heart: one scroll up and one scroll down above the portal. Flank with
two columns, crown same with twisted saint each. Finished. Next,
please.

I reach an elbow made by the street opposite the Palazzo Trecchi
and sit down at a café table.

Once seated, I find myself in an alien climate. There is no blan-
dishment, no subtle service from the waiter. Instead I am served by
the *padrone* in person, who is an animal of quite a different colour.
He is to the waiter what the tiger is to the lamb. He places the coffee
tray before me with a somewhat contemptuous smile. It is the contempt which a man such as he has for every woman. It is the contempt of the seducer.

As I watch him, in his jersey of dark wool and his tight-fitting old
trousers, prowling among the tables or sitting down to talk with one
of the guests, I am reminded of a little poem by Goethe. The meaning is something like this:

"Approach women gently and, upon my word, you will win them.
Though, if you be bold, you may meet with even bigger success.
But he who feigns to be indifferent
Whether he charms or whether he moves –
He will offend and it is he who will seduce."

Yes, there is that lordly indifference about the *padrone*. As I pay
I say: "There don't seem to be any tourists about. Are there ever
any?"

"Oh, yes, lots of them. But not now, in the nasty season."

"For me the season is not nasty," I say; "for me, Italian April is lovely and warm."

"Ah, yes, perhaps. But for us it is cold."

"Of course," I say, "especially for you, as you are from Sicily."

It is for the first time that he looks me fully in the face with those Sicilian eyes which make my heart miss a beat. How well I know them, those southern eyes, already Arab in their splendour, dazzling with the contrast of light iris and dark lashes. His eyes are grey-blue, like a flash of water glimpsed between black trees.

"How do you know I am from the south? The way I talk?"

I laugh. "No. I just knew as soon as I looked at you that you were from Sicily."

I cannot tell him that, looking at him, I see behind his figure the African sea under the night sky barred with moonlight and spangled with the lamps of the fishing-boats.

"You are right. I am from Trapani."

He is very astonished, and there is no end to his astonishment. He stops every passer-by in the street and tells him: "Just imagine. The foreign *signora* knew that I am from the south. Just like that. By looking at me."

As I prepare to leave, he asks: "And can you find your way about in Cremona?"

"Oh, yes."

"Will you not get lost?"

"I don't think so."

Alas, I know the trend of this conversation only too well. And sure enough it comes.

"Now, I, *signora*, I live in Cremona. I don't get lost. But I would like to lose myself in your arms."

I curse myself for my low tastes and leave. The non-existing history of Cremona is waiting for me.

The museum is another of those dark brown self-effacing palaces. Professor Gualazzini waits for me at the foot of a brown marble staircase of such dimensions that three grand pianos could be moved up or down on it, simultaneously.

They are stairs built to give one an inferiority complex. I am reminded of Dante's "It is bitter to climb the stairs in other people's houses," which was the complaint of the exile. But I am not an exile. I did not have to flee from London to escape being burnt alive because I made propaganda for the wrong political party.

Here it is the other way round. It is this palace built in the sixteenth century which is an exile in our twentieth century; it is yesterday stranded in our to-day. And it must be bitter for those stairs to be climbed upon by people like me who have never had authority and power – not even over Lumpi, my old dachshund.

The professor is a short, dark-haired man of about forty, slight of build and with a lean, small-featured intelligent face. He talks fast with a contained liveliness and, unlike his father, he exudes no threat of my having to repeat the lesson. Obviously he is used to undergraduates who do not attend to his lectures.

The stairs divide at the top into two majestic branches, one, I am told, leading to the library, the other to the archæological museum and to the picture gallery.

Here we are met by two gentlemen, one the head librarian, the other the keeper of the gallery. They both look alike; short, plump, bespectacled, fair, with that unsatisfactory fairness, like the badly baked Cremonese rolls. They are a cross between owls and bread rolls, alarmingly human, in the way owls are.

During my youth I never had any particular feelings for owls, because I never had anything to do with them. But when I was in my teens I had a craze for coining sentences which seemed very witty to me at the time. Those sentences were on the pattern of "Stockholm is the Venice of the North", which is nonsense, of course, because Stockholm is not like Venice; Stockholm is exactly like Stockholm. And thus I created the statement: "The owl is the cat of the air." Some time later the cat of the air came into my life. At that time we lived in a house in the country, and an owl flew every night at half past eleven into my mother's bedroom.

First it would sit on the foot of the bed and stare at my mother in a terrifying manner: "I wouldn't mind so much if it looked at me like a bird, but it looks so horribly human." Then the owl made attempts to come and sit on my mother's head, and my mother made attempts to stop this happening.

The obvious thing would have been to close the windows, but my mother would not hear of it.

After three nights of tussle between the owl and my mother, my mother used to go to bed with an opened umbrella and the owl came and sat on the umbrella. Even this compromise was too nerve-racking for my mother, and she used to get out of bed, leave the room, and spend the night on a settee. These broken nights frayed her nerves to such a degree that my mother would say to me when we were sitting over dinner: "You know, my head is in such a whirl that when I look up I don't know whether owlie is sitting here with me, or you."

One afternoon the gardener called me to come out and led me to a trellised wall, and there was owlie sitting a few inches above my head and yawning into my face, looking very sleepy and very learned. This was the last anybody ever saw of owlie. The gardener said afterwards he was not surprised, he was sure that owlie had died, because he had looked ill already that time in the garden.

I never believed the gardener could tell whether an owl looked well or ill. I think it was sheer swank. But I could not contradict the gardener, because I could not prove anything to the contrary. Later on that year, at Christmas, my mother bought herself a miniature owl made of silver, to carry in her hand-bag. She said it would bring her luck at bridge. This belief of hers was as inexplicable as owlie's disappearance, and in the face of it even the gardener's wisdom failed.

During the introductions I am absent-minded, occupied with visions of the head librarian sitting on the foot of my mother's bed, and the keeper perched on the umbrella above her head. Both owls say that they will take me round their respective beats whenever I call on them.

"Do you know the reading-room in the British Museum?" asks what must be the library owl.

"Yes, I do."

"Do you like it?"

"I am devoted to it."

"In that case," says the librarian, "you will be interested to hear that it was designed by a Cremonese called Panizzi and built under his supervision, and that he himself was head librarian of the British Museum for many years. His statue is still to-day at the entrance of the reading-room; haven't you seen it?"

Of course I haven't. That is to say, I must have seen it without having noticed it.

The librarian is grieved to hear it, but the professor makes an airy gesture as though to say that he never had a high opinion about my capacities and that, therefore, no proof of my ignorance shall ever surprise him. I like this attitude of his. It is restful and charitable. I know that, before coming here, I should have mugged up something about the Guelfs and the Ghibellines, in order to be able to ask intelligent questions, instead of coffee-housing and composing advertisements for B.O., and it is good to know that no intelligent question will be expected of me.

The professor leads me through a Renaissance wing and through a Baroque wing and through a modern wing built in the Mussolini era and through another Baroque wing, where the rooms get of a more modest size progressively.

He unlocks a door concealed in a panel and we enter a little study, deliciously furnished with black and gilt, French pieces in the Chinese Rococo manner, with slight ladies' writing-tables and dressing-tables and sewing-tables which now serve as cabinets for files and other papers.

The chairs are also French, but of the Louis-Philippe period, and, as they are really imitations of the Rococo-*chinoiserie* style, they fit in a most piquant way with their curly legs and black lacquer inlaid with flowers of mother of pearl. It is an idea for decoration which I have never seen before, to place side by side two versions of the same thing done in two different periods. In this case the idea gains yet an additional twist, because the Rococo pieces were made originally to imitate genuine Chinese furniture.

There is also a small grand piano and a spinet.

The professor makes me sit behind a desk and sits down at the side, as though he were a visitor.

"Make no mistake about it," he says, "Cremona was once a very important place."

Of course it was. I can feel it in my bones.

"Cremona is of great antiquity."

"Etruscans?" I ask, feeling that I am not so bad, after all. It is not everybody who has heard of the Etruscans.

"I have no idea," he says; "perhaps. And perhaps not. One cannot be sure."

He starts with the year 218 B.C., when Cremona was founded by the Romans as an important military stronghold and a thorn in the flesh of the Gaulic tribes who were living in that part of the country. At first Cremona was only a big Roman garrison town. In those days the Roman soldiers took along their families, just like British sergeants used to take their wives with them to India or still do to Gibraltar. The Romans did this partly to keep the soldiers happy, and partly because, in this way, the men not only held the place, but colonized it at the same time. They bought houses and properties for their families, settled down, intermarried with the locals, and spread the Roman way of life.

Now, in the day of Virgil, Cremona was already a very prosperous town, under Roman rule though not belonging to the Roman Empire yet. After the battle of Philippi, there was a lot of requisitioning going on, by the Romans. For one thing they wanted to reward the soldiers who had fought at Philippi and defeated Cæsar's murderers, with plots of land and houses, and also they needed more ground for enlarging the garrison. This meant that they took hold of a great number of farms and fields belonging to the native population, and chased the former owners away.

This also happened to Virgil's parents. They were peasants and quite substantial people in a small way, who farmed their own estate. They were Cremonese, but moved to Mantua before Virgil was born. Nevertheless, when the Roman administration started their grabbing campaign, Virgil's parents, too, lost their property, because Mantua is near Cremona and the Romans were spreading themselves all over the place. Virgil, through his parents, had great ties with Cremona. He studied for some time in Cremona and took there his *Toga Preatesta*, which was assumed by young men as a symbol of having reached their maturity. As he spent his youth in Mantua and Cremona he could not forget those fields and pastures which should have been his by right, and the thought of his loss preyed on his mind.

He moved to Milan for further studies, and then to Naples. After this he went back, and lived in the country near Cremona, with a rich landowner, and at last he managed to get to Rome and was introduced to Maecenas. He became hanger-on at Maecenas's palace, which was the only possible way for poets to make a living in those days, and from that time on he was famous and respected.

But he still could not get over the loss of his parents' estates. He began to sue the Roman military authorities for restitution. A friend started a political mud-flinging campaign in order to help Virgil, whereas Virgil himself began to butter up Alfeno Varus who was in charge of the requisitionings. He probably even had an interview with Octavian in person and he got his farm back—that is to say, on paper. When he went there to take possession of it, the tough old sergeant who had moved in, not only refused to let go, but ran after Virgil with a drawn sword. Virgil hid in a shop, got out through the back door, jumped into the river and swam to the other shore. Once back in safety he started pestering the authorities once more and pestering them very beautifully in the shape of

song and counter-song between his famous shepherds in the *Eclogues*.
This litigation and the sense of loss poisoned the whole of Virgil's
life. His famous gentle melancholy, which lends itself so superbly to
pastoral elegiac poems, and which was imitated by all Europe in all
ages, was not the picturesque pose which one might think it to be.
His yearning for the delights of nature was very real: he yearned
for his own particular plot of land.

It is true, of course, that the Virgilian shepherds are drawing-
room shepherds, but they could not have survived till to-day if
they had not come out of an eternal drawing-room. They will live
as long as sophisticated society people are fascinated by the charms
of country life. Their most famous sister was Marie Antoinette,
when she played at dairy farming in Trianon, milked real cows and
churned butter from real milk.

On the other hand, I would say that Virgil could have gone and
bought himself a bit of farm land, in later life, when he was doing
very nicely in Rome. After all, he must have made a very good
living out of his poetry, being in court circles, in the swim of
society, patronized by Maecenas and highly thought of by Augustus,
the Emperor. I am sure that I am not the first person to think of this.
I am convinced that Horace and all his other friends gave him similar
advice, but he would not listen.

I imagine this would have been one of those solutions which one
always suggests for other people's troubles, and which seem so
simple and obvious but which cannot be accepted by the person in
trouble himself because it does not go to the very root of the trouble.
Virgil preferred staying in the capital and eating his heart out. That
he did eat his heart out is known to all. He leaves no doubt about it.
In Eclogue Number 1, for instance, and in Number 9, the two charming shepherds do nothing but complain about the evil of requisitioning farms from private owners. During his last years he went
to live in the country near Naples, which just shows that he wanted
to nurse his grievances. Why didn't he go and live on the banks of
his native Mincio instead, among the barren stones, the slimy

marshes, and the bitter willows, over which he had shed his heart-blood in the *Eclogues*?

After the fall of the Roman Empire, Cremona was still an important garrison town in the West Roman Empire, with Ravenna as capital. For years it held out against the Longobards, but in the end it was destroyed by them.

After this the history of Cremona becomes messy and complicated, to a degree which would astonish the 'king of the dead news'. When the Guelf and Ghibelline row started, Cremona was asked by other Lombard cities to join the league against the Ghibelline party, that is to say, against the Emperor. Cremona agreed, but when it came to fighting she kept out of the battle and not only the Lombard cities hated her for it but also the side of the enemy. This is life.

In 1240 the Holy Roman Emperor Frederick II made Cremona his place of residence with his harem, court poets, court philosophers, court musicians and all, and thus it became one of the most interesting towns in Europe. The Emperor himself made charming little poems in Sicilian, which was his mother tongue, and they were despised by Dante because they were not written in Tuscan Italian. But still, even Dante admitted that the Emperor's court gave birth to Italian poetry.

This may be true, but I doubt it. I think that most of the stuff which was turned out in those days in Italy was nothing but a re-hash of troubadour French love-songs, and quite worthless. I would never go by Dante's judgment. He was not a reliable judge of poetry, in my opinion. This is not astonishing. Goethe, too, was a poor judge of his contemporaries. Goethe, for instance, was unimpressed to the point of nastiness by Beethoven, but thought the world of a Berlin composer called Zelter, of whom no one has heard since. Similarly, Goethe was frosty and unhelpful to Schopenhauer and, during the well-known interview with Heine, Goethe was to Heine what the spider was to Miss Muffet. Heine wrote quite rightly afterwards that for a contemporary artist to be praised by Goethe meant to have been given a certificate of mediocrity.

Frederick II must have been one of the most extraordinary persons who ever ruled. He was a German who spent most of his life in Italy and Sicily, not ruling the whole of Italy but only the bits and pieces which he could grab.

As he was born from a Sicilian princess while Sicily was under Norman rule, he assimilated the Oriental spirit, which expressed itself in a way of very colourful living, with a full-blown harem, though officially he was a Christian. To-day we should say that he lived a full life.

But he was not as Christian as all that. As far as I can make out he was excommunicated at least three times because of his quarrels with various Popes. The Popes also tried twice to get rid of him by finding another Emperor to set up as an anti-Emperor, but they never succeeded. I think that this reckless excommunicating is silly. It is bound to lose its effects after the first time.

Frederick II had an illegitimate son by a lady of Cremona. He was called Enzio, and I think he was his favourite child. Anyway, Enzio was much more loyal to his father than the proper sons, who always quarrelled with the Emperor.

Enzio got married to the Sardinian princess Adelasia and became King of Sardinia. The Pope tried to prevent the marriage and when he couldn't, the Emperor became once more excommunicated. I cannot see the point of it. It is terribly unfair. Why didn't the Pope excommunicate Enzio? Then the Pope captured Enzio and the Emperor was going to hit back by besieging Rome but in the last minute the Pope died and so it was not necessary any more. But later on the Emperor quarrelled with the next Pope and besieged Rome twice. There were many more ups and downs, and Enzio came to a bad end, being captured by the Bolognese during one of the campaigns of the Lombard cities. This was the last straw for the Emperor. He could not get over Enzio's death and lost his appetite for any more fights, and he withdrew to Palermo and died there.

Dante himself passed through Cremona during his wanderings in exile. It is not known how long he stayed – it was probably just a passing visit, but he found sufficient time to engage in a violent quarrel with Cavalcabò, one of the nobles of Cremona. The Palace Cavalcabò still stands. It is one of those well-bred buildings whose beauty derives from superb craftsmanship and proportions, with no trimmings, substantial and discreet, like a well-tailored suit. The Cavalcabò family still live there.

Cavalcabò was 'black', that is, he was Guelf and supported the Pope, whereas Dante was 'white' and supported the Emperor. This is, of course, just what one would have expected from Dante. He would quarrel with anybody if he possibly could. It was merely a matter of giving him enough time.

The professor tells me that Dante's faction, the Whites, were called, in Dante's time, the 'accursed faction'.

"Was it true?" I ask. "Did very nasty people belong to it? Or was it called accursed because it was against the Pope?"

The professor regards me with astonishment. "Oh, no. It was only called accursed because it lost."

Anyway, though Dante was 'white' and had to keep out of Florence because of it, he very soon made himself unpleasant with other influential Whites who were his fellow exiles, and decided that the only thing for him was to form his own party. If he had lived to-day, he could have held his annual party meeting in a telephone box.

He roamed Italy, and was for ever after sorry for himself. He did not seem to remember that, while the Whites were in power and he was a prior of Florence and sitting pretty as one of the six of the *Signoria*, he had thrown out all the leaders of the Blacks. I feel that if he couldn't take it, he should have kept out of politics altogether. With him it was a case of "Wash me but don't make me wet."

François I, King of France, was beaten by Charles V in the battle of Pavia and was imprisoned for a time in a tower in Cremona. The tower still stands. From there he wrote a letter to his mother, containing the famous words: "*Tout est perdu fort que l'honneur.*" This is a very nice example of how to keep one's self-respect.

"And now," says the professor, "we come to a point of Cremonese history which will interest you more than anything else I have
told you so far."

It was like this: In the beginning of the eighteenth century
Cremona was under French rule, with a military governor called
Villeroi.

At that time the Austrians had Prince Eugène as their field-
marshal. He was the greatest soldier they ever had. Actually, Prince
Eugène had first wanted to become a priest, but later on he had
decided to join the army. As he was French, a native of Savoy, he
went to the King of France to offer his services. Prince Eugène was
a small, slight, ugly young man, and when he presented himself to
the King, the King started to laugh and said something like: "What,
you miserable little seedy weedy *abbé*, you want to be a soldier?
This is priceless."

So Prince Eugène went off in a huff, and went to the Austrians,
who took him on, and he became one of the greatest military
leaders of all times. The French King was livid about it, but then it
was too late.

One of Prince Eugène's campaigns was against Cremona, during
the War of the Spanish succession, when he planned to take Cremona for the Austrians. On the second of February, 1702, he reached
the town. He did not have to fight a battle, because the French
military never expected him to come, and the garrison just folded
up when they saw him. Thus he took Cremona without making a
disturbance, and the governor, General Villeroi, never showed his
face. By the time it was all over it was already night, and Prince
Eugène thought the time had come to get hold of Villeroi and to
acquaint him with the news.

Prince Eugène took with him only a few men, and they crept in
the dark to the governor's residence, which was the house of Stradi-
varius, the famous maker of violins. They entered the house,
walked into the bedroom, and found the governor in bed but not
asleep, and in the company of one of the ladies of Cremona, and

Prince Eugène made him his prisoner there and then. This incident became known as "the Surprise of Cremona". The General became the laughing-stock of the whole of Europe, and innumerable pictures were drawn, lampoons and songs were composed, and mock heroic epics were written to commemorate the episode.

"This is the true 'Surprise of Cremona'," says the professor; "mark it well. Because you will not find it recorded in English books of history."

"Do they suppress it?" I ask with indignation.

"I did not know you cared so much for historic truth," remarks the professor. "No, they do not suppress it. They cannot do so. Because it is a decisive point in history. They mention the 'Surprise of Cremona' and explain that the name is derived from the fact that the garrison was caught napping."

The day after the Surprise the French got on their feet and gave battle, forcing the Austrians to retreat, which they did, taking General Villeroi with them. One of the French couplets of the time runs thus:

> Français, rendons grâce à Bellone
> Notre bonheur est sans égal;
> Nous avons conservé Crémone
> Et perdu notre Général.

But the Austrians got Cremona in the end. Their administration was very well liked, and they stayed till Napoleon walked in. He stole a lot of valuable pictures as he did everywhere else and carried off one of their most prized medieval documents, a translation by Gerardo di Cremona of an Arab treatise on astronomy. But the French didn't keep it. It is now in Berlin, probably stolen from the French by the Germans during the Franco-Prussian War.

After Napoleon had been put out of harm's way in St. Helena, the Austrians took over once more, but this time they were not as nice as before. Metternich's police were very active, always on the look-out for insurrections, and because they were looking for them they got them and life was hard.

Cremona was very glad to get out of it, and put herself under the house of Piedmont. Three years later, in 1861, Italy became unified, and that was the end of Cremona's own history.

"There is only one remarkable thing in our own days about Cremona," says the professor; "in Mussolini's time there was a paper in Cremona which was the only journal which could write freely."

Here I must say that a short while before, during the conversation about Napoleon, I believe, the door opened and in walked a tall, skinny young man. He nodded to the professor and busied himself in the other part of the room with some papers he took out of a lacquer cabinet. I could see that he was listening to every word and waiting for an opening to join our talk.

And now, as I ask: "How did they manage that?" he comes up to us. He has black wavy hair, a blotchy skin, and a goat's profile, with a short nose curving between a receding forehead and a receding chin. He is introduced as Professor Nicodemi, lecturer of musical palaeology at the University of Pavia. In his smile he bares long teeth and unpleasantly pink gums, like a goat ready to browse. I do not know what palaeology is, but I feel that gums should be had and not seen.

He says: "The paper got away with it because the editor was Protestant and played on the religious angle while hitting at Mussolini all the time."

Professor Gualazzini makes an airy gesture, as though to say: "Just the sort of explanation the fool would produce. What do you expect?" It is obvious he does not like the Pal, and that I shall not get another worthwhile word out of him now. The Surprises of Cremona have been put back into his bag.

Now the picture owl and the book owl come in too, and the professor retires with them to one corner of the room, determined that I should get a dollop of musical palaeology.

Soon I begin to understand the Pal's eagerness to talk to me. He tells me he has been studying English for two years, and naturally enough he wants to reap the fruit of his endeavours. At once I find myself giving a lesson in colloquial English.

He would be very happy to show me the town.

"How very kind of you," I say, "if it won't be too much of a bore for you?"

"Bore? What does this mean? It will be for me similar to going to the dentist? Like the dentist's bore?"

"Not quite," I say. "The dentist drills, but that doesn't mean he can't also bore. Actually, I once left a dentist because he bored me to tears. The one I've got now is much brighter. What I meant was 'dull'."

"Ah, yes, dull. And you can also say 'bore'?"

"Yes."

"They are the same?"

"Yes, I think so."

"And they are both correct?"

"Oh, yes."

The Pal grows thoughtful. "But which of the two expressions is of the greater elegance?"

This reminds me of Ploetz, Dr. Charles Ploetz, one of the vicarious tormentors of my youth, who wrote the most comprehensive French grammar in existence. This work was so maddeningly comprehensive that it contained all the exceptions to all the rules, and all manners of expressing the same thing in different ways. Ploetz's last words were: "*Je meurs*, but it is equally correct to say *je me meurs*."

Still, I have promised to be fair to goats in future.

The Pal asks me to come to a party which he is giving on the following day. He will play some music, pre-Gregorian chant. A few friends of his are coming, too. The party will be held here, in this study. I accept. I would much rather be asked out to dinner.

That night, at the Padovana, I start dinner with a salad of *finocchi*. This is a round, whitish-green, fascinating vegetable, wrapped up in layers of itself which overlap like the tiles of a roof. At the top it sprouts four pale, reeded stems which bear dark green leaves, delicate, like feathers made up of needles, reminiscent of the foliage of wild asparagus. Only the round part is eaten, boiled or raw, sliced, with oil and vinegar. It has a cool, clean, nutty flavour.

After I have finished the salad, the *padrone* appears, rolling a trolley towards me. He comes, I see, I am conquered. On the trolley there is a composite dish. It is called *bollito misto*, and is the counterpart of its better-known brother the *fritto misto*. Whereas the *fritto misto* is all golden, dry, crinkled, and crisp, the *bollito* is silvery smooth and watery. Who shall say which of the two is more glorious? They must be taken according to one's mood, like the Sun and the Moon.

The *padrone* carves me a slice of boiled tongue, a sliver of boiled chicken, a chunk of boiled beef, half of a boiled calf's knuckle, and a round of a large boiled sausage. There are two sauces to go with it, the *salsa verde* and the *salsa rossa*. Intelligent as he is, he does not ask me which of the two I prefer. He knows I shall want both.

The green sauce is an enticing mixture of aromatic herbs, smoothed with oil and sharpened with vinegar. The red sauce is of an evenly thick consistency and cannot be analysed easily. Here is the recipe as told me by the *padrone*:

"Chop a shallot and fry in oil till it blushes. Add fresh tomatoes and minced carrots and butter and simmer for about twenty minutes. Add minced fresh red peppers and simmer for another ten minutes."

For those who cannot be captivated by either of the two sauces there is another still more picturesque choice, called the Mustard of Cremona.

This is a dish of fruit candied in syrup, to which a dash of pepper and mustard powder has been added. It serves as sweet spice to the mild meats and sets them on fire, in a cool and lovely way, like moonlight burning on water. The fruit is luminously transparent, like semi-precious stones. I am given a plateful. There are several cherries, unevenly rounded like antique corals; a green pear of the size of a walnut, with the black pips shining like onyx; a larger pear of the colour of rose-quartz; a green fig clouded like a flawed emerald, a curved strip of pumpkin, reddish brown and veined like chrysopase, and the half of an apricot which could have been carved out of a topaz. They are almost too splendid to be eaten. Before starting, I ponder over their many-hued flamboyance, and come to the conclusion that the colours of the Mustard of Cremona are those found in Veronese's paintings. It is an exceedingly *raffiné* dish, a Baroque dish, sweet, full-bodied, glowing and tingling. Life is beautiful.

I must add that the dining-room of the Padovana is well suited for the eating of the Mustard of Cremona, because it is a sombre room. Dark, rich colours like those of the Mustard are at their best only in dark rooms. This is a principle of interior decoration which is, unfortunately, ignored to-day. People always think that they can brighten and lighten a dark room by furnishing it in pale pastel shades. This is nonsense. The pastel shades merely appear grey and watery, and are swallowed up by the surrounding darkness. Only strong, deep colours can stand up to a dim room. On the other hand, they are apt to look garish when put in a light room, and quarrel with their surroundings, whereas pale colours come into their own and expand like delicate flowers. One should always team the dark with the dark and the light with the light. It all boils down to the Platonic principle that "only the like can understand the like".

In the morning the Pal calls at my hotel and takes me sight-seeing. The cathedral square and the two streets leading towards it are crammed full with men who stand about in groups plotting evil deeds. The humming of their voices gathers and pervades the square like the rushing of the wings of revolution. A quaintly sinister touch is added by several youths, weaving in and out among those groups. These youths are silent, and their bodies are entwined by strings of sponges. No one glances at them, let alone buys a sponge. Needless to say, they are not sponge-sellers. It is they who carry the ammunition concealed on their bodies, and soon they will tear off their silly mercantile disguise and lead the assault. I shudder, and ask the Pal for an explanation.

He says: "It is market-day to-day. It is a day of merry-making."

"And the men?"

"These are the peasants from the vicination."

"I can see the peasants from the 'vicination,' but," I say, "where is the market? Where are the wares? They can't all be selling themselves?"

From the Pal's explanation I gather that the day of merry-making is of an abstract nature. They come together, tell each other what they've got at home, and sell it. They seal the deal by shaking hands, and sometimes they even have a drink together. But this goes only for the important deals. In the case of trifles they do not even shake hands. I can quite understand the reason for these differences. The more emotion one feels, the more there is the need for ceremonial. In Sicily, for instance, where the men engage in duels with knives, carried on till one of them is killed, the two adversaries embrace and kiss each other after having agreed on the time and place of the fight.

We leave the square and walk through side streets till we get to St. Agatha. "Please, observe the façade. Is it not of the greatest elegance?" The front of St. Agatha is, of course, another tiresome piece of provincial Baroque. Inside the church, two panels of thirteenth-century frescoes are still visible.

There is the picture of a young woman, pale and fair, in a yellow, pleated robe. St. Agatha, I presume. She looks exactly like my Aunt Alice after death. Here I must explain that my Aunt Alice had the theory that everybody dies once a year. She lived up to it. Usually it was after *pâté de foie gras*.

My Aunt Alice may have looked pale and saintly on such occasions, but her character would have shocked St. Agatha. Once, my Uncle Ernest went on a business trip to Rumania and brought back a pot of caviare. He was my mother's and Aunt Alice's brother and, strictly speaking, he should have divided the caviare between both of them, but he and my mother were always quarrelling and so, in order to annoy my mother, he gave the whole pot to Aunt Alice. It was put in the ice-box in the pantry, and every morning it was served to Aunt Alice in bed, with the coffee.

My mother and I used to gather by her bed and watch her, with eyes glittering with fury, but she continued to eat and never gave us so much as a grain. She never died from it, either. My mother rang up our family doctor, who knew Aunt Alice's inclination towards dying, and she asked him if caviare wasn't frightfully unhealthy; but he said no, it was a most valuable food, full of lecithin and phosphoproteids and lipoids.

"In that case," said my mother, "surely, we should all eat caviare. Or, at least, we should eat it whenever we get the chance?"

"Not necessarily, dear lady," replied the doctor; "if you want to replenish your lecithin you do not have to eat caviare. You will be glad to know that an ordinary egg-yolk holds the same virtues."

All I can say is, that, if my mother had had as much gift for diplomacy as our family doctor, she would have been given a pot of caviare for herself.

We go to see the Palazzo Foddri and the Palazzo Raimondi, both fifteenth-century palaces. They are built in that supremely simple good taste which I have seen nowhere else, before or after. The walls are of deep pink brick, and beneath the eaves there runs a frieze of terra-cotta: fat, close-leaved garlands encircling medallions of women's heads carved in semi-relief. The special thing about it is that the brick and the terra-cotta are of exactly the same colour-tone, which gives the impression that the entire palace – walls, roof, and decoration – have been made out of a single piece, and one is awed by the typically Cremonese mixture of well-bred reticence and ferocious dignity.

Afterwards we have white coffee in a bar, and the waiter sprinkles powdered chocolate on the frothy milk in our cups. This, too, is a speciality of Cremona.

In the evening I take myself to the musical party. This is a fair way of expressing it, because the I and the self are not in harmony, the I being bent on studying Italian social life and the self inclined for coffee-housing.

I find the other guests assembled in the street in front of the museum, and as soon as I come we all go in. The reason for this gathering outside is that, at night, the door must be kept locked. And who would want to go several times up and down those stairs, in order to admit late-comers?

The Pal introduces us. It seems that, like him, they are all fond of medieval music and speak English.

There are two young women, one plain and soulful, the other pert and pretty. The pretty one is married. Apart from her husband, who is a doctor, there is another young man, prematurely bald and comfortable-looking.

While we ascend the stairs the pert woman attacks me with questions. Buzzing and inopportune, like a bluebottle, she rushes at me with a new question as soon as I have brushed her off.

"Do you know Gray's 'Elegy in a Country Churchyard'?"

"Yes."

"Do you know East Barnet in London?"

"No."

"But you live in London, don't you?"

"Yes."

"But you don't know East Barnet?"

"No."

"Do you know a poem by Byron called 'A Roman Night'?"

"No."

Now that we have reached the head of the inferiority-complex stairs the bluebottle's husband joins us. He, too, seems to have East Barnet on the brain. His remarks are as follows:

"Is it not truly wonderful to think that in a great city like London there can be found a place like East Barnet? After one has been to the City and the West End, is it not truly astonishing to reach East Barnet, so green, so harmoniously laid out, so peaceful, forming such an amazing contrast to the teeming city of London?"

I sample the conversations of the others. They are all bores, though each a bore in a different way. The bald friend is the best, because he is restful and has no ambitions aimed at Gray, East Barnet, and Lord Byron.

The Pal asks me if I know a Mr. Pearson, who is the head of the College of Pipers in Glasgow. I remark that Mr. Pearson is darker to me than any Roman night.

He fastens on to the Roman night. Would I be astonished if he told me that the music of bagpipes goes further back than any Roman night, that is to say, it has come to us from ages before Rome was founded?

By now my cruel streak is aroused. Neither the Pal's looks nor his talk are of a nature which appeals to women and, to verify this impression, I ask him whether he has got a girl friend.

No, not really, but there is a young lady in London with whom he corresponds in English. She lives in East Barnet. He has never met her. Do I know East Barnet? He has never been to England at all.

I imagine that this pen friend was procured by the bluebottle's husband. All blessings seem to flow from East Barnet. He asks me whether I do not think it nice to keep up a friendship by letters. I make no comment.

But while we are bidden to take our seats and the Pal clings to the piano, discoursing about the harmonic laws of pre-Gregorian music, I make up a verse:

> "Love without approximation
> Holds for me no fascination."

Owing to this wayward mental activity of mine I am unable to say anything about pre-Gregorian harmonics, but I notice that the ladies' shoes are pointed, whereas mine are rounded at the toes, and I wonder whether their footwear is out of date or whether it represents an *avant-garde* trend which will sweep the world of fashion.

Now, after we have been conditioned to awe and reverence, records are put on the electric gramophone. They are the latest thing from Paris, and are very expensive.

It is all *a capella* song, very noble and exceedingly dull, like chestnut purée with whipped cream.

The only enthusiast is the bluebottle who, afterwards, leaps up excitedly, exclaiming: "*Che cosa, che cosa.*"

On the following day I go once more to the Sicilian café. A man enters with a terrier at his heel. The terrier's fur is dyed rose-red. Afterwards I ask the *padrone*: "Did you see the red dog?"

"Ah, yes, I know him well."

"What's the matter with him? Is he ill, and has to be rubbed with a coloured ointment?"

The *padrone* is delighted. "No, *signora*, that dog is as healthy as a dog can be. His master is red, that is to say, he is a Communist, and so the dog has to be red too. Is it not interesting to be in Cremona?"

"Very."

"Have you seen many interesting things?"

"A few."

"Have you seen the *torazzo* by the cathedral?"

Of course I have seen it. It is the square-built belfry standing to one side of the cathedral, tied to it by those corset laces, the arched colonnades. Like so many campaniles, it has one window at the bottom of the tower, then two, then four, in order to counteract the optical illusion that tall buildings taper upwards.

"It is the highest tower in Italy," remarks the *padrone*. "Would you like me to come up it with you?"

I know that it isn't colloquial English he is after. I say: "No, thank you, I'll do it alone one day when I feel energetic. Just now I'm too lazy."

"But you cannot go up alone, *signora*."

"Why not?"

"Because it is forbidden. Last year four people threw themselves from the top of the *torazzo*, that is to say, each time one person went up there alone, and since then there is a law that one must go in company."

Then, after a pause: "Foreign ladies often travel alone, I know. And then, they find company; they can't help it, it is only natural. What are they to do, when, for instance, they want to see the *torazzo*? I understand. But I would rather kill a woman of mine than see her walking with another man. Do you understand me?"

"Of course."

"When a woman is dead I know at least where she is and what she is doing. Would you not agree?"

"Of course."

"And a woman who is not worth killing is not worth having at all. Would you not agree?"

God, yes, he is right. And what he says is not mere operatic breast-beating out of *Cavalleria Rusticana*. He means it. I know his type. They really do kill.

In the morning I go to change a traveller's cheque. The bank is part of that modern block running alongside the whole length of the public gardens, called the Galleria, no doubt after the Galleria in Milan; but in this case the glass-roofed street inside the house does not form a cross, but cuts diagonally from one corner of the building to the corner opposite. The Galleria in Milan is a monster, with a monster's grandeur, inspired by the same love for vaulted glass roofs which called into being the Crystal Palace and Victoria Station. But the Galleria of Cremona is of quite recent date, and lacks the generosity of the nineteenth century. Upon entering it I feel that I have been swallowed up by a whale, and shall come out mangled by all those shopkeepers who stand grinning in front of their shops in the milky light beneath the glass vault.

I enter, present my cheque, and a shiver runs through the bank. Various gentlemen leave their counters to peer over the shoulder of the clerk who is holding the paper. Doors at the back open and there come forth other gentlemen who, during a normal banking day, were never meant to be revealed.

I hand in my passport, and now the two documents are being

carried about from one table to the other, from one counter to the other, by men with panic-stricken features.

"You have it."

"No, you give it to him."

"No, he doesn't want it."

"Here you are, you'd better deal with it."

"I've had it once already, you fool, what am I to do with it?"

And this is the bank which has a notice in the window saying that foreign business will gladly be transacted. They transact it as gladly as handling a tarantula spider.

In the end, ironically enough, it is the youngest of the clerks who grasps the tarantula. He digs out some printed forms, fills them in, and tears them up once they have been written. This is a well-known creative process known by writers as 'warming up'. At last he is satisfied with his work. He hands it to the others, who now are very knowledgeable. The layout is criticized and amended. The end is near.

I am given a metal disk with a number stamped on it, sign the cheque, and go to the cashier's grille. While he pays me, my passport does yet another round from hand to hand, a sort of farewell visit. By now, all the bank knows my age, and I have a horrible feeling that, later on, they will tell each other how old they thought I was and how far they were off the mark. For all I know they may already have established one of their colleagues, with a book, accepting bets.

My passport is returned to the cashier, but it is not given to me until I have answered all his questions. What have I seen up till now in Cremona?

First things first: I start with the donkey and end with the Perugino Madonna in Sant' Agostino.

"It is not a good Perugino," he says. "Nevertheless we are proud of it, because it is the only one we have got. You must see San Sigismondo, however. It is not easy to get there, it is outside Cremona, but I beseech you to make the effort nevertheless, however."

When I get back to my hotel I look up San Sigismondo in the guide-book. The guide-book does not beseech me to make an effort. Far from lavishing a star on San Sigismondo, it has printed the name in small italics, which means: "Go there if you want to kill time." I think I will go there nevertheless, however. It is not every day that I have been beseeched.

When I come downstairs Medea tells me that Professor Nicodemi has rung up to say that he will fetch me after lunch for an excursion.

"After lunch." I say to Medea. "After lunch, with the accent on 'after'. Do you see what I mean?"

I am in two minds. The last time I saw the Pal he pestered me to place a quotation by Donne, till I felt like saying: "Go and catch a falling star."

No doubt, one should avoid English-speaking Italians. The saying "Un Inglese italianato e un diavolo incarnato" could be countered by "Un Italiano anglifiato e un seccatore nonsurpassato". But I shall try to make him take me to San Sigismondo.

He arrives in a car, with the bald friend, and I do not have to beseech him – he intended to take me to San Sigismondo in any case.

We drive away, seen off by Medea, the luggage boy, and one of the waiters, who tell each other in loudly whispered stage-asides: "Ah, our professor, he is a nice man, a dear man, a veritable treasure." Looking back, I see them still standing in the porch, as though waiting for the cue to break into a terzetto.

From narrow streets and cobbles we emerge on to a wide, smooth highway which leads to the Po. The greatest river of Italy has a rude name, but the Italians do not know it. They pronounce it in a very short way, as though spitting it out, with an open o like in 'rot', 'bosh', 'tosh', and 'poppy-cock'.

The road is dreary. It is lined by necessary and unpleasant buildings, which usually are on the outskirts of a town, like prisons and loony-bins and electricity works and homes for neglected children and homes for imbecile children. The electricity works looks much more like a prison than the prison.

The Po is much larger than I had imagined it. It would be majestic if it were not so bedraggled-looking. Its banks are all frayed and shredded, like old shirt cuffs, and, besides, it does not know where to stop. What I have taken for the shore on the other side turns out to be a tongue-shaped sand-bank, merely splitting the river, and beyond it there are islets strewn about like splinters, and strips of marshy ground where the Po keeps looking at me with glittering eyes between high sedges. In other words, the Po cannot make up its mind whether it should let go or not. And every time you think you have got away from the river there is yet another water arm encircling a reedy, willowy stretch of bog.

The water of the Po is a dull blue, neither pale nor deep. If one were to paint it one would have to underpaint with grey-brown.

While we are driving over the enormously long bridge I get the impression that the Po tries to be blue, but there is not much pleasure in being blue these days.

The Cremona side of the Po is Lombardy. The other side is Emilia. After ten minutes of Emilia we stop. We are supposed to go for a walk. I cannot see the point of it. I can never see the point of a walk. We drag through clumps of rough river grasses and through sandy patches pitted with holes and take a footpath criss-crossed with the skeletons of uprooted brambles. They have thorns which would gladden the heart of Graham Sutherland. This is just the sort of walk which I like, especially when I am wearing high-heeled lizard-skin pumps and sheer stockings. The Pal and the friend have a manly talk about the car and its virtues, and I stumble along trying to avoid all those snares with which the nature of Emilia tries to entice my stockings. Then I stop. "I've had enough," I say.

"But we want to take you to that point over there, it is so beautiful."

What can I do? One must not look a gift outing in the mouth. And so, we continue.

It is not the thorns which are my undoing in the end, it is a last year's burr. In my cat-of-the-air days I would have said that the burr is the hedgehog of the plant world, just as the sea-urchin is the burr of the ocean. In those days I did not have to buy my own silk stockings.

We reach the 'point', which is the extreme edge of the thorny path, affording a view of the – any way – ubiquitous Po. Here we sit down, and I empty the sand from my shoes and contemplate the yawning Po and my yawning ladder alternately.

The Pal says, surely, what is a stocking? It can be bought anywhere. I nod in silence. This is true, I know, but he will not buy it for me.

"And furthermore," says the Pal, "surely, an excursion like this must be worth it? Surely, one must pay a price?"

Idiot! No wonder he has not got a girl friend.

We go back to the car and drive through the green, cheerless country-side lit by the cool April sun. It is the richest soil of Italy. Strange, how the most fertile country is also the most unattractive. For beauty, one must go to barren land.

We drive through Busseto, which is Verdi country, past the house where Verdi lived for thirty years. It stands in the shade of unkempt trees, modest-sized, the walls once yellow, the shutters once green; it belongs to an age when green shutters stood for a certain way of life. There is nothing more melancholy than the sight of faded green shutters.

We get to Fidenza and halt before the cathedral, in a square surrounded by proletarian blocks of flats, partly destroyed during the war.

The cathedral is Romanesque, a homely body of red brick with bulging apses, which I like. On the walls there are tiny carved reliefs with the four seasons. I prefer the one which is Winter. It shows a family sitting by the fire, with hams and sausages hanging from the rafters. It is good to see that already in the thirteenth century they had the ingredients for the *bollito misto*.

The portal is flanked by two stone lions. I have seen many such lions guarding many such portals in many such cathedrals in Italy, but I have never seen a more amiably half-baked-looking pair.

The Pal tells me that if I put my hand into the lion's mouth I shall never have a sore throat. I rather like him for this. I should have expected him to say something like: "The people in their ignorance imagine that – "

To make sure, I put my hand into the mouth of both lions.

As we turn the corner a side door opens and a stream of choir-boys pours out, in white cassocks bordered with lace two hands deep, and sashed with black and gold brocade. Then a few priests.

"It's the new Bishop of Cremona," say some people near us; "he has come to us for the first time to hold a service."

The Pal wants to go, but I will not budge. I am very fond of bishops. And here he comes. He is so fat that he moves with difficulty, impeded by surplice, cope, and stole, like a huge baby in swaddling clothes. The people right and left kneel down at his approach and lower their heads like a field of corn bowing under the breath of the wind. The Pal turns away, his lips folded back in a disdainful smile, like a goat which has bitten off a bunch of nasty herbs.

The Bishop is not a reckless blesser. He moves along warily and takes his time, bestowing one careful blessing after another. He comes nearer. Suddenly he is no more an inordinately fat man with a smile studied in front of the glass. He is the vicar of God. I find myself sinking to my knees and receive his blessing. I am forgiven everything.

I rise and walk to the car, where the Pal is waiting with the bald friend. The bald friend says: "You look so extraordinarily content." I am. I did not know myself that there was so much inside me which clamoured for forgiveness. Why must we go through life weighed down by the stones of guilt we have picked up on the wayside?

We drive on till we come to San Sigismondo, a large, grey, dowdy church, standing by itself like a dowager Royalty left behind by her court. We go inside, and find ourselves surrounded by the gorgeous scenes of Baroque ballet, in bright, cool colours, orange, azure, and coral-red. The frescoes are all done by the Campis, and it is no good trying to sort them out. They were a family who bred like rabbits, and all painted. They have depicted incidents of the goriest biblical butchery, but this will not put you off. Everything is in delicious movement, even Abraham's sacrifice of Isaac is pirouetted. And you know quite well that as soon as your back is turned the voice of the ballet-master will flute: "Aby, dear, how often must I tell you that if you raise your right arm to point the knife at Izzy's breast, you must put your left foot forward, pointing the toe to the centre, otherwise we lose the balance of the whole design?"

On each of these compositions, most of which are built up on a flight of steps, there is, on the lowest step in the foremost centre, a small dog, each time of a different breed. San Sigismondo should be popular with the British. It is almost as good as going to Cruft's.

We wander from the nave into the aisles, where the dancing continues in a more cramped space. Where there is no room for a complete *pas-de-deux* there are biblical figures on their own, sitting on window-sills with fine vistas behind them, with a curtain painted as though fluttering in the breeze, and in such a way that their limbs seem to reach out towards the beholder. This is Baroque in the grand manner, magnificently brazen, restless, deceitful.

One day I will write an anti-guide-book, in the same spirit as the medieval Popes set up anti-Emperors when the actual Emperor did not please them. And San Sigismondo will get the star which it deserves, and I shall call it "a highly rewarding excursion". Upon leaving I reflect that it would be better if bank cashiers wrote guide-books and writers of guide-books cashed cheques.

On our way back we stop at a large country house near Busseto. The bald friend wants to call on the family. Through the narrow hall we are led into the dining-room, which also serves as sitting-room. This is a typical feature of Italian domestic life. Instead of having a living-room with comfortable arm-chairs, like the English, and with a dining-table put somewhere in the background where it will not be in the way, the Italians who have no proper drawing-room go in for a huge, patriarchal dining-table and hard dining-chairs, and sit on them all evening.

Every nation has its own way of making itself uncomfortable. The English like to have lots of separate bedrooms and huddle into one single sitting-room during the day, where they get on each other's nerves. They sacrifice the comfort of their days to the comfort of their nights.

The Central Europeans, on the other hand, want to have as many sitting-rooms as possible, so that each member of the family can work and receive friends in full privacy. Thus, one might find in Vienna a four-roomed flat with not a single bedroom in it. Each of the four sitting-rooms has a divan and is transformed into sleeping-quarters at night, which involves daily acrobatics of folding up tables, letting down hidden cupboards, doubling up eiderdown quilts and shoving them into the oddest hiding-places.

The French are more for show and less for utility. To them it is not enough to have one drawing-room, they must have two. There are occasions in French life when it is proper to receive in the *petit salon* and others when it is *de rigueur* to forgather in the *grand salon*. When there are no guests these *salons* lie fallow. Life without the *grand salon* and the *petit salon* is a dog's life. The French will rather cram their beds into passages and boxrooms than forgo their dignity.

Upon entering, we find an old couple in the dining-room, and while we are being introduced, more and more members of the family appear from various doors till there are about fifteen people assembled. It is like a farcical scene on the stage, something in the vein of the third act of *Der Rosenkavalier*, where Ochs sets about seducing a country wench thinking that he is alone with her in the tavern room, and all the while panels are slid apart and heads pop out and doors open and shut and admit each time a few lookers-on, till in the end the place is as crowded as Lyons Corner House at tea-time.

I try to sort them out. The old man and his wife are rich peasant types, he in tweeds and breeches and jackboots, she in old-fashioned black wool, with a crocheted woollen shawl drawn over her shoulders and fastened with a garnet brooch.

Then, there are two of their daughters. One also in black – but what a black – of a cut and simplicity which only the 'hautest' of *haute couture* can produce. She wears pearls of such beauty that, if my mother had been present she would have said afterwards: "Did you see those pearls? I should have liked to have torn them from her throat."

The other daughter is equally elegant, in sky-blue, closely pleated silk, and adorned with a set of bracelets, ear-rings, and clips which might have come from Cartier's. Further, there are sons and sons-in-law and daughters-in-law and Heaven knows what other aberrations of which family life is capable.

The furniture is mid-Victorian, windows darkened by plush and bobble fringe, cabinets hideously inlaid with coloured woods and mother of pearl, and chairs with carved and pierced splats which force one to sit upright. It is a room made to harbour flowers made of feathers or of shells or of wax. This impression is so strong that, in order to say something to the old woman, I point to a spray of blossoms in a vase, saying: "Aren't they lovely?" really meaning "lovely specimens of artificial flowers," and I am shocked when she replies: "Yes, they come from the magnolia tree in the yard." They are real, live magnolias. A sacrilegious sight.

We get vermouth from a straw-covered bottle of such size that it has to be lifted by a son-in-law with both arms.

The talk is about somebody who has got married to someone else against all expectations – has there ever been a marriage which was not surprising? – and the oil-wells in Cortemaggiore and the Cremonese school of painting of the fourteenth century. The old man talks like a mixture of Berenson and Roger Fry about the Cremonese school, and he also talks about the oil-wells like these two art critics might have done—that is to say, he knows his art and hates his oil. On the table there are a book of poems by Jacques Prévert, who is an *avant-garde* Parisian poet, seed catalogues, and a copy of the latest *House Beautiful*.

Children weave in and out, some dressed, some in night-gowns, some in the process of being undressed. Servants are shrieked for and are told to fetch I don't know what. Dogs are patted and kicked out. I keep wondering what sort of life these people lead, three generations sharing this house in the middle of the country, sitting about in this middle-class room of the last century in their outrageously elegant clothes as though waiting for the beginning of a party which will never take place.

They are not aristocratic. Their past is still with them, they are still drinking out of its glasses and dining off its tables, and it is not closed in by faded green shutters.

We stay for half an hour. From the nature of their good-byes it is clear that they did not expect our call, which means that they did not even dress up for us. And now they will soon sit down to dinner, strictly *en famille*. I shall never understand.

We drive back by night-fall, and in the distance we see one of the derricks of Cortemaggiore, curved in like a Chinese roof and outlined by strings of small lamps.

To-day is Good Friday. When I travel I never know the date, but in this case I knew it was coming sooner or later because the shops have been dressed up for Easter. Easter chickens and Easter eggs are represented but not predominant. Brooding hens are more popular, sitting on nests and hatching socks, ties, spare wireless parts, or whatever else the shopkeeper wants them to hatch. In the pastrycook windows there are fish of sugar or marzipan swimming on billows of paper-wrapped sweets. But the outstanding harbinger of Easter in Cremona seems to be the cake of *brioche* pastry, baked in the shape of a pigeon lying flat with outspread wings, with raisin eyes and almond feathers.

I hope that this description of shop windows at Easter is sober and mature. It reminds me of the days when I was a schoolgirl, and my mother used to beg me to allow her to write my school essays. Indulgent as I was I always let her do them, till, one day in autumn, at the beginning of a new term, when I was twelve years old, we were set a theme called "the shopping streets at Christmas-time". It was an easy theme, given purposely by the teacher of literature, because we had not yet started on anything serious.

I came home and told my mother about it, trusting that it was within the range of her capacity. She started writing at once. I copied it and took it back to school. I was given the mark 2, which was the second best, but underneath the 2 the teacher wrote: "Has worked hard and obtained pleasing effects, but shows a childish enthusiasm and immaturity." I went home furiously, and my mother wept when I told her that this had been the last time that she was given a chance to exercise her bent for writing. I never had trouble of that sort afterwards, with my school essays.

I go to the cathedral. Very good show, beautifully produced. There are about three hundred yards of choirboys, ranged to the left and curving behind the altar, where they disappear out of sight. They kick and scuffle for all they are worth. On the right there is an impressive assembly of priests, some in black, some dressed up in colours resplendent with embroidery. I am sorry for the black ones, they must be livid with envy. To one side, in front of the altar, there are three young men in white surplices, singing.

When I enter they are just singing the story of Christ's interview with Pontius Pilate, and Christ's exceedingly ambiguous answers. The rôles are divided between them. The mild baritone in the centre is the narrator, smooth, urbane, and dispassionate, like a B.B.C. commentator. The metallic baritone is Christ, the melting tenor is Pilate.

No, it is not possible, I tell myself. It must be the other way round. This truly celestial, high sobbing voice must be Christ. Is my Latin as shaky as all this? I will follow more attentively.

The narrator has got to the clamouring Jews, "Crucify him,

crucify." The clamouring Jews are done by the scuffling choirboys with great liveliness. The story moves on. The narrator takes over once more, and tells of Pilate writing at the foot of the cross. Now I must listen carefully. And, sure enough, the angelic high voice bursts forth, sobbing: "I have written what I have written." I was right after all – it is Pilate who sings like an angel.

This is quite wrong, of course. Pilate was an impeccable high Civil Servant, nothing unearthly about him. He was born in Spain and was allowed to take his wife with him to Judaea when he was sent there as a Roman governor. The wife is mentioned in Matthew.

This was exceptional in those times. Generally, wives were not allowed. That Pilate was allowed to take his wife with him to Judea is possibly due to the fact that she had been, when a child, one of the child-mistresses of the Emperor Tiberius. It is even possible that she was the Emperor's own daughter and that, when he divorced her mother, the mother sent him the child to be "educated". Those child-mistresses when grown-up were very difficult to get rid of: nobody wanted to marry them. It probably helped Pilate in his career as Civil Servant when he took this girl as his wife and he may have entered into the marriage for this reason.

Pilate was on very friendly terms with some of the Jewish High Priests, but this would never have swayed him in the favour of the Jews, when the trouble with Christ started. He did not give in to the Jews because he was in sympathy with them—he never was, he liked only a few of them personally – but because he could not afford another uprising, all because of a new religion. New religions were two a penny in those days. I think he retired to the south, when he was pensioned off, to Naples or Sicily, which was ideal for elderly retired gentlemen, because of its wonderful climate and landscape. Pilate is my favourite figure in the New Testament. He is the model of a detached, fair, and judicious colonial governor who hesitates before making a move and prefers tact and negotiation to violence. His question: "What is the truth?" sums up all that can be

said not only about all religions but about all beliefs. I do not think
he said it cynically. I think it was a cry from the heart, the perfect
expression of the human predicament.

The story comes to an end, and I leave. The roles were miscast.
Jesus should have been sung by Pilate, and the other way round. If
I were not so lazy I would write about it to the new Bishop of
Cremona.

I sit down in the café in the cathedral square. It is teeming with
people. It is as crowded as Piccadilly Circus. For a while I look on,
very impressed, till I begin to understand that the crowds do not
work on the same principle as they do in Piccadilly Circus. In the
Circus people come, cross over, and are gone. Others take their
place. Here in Cremona they work like a stage crowd: they appear,
walk across the square, disappear, walk round the back of the
cathedral and emerge again from the other side.

In the afternoon the Pal calls. I tell him that I shall leave on the
following day and he asks me to come to his study in the museum
in the evening, for more medieval music, as a farewell.

For a while we wander through the streets and watch a procession.
The baldachin above the Viaticum is carried, to my surprise, by
four Carabinieri who, to honour the occasion, have replaced the
rosettes on their two-cornered hats with stiff bunches of grey plumes
like glorified shaving-brushes.

"Dearest Edith," says the Pal, "let me hold your hand as a sign of
friendship." I do not think it is a good idea.

Afterwards I go to the Sicilian café in the elbow of the street. The
padrone is dressed in black, because he too has been to Mass this
morning. He asks me to come to-morrow to say good-bye, and
I reflect sadly that he would never ask me to let him hold my hand
as a sign of friendship. For one thing, he would not trouble to ask,
and for another he would not be interested in friendship. The Nico-
demis of this world will never learn.

In the evening I go to the museum. The Pal wants to put on some
more of the chestnut purée music. I know he means well and I know

I should listen with good grace, but I am nervy, as I always am on the eve of a departure.

I say: "You know, couldn't you play something else? This pre-Gregorian chant bores me to tears."

He looks up. "Does it? It bores me, too, you know."

I feel shattered. "Does it really?"

"Of course it does. It is so limited in its range, you know."

He opens the piano. "What shall I play?"

I ask for Gluck's *Orfeo*, one of my favourites.

He finds the score and plays, right through the whole opera. He plays superbly. My God, he can play. From a pimply goat he is transformed into a passionate human being with flashing eyes. I feel ashamed of myself, of all the spiteful thoughts I had about him in the past.

He plays the *Erlkoenig*, with its accompaniment, which is almost unbearably exciting. Then he gets out the score of *Norma*, and chases along to the *finale*, which crashes through the marrow of one's bones. He sits back exhausted. I am exhausted, too.

"You know," he says, looking at me sadly, "music is a disease." Then, as he tidies up and closes the piano, the transfiguration is gone. Once more he is preoccupied with the English language and expressions of the greatest elegance.

He asks me if I will write to him. Like hell I will. And if he writes to me, will I correct his letters and send them back to him?

What's the good? He is as he is. We are all of us made up of bits and pieces. I, too, was ashamed of myself a while ago, and now I have hardened again.

In the morning I telephone to Professor Gualazzini to thank him for his kindness and to say good-bye, but it appears that once more he has broken his father's heart and has gone his own secret ways.

The Sicilian *padrone* is waiting for me. I get a coffee and a Marsala on the house, and I tell him that when I went to Marsala last year I wrote postcards to all my friends, saying: "I am now in Marsala where it comes from."

And so we take leave. He presents me with two bars of *torrone*, a hard, brittle sweetmeat of burnt sugar and coarsely chopped almonds. "It is a speciality of Cremona," he says.   And now I recall those postcards which I have seen in all shops, with a composite picture of the cathedral, a pretty girl with a big bosom, and a bar of *torrone* and the legend beneath it: "The Three Specialities of Cremona."

He does not say: "I hope as you eat the *torrone* you will remember me."

And I do not reply: "I do not need the *torrone* to remember you by." I know I shall never see him again and he knows he will never see me again. I have not walked the streets of Cremona for nothing; I have not looked upon its palaces in vain, reading their message: "Let's be quiet, shall we?"

"Yes, let's be quiet," I think, and pass on my way.

In the hotel, when I ask for the bill, I find Medea and her husband side by side, as meek as lambs. Italian hotel-keepers are scrupulously honest, and when they err it is usually to their disadvantage. I ask them if the bill includes my breakfasts and it turns out that they had forgotten to charge for coffee and egg, butter and *brioche*.

Medea's husband shrugs good-humouredly, saying: "If only all our guests were like the *signora*," and puts it right. I am relieved. Clearly, to-day is not a day for rows.

Then it occurs to me that there was that telephone call to Professor Gualazzini: "I also made a call," I say.

At once Medea's husband is transformed into a lion. "You made a call," he roars, not at me, but at his wife, "the *signora* made a call. And where is it, where, I ask you? Where was it written down? Where is it to be found? Did you intend it to be effaced like footsteps on the sand? The *signora* makes a call and on the contrary of which you go and twiddle your thumbs. Ah, women, women."

It is no use telling him that his grammar is all wrong, its wrongness hinging on that unfortunate "on the contrary of which," because now Medea seems to have grown in stature and gets ready to invoke the gods. The drama is well on its way, slain children, poisoned gown, dragons, and all.

It is the luggage-boy who alone has kept his head.

"*Per carità*," he says to me, "tell me where to you made this call so that we know how much to charge."

"To Professor Gualazzini," I say.

The luggage-boy puts his hands to his mouth, forming a funnel to increase the sound of his voice and, like a sailor shouting to his mate above the turmoil of the waves, he yells across to the ill-matched and vociferous couple: "It was only a local call."

What a brain that boy has got. His words work magic. Medea's husband throws my bill on the counter and turns away with quiet disgust. "It is nothing, *signora*. We do not charge for local calls."

He seems to have lost all appetite for being an hotel-keeper. Medea, too, has become dispirited. "Life holds no beauty for me," she remarks. "I pray for the day when our Lady above will call me to her," and she leaves.

I fully appreciate the subtlety of her words, insinuating as they do that it is a female deity who holds the threads of our lives.

It is left to the luggage-boy to take my money, receipt the bill, and give me change. I think he is wasted in Cremona. I think he should go to Venice or Taormina. With that brain of his he is bound to go a long way.

PARMA

In the train I reflect on the pictures of the Cremonese school which I saw before leaving. There was, of course, a whole, big roomful with the various Campis; I counted six different Christian names, and then abandoned my attempt to penetrate into the labyrinth of their family relationships. They are all tremendously professional in the best meaning of the word and, as is shown, they will tackle anything and illustrate any subject for any purpose.

This reminds me how, during the war, there was one branch of the War Office which put on its walls morale-building posters and slogans. One of these read: "Give us the tools and we'll do the job." And another following on to this: "We'll do it. What is it?"

Beneath it a wit had written: "We did it. What was it?"

Now, the Campis' motto could have been: "We'll do it. What is it?" Whereas the motto of some contemporary painters—whom I should love to mention – could be: "We did it. What was it?"

Near the Campi room there was a huge picture, somewhat later than the Campis, I think seventeenth century: a heroic knight on a white charger amidst magnificent autumnal foliage, the horse wading through the gold and the red. When I expressed my admiration, the picture owl said: "You can hardly call this a picture. It is mere *décor*." He was also quite unenthusiastic about some marvellous Madonnas of the fourteenth century, done by masters whose names I had never heard of. Only politeness stopped him from yawning into my face, the way owlie did that day in the garden. I have the impression that among owls it is considered good style to admire nothing. For a historian of art, beauty and ugliness do not exist. There is only the important and the less important, and the trend which created an influence and the trend which led to nothing further.

Those early Madonnas were done in the way I like: the Madonna in the middle, generally on a throne, and on either side, a bit beneath her, a saint. The Madonna has a gown of red and a mantle of blue. One saint is dressed in yellow and the other in green. It is the old, well-tried recipe which Raphael picked up and raised to the greatest heights.

In these pictures the master does not try to be clever, nor does he try to produce something new and problematical. And he created a work of purity and clarity and serenity which is extraordinarily soothing to me. As Plato said, only the like can understand the like. And whenever I look at a picture like this, I feel that I, too, must have a small share of purity and clarity and serenity, otherwise the painting could not reach out to me and draw me inside and make me breathe for a while the luminous air behind the blue hills. This is why I can never make friends with people who do not care for that type of art. And though I never ask anyone, upon making an acquaintance, about his feelings for Raphael, I can generally guess with accuracy and find that I have been right. This is as good a way of judging people as most others, but though it works for me I could never recommend it.

I get out at Parma. My idea of Parma is Edwardian, derived from tales of my mother's youth.

Parma means Parma violets, a large bunch of them pinned to a lady's fur. The garment is a stole or a cape. And the fur from which it is made is, of course, chinchilla. Already in my childhood it was a legendary fur, almost extinct. I saw it on only two occasions, when it had the shabby nobility of an old Rolls-Royce. But its name had a whispering, sibilant enchantment recalling the rustle of taffeta petticoats, the crunching of sugared almonds.

Those were the days of *demi-mondaines*, and I imagine that those ladies used to wear huge compositions of Parma violets, fastened with a long slim brooch set with a single black pearl, arranged on an ivy leaf and with the stems wrapped in silver paper. The decent women wore bunches of a modest size.

Parma violets could be worn one day only, because they lost their

fragrance when put into water. They were the true flowers of lavish-
ness.

In Parma the houses are pale grey and white striped, like chinchilla; the windows are draped with violet-blue, and the squares are
steeped in the twilight of the fading day, with veiled ladies hastening
through the blue hour, the violets on their throats already wilting,
to reach their lovers, who will not wait after the violets have
exhaled their last breath of scent.

I take a taxi and drive to the hotel with the strange name of
"Button". It lies near the main square, behind a grey Renaissance
palace which has suffered from architectural small-pox; that is to
say, its walls are pitted with square holes. The driver tells me those
holes are provided for the pigeons. Though I cannot think of a
better explanation, I do not believe it.

One part of the *piazza* is formed by a long, yellow building with
a clock-tower in the centre; on one side I can see a tiny Baroque
façade, also yellow, surmounted by a grey dome. The general
impression is grey and yellow, grey and yellow, as far as the eye can
see.

It is not the yellow of spring, like primroses and crocuses, or the
yellow of late summer, like ripe pears and ripe corn. It is the yellow
of old age, of yellowed ivory, yellowed prints, yellowed kid gloves.
I was not so wrong after all. The grey and the yellow, the colours
of Parma, are those of old chinchilla, when the white has faded and
the grey has remained.

The hotel is grander than the hotel in Cremona. There is a car
park, and an attendant in top hat and livery of chinchilla yellow.

At the reception desk I find an old lady who smokes a cigarette
from a long black holder, which gives her an air of devilment, and
a cowed, thin youth in porter's livery. This, too, is a family set-up,
owner with grandson.

In Italy, most hotels are not only owned by a family but also
staffed by it. Here, for instance, the old lady acts as day receptionist,
one of her sons as night clerk, another son as accountant, a daughter-

in-law as catering member, the grandson as porter. Only the large hotels *de luxe* are owned by companies and then very often they are foreign, Swiss or German.

There are three lounges and a bar, all filled with business-men, who tell each other how much they paid for their cars. The air is thick with smoke, the wireless emits two different programmes at the same time, one superimposed on the other, and the barman rattles cups and glasses. An occasional hiss from the coffee-machine provides the punctuation to this symphony of restlessness. As I walk up the stairs I reflect sadly that it is not surprising that so many people to-day have no time for Raphael. They mistake his seraphic calm for emptiness.

My room has non-committal blond furniture, the water is very hot, and the price moderate – only slightly more than at the Roma. My window gives on to a cul-de-sac forming a tiny, irregular square with two small palaces and a restaurant screened by a green hedge – a sleeping beauty of a restaurant. One would never find it if one looked for it. It is called Fontana.

My guide-book tells me that "the cathedral in Parma is not to be missed". I have not yet seen the cathedral. On the other hand, I saw about six cafés on the Piazza Garibaldi, one flowing into the other, and to be told apart only by the blossoming of different coloured sunshades, forming a floral border after my own heart.

I grow very proverbial: What the eye does not see the heart does not grieve over. Therefore, I shall not grieve over the cathedral, but I shall grieve over the cafés if I do not visit them. Also, the cathedral will still be there to-morrow, but I cannot drink to-morrow to-day's vermouth. And here is another proverb: Never put off for the morrow what you can do to-day. This, clearly, must have been coined for coffee-housing. Let me never in the future deplore my lost opportunities. Let me never ask: "*Mais où sont les apéritifs d'antan?*"

On my way to the *piazza* I pass the pock-marked palace and find several newspaper stands housed under the arches of the *loggia*. I buy the one and only copy of the *Continental Daily Mail*, and begin to read it over my white vermouth. The *C.D.M.* is edited in Paris, and, therefore, most printed readers' letters have some bearing on France. Year in year out these letters are the same. They say how nice the French are and how nasty the French are, how generous and how mercenary, how good French cooking is and how atrociously over-rated. Also, the inevitable reply: "If 'Disgruntled' finds French cooking liverish, let him stay in England. I, for one, can assure him that the French have brought cooking to such an art that it can withstand . . ." and so on. Signed "*Vive la France*". And then there is the crossword puzzle. Last year and the year before I was able to fill in all the squares at the end of two months in Italy, working up from a start of about a half. Now I see that the level has risen to un-dreamt-of heights of refinement. There is hardly an entry to which I know the answer. What, for instance, do you call money given to shipwrecked sailors? As our cook would have said: "Seeing that I've never done it, I'm sure I couldn't say."

On the next day I find, to my delight, a reader's letter complaining about the crossword puzzle. "Only a warped and perverted mind could find the answers to the clues," and he laments the past days of the golden age when all was idyllic ease and simplicity. I also check up on the solution of the previous day. It is "sinking fund". What a pervertedly far-fetched solution. As warped as the raft on which I hope they all sank.

At dinner I am very hungry. I start with *fettucine al ragoût*. They are long, flat noodles, less difficult to negotiate than *spaghetti* because they are two-dimensional, whereas *spaghetti* are three-dimensional and can, therefore, evade you in three ways, instead of only two, like the noodles. The *fettucine* are hellish, just the same.

At first I wind them round the fork and find that they behave like the crowds in the cathedral square in Cremona: while one end is being wound up, the other end – which I believed already secured – strays loose and expects to make a come-back once more. I get tired and just shove them into my mouth. It is no use. A non-Italian can-not look dignified while eating *pasta*. The wise traveller will eat his starch of such reduced size that it is almost one-dimensional, like a dot, such as *pastina* or rice. Or, he can go to the other extreme and eat *pasta* compressed into towering shapes, like the *lasagne al forno*, which consists of layers spread with meat sauce and baked into a cake, which can be divided into morsels to one's liking.

To-day is my birthday. "Would you like a whole carafe of wine?" I ask myself, tenderly. Yes, I would.

And now to the cathedral. I fortify myself with another glance into the guide-book. The guide-book calls it "impressive". The word "impressive" is always a bad sign. It means that the guide-book writer has scraped the bottom of the barrel, for want of other words. An impression can be good or bad: so it lets him off nicely.

As soon as I enter the cathedral square I get a shock of revulsion. Talk of functional. I did not know that the twelfth century could produce anything quite so beastly.

This is what must have happened, I think, as I gaze at the inordinately high front rising in a stepped-up outline, reminiscent of the stepped-up gables of the old warehouses on the Trave in Lübeck. The citizens of Parma thought they must have a cathedral because all the other towns had one, too. The architect they commissioned for the work did not believe in God in the way most people believed in God at the time. I imagine he thought of God as a sort of mathematical formula, in the manner of early Greek philosophers, like: "God has the shape of a spiral, winding higher and higher but always returning upon itself"; or: "God is his own prisoner" or: "the essence of God is geometry." Anyway, something utterly cheerless like that.

Besides, he was not really interested in God at all. Also, he had no time for saints and angels. He would have much rather built a factory, but there was no demand for factories in those days. So he got down to it and made a design straight up and narrow and coming to a point at the top, the plainest pattern he could think of.

At the time it was fashionable to have little arched colonnades strung like galleries round the walls, supporting exactly nothing. So he stuck those on, saying, "Thank you for nothing", and framed the stepped-up top with them as well, till it ends in a point. It was also fashionable in those days to put stone lions in front of the portal, guarding the steps leading inside, and, therefore, he shoved in a couple of lions, and very bad-tempered beasts they are, too, and constipated-looking. Thus the Parmesans did not get a cathedral but a factory for praying, a storehouse for absolutions, and a distribution centre for the spreading of the glory of God.

I step inside – I might just as well. But how beautiful it is. Every inch of wall is covered with paintings, and the ribs of the vault are banded thickly in gilt. In the cupola above the choir there are frescoes by Correggio and I stand there like the ox in front of the gate. They look wonderful. That is to say, they make you feel as though you were asked: "Would you like some of this cake?" and you would reply: "I'd love a slice. It looks wonderful." In other words, the Correggio paintings look wonderfully promising, and I am sure that they would look wonderful if I could see them properly.

It is always the same with church paintings. If they are on the wall more or less at eye-level one cannot see them because it is so dark, and when they are near the light, in the dome, they are so high up one cannot see them either.

For a while I fight against the crick in my neck and gaze into Correggio's exceedingly pleasant heaven, sky-pink, sky-blue, and clouded white, with cherubs strewing flowers in all directions. It is a rendering of the Assumption, and seems deliciously lively.

On the high altar there is a row of Baroque candlesticks, gigantic and wrought of silver, resting on scrolled three-legged supports. It is a sight which would warm the heart of any Mayfair interior decorator. It is a pleasant surprise to see them just for once in their proper place and being used for what they were meant to be used, instead of seeing them deprived of their lily-white tapers, wired for electricity, over-hatted with a lampshade, and shedding light on a stock-broker's evenings.

Slightly behind the cathedral I find San Giovanni, a big, hefty church, wavering between Renaissance and Baroque. No doubt it was put there, so near the cathedral, to vex the church-going public.

Inside it looks like a drawing-room with the pillars clad in red figured damask, too polite for words. Again there are some frescoes by Correggio and Parmigianino, practically invisible.

The next item on the menu is the baptistery. It is twelfth-century, and of course it is octagonal. I have never yet seen a baptistery of that period which wasn't. I should be quite prepared to be resigned about this if I knew the explanation for it. Last year, in Brescia, I went to see the town with an archaeologist who specialized in this period in the north of Italy. While we were looking at some frescoes it suddenly occurred to me to ask him about this octagonal business. He said: "When we get out of here I will tell you." We left, and when I asked him again he said he would tell me after we had seen the Victory by Praxiteles. After the Victory he said he would tell me after we had seen the Cross of Galla Placidia. We left and, in the street I reminded him of his promise. He said: "I don't really know." This attitude of his reminds me of what I have read about the arrangements of Egyptian temples: from a large hall containing statues of many gods one comes into smaller and smaller rooms with fewer and fewer gods, till, in the end, one stands in a tiny room which is empty.

The baptistery is to the cathedral what the dot is to the exclamation mark. It, too, is built in the plainest possible manner, with four rows of colonnades ringing round it, one above the other. The walls are dark, high, and narrow. It is hardly more engaging to look at than a block of council flats. I could imagine it being entirely occupied by dentists, the colonnades being used for airing bibs and forceps.

The only ornament is a sculptured frieze of fawns and roe deer, rather charming, but placed so low down on the walls that one does

not notice it at first. Heaven forbid that the architect should have
been accused of seeking to create cheap effects and of pandering to
the popular yearning for the pretty-pretty. It is clear that he had the
medieval equivalent of the modern obsession peculiar to the American male: the fear of being thought a 'sissy' and the desire to be
a hundred-per-cent he-man with architectural hair on his chest.
Very well, I will say this for him: structurally, there is nothing sweet
and lovely about either cathedral or baptistery.

The door is closed and I, according to instructions from the guide-
book, fetch the custodian from a house opposite. This is a kind way
of putting it. Shame on the guide-book. It says: "If closed, apply to
custodian at No. 2." Actually, it is No. 3.

The custodian, like most of his breed, is a pensioned-off old
sergeant. He is stoic in face of my request. I know that he will spare
me any drivel about the baptistery and that he will accept his tip
without thanks. He takes the keys from a nail, picks up a copper
vessel and fills it with water from a tap in the hall. When we enter
the baptistery he empties the water into the font in the middle.
This octagonal basin is hewn out of a reddish-brown monolith, and
was used for bodily immersion. It is not used any more, so why is
it kept filled with water?

Perhaps because water is the keynote of the whole place. As one
comes in one has the feeling of having become a plain fish in an
aquarium filled with jewelled fish. The eight outside walls have been
transformed into sixteen niches which surround me like the walls of
sixteen gigantic waves, curving and rising towards me, ready to
overwhelm me, flowing with kings and saints on a ground of
watery blue.

Each niche is divided into panels of quite arbitrary size, large
and small, square and oblong, all jumbled together. It is as though
a child had started to draw a picture without planning it first and
then, when it found still some space left on the wall, had added
more and more pictures till it had used up all its paint. But, some
child, some pictures. They are done by the Giotto school – or

perhaps not – but I can't think of anything else, and the way the figures stare at you, all facing you dead face-level, increases the feeling that one is being stared at by swarms of gorgeous sacred fish.

Then, raising one's glance, one meets more saints and kings staring down from the eight-fold vaulted ceiling.

Only now do I realize how beautifully urbane are people like Correggio, who make their saints look at each other so that they do not trouble the beholder. This ceiling, done three hundred years before Correggio, is over-powering in its Byzantine, insistent no-nonsense glory. Quite uncompromising.

Each saint looks down at me, firmly fixed in space by a gilded outline, and seems to say: "I am the well-known Saint So-and-so. My credentials are impeccable. Here is my saint's emblem. Here is my staff. Here is my martyr's crown – see? Here is my halo. But – who are you?"

I feel uncomfortable. How very different from the sophisticated creatures done by the Campi crowd in San Sigismondo. These were so busy to put themselves into the best possible poses for elegant funeral pyres and fashionable toastings on the rack that they were fully occupied with their doings and did not ask awkward questions. But then, they were painted in the late sixteenth century, and were spell-bound by the technique of foreshortening and perspective, of leaning backward and twisting forward, and this distracted their attention from the beholder. Though in the process the fear of God seems to have got lost. One cannot have everything.

I get out of the baptistery, or rather, swim out. I am still dazed, and decide to go to the hairdresser.

Here in Parma, as in most Italian towns, I have noticed the sleekly groomed heads of the women. They all look as though they had just been to the hairdresser and, not only this, but as though they had been to the best Parisian hairdresser.

Elsewhere, so many women have their hair dulled and frizzed by perms and nightly putting into curlers. The hair of the Italian woman flows in a smooth curve from the forehead to the nape of the neck.

Any fool can have curls, each curl standing on its own and destroying the general outline. It is much more difficult to have a sculptured head. How do the Italian women achieve it? Looking at them, one knows that the classical tradition is still alive.

As soon as I sit down the hairdresser gets out his scissors and snips away.

One must never tell an Italian hairdresser what to do. It would be like telling Raphael how to arrange his figures in space. One must never argue with the Italian hairdresser. He has argued with petulant women all his life and is invincible. One must also never deprive him of the pleasure of telling you that the individual who did your hair previously was a vile irresponsible brute who should have been cut up into strips and fed to the pigs.

Like most of his kind, once the hairdresser starts cutting he does not know when to stop. But does anybody, ever? Watching myself shedding enough hair to stuff a pillow, I venture to remark that I am going to look like a plucked chicken.

"Perhaps, *signora*. But like a fashionably plucked chicken."

I prefer to close my eyes, it makes me giddy looking at this hairy massacre. The superiority of the eye in regard to the other senses lies in the fact that one can close it.

And still the scissors continue to click. I say, breaking my own rules: "Don't cut off too much."

"I really wanted to stop just now, *signora*. But as you insist I will take off a little bit more."

At last I rise, tamed. I am sorry to say that my hair looks enchanting. I express my gratitude.

"I know you, *signora*," says the hairdresser; "you have to be forced for your own good. Now you are pleased. But if I had told you before that you would be pleased you would not have believed me." He is quite right, too.

On the following day I go to the Pilotta. This is the Farnese palace and is called Pilotta after the name of a Renaissance ball game, rather like tennis, which used to be played in one of the courtyards.

It is an immense building, plain and grey, with small windows which look inadequate. But then, elephants, too, have small eyes. From those small windows one can guess that the Farnese family felt none too secure when they took over the government of Parma. I can see the first Farnese Duke of Parma walking up and down in his frescoed rooms and biting his nails and wondering if it would be safe to ride out this morning. The palace is really a fortress, though situated on flat ground and lacking gunpowder towers and crenellations. It is a fortress built for defence, not for aggression.

The Farnese family got into Parma because there was a Pope who was a Farnese, and he asked Charles V to create the Duchy of Parma and Piacenza and to give it to his son. The idea was that the Duchy would be a thorn in the flesh of France and Spain, and would prevent their getting too powerful. Charles V did as he was asked. In those days nobody minded if Popes had sons. It was only in later days that the Popes got coy and called their offspring 'nephews'.

This reminds me of a story about a Pope who died not so long ago. As soon as he was installed in the Vatican he celebrated an orgy of what is called nepotism, and found offices for all the members of his family. There was one problem child, a young man who was not over-loaded with brains, and no one knew what sort of work to give him. In the end the Pope found an employ suitable to this young man's intelligence, and gave him the office of waker-upper, that is to say, every morning the youth had to come to the Pope's bedroom, knock, and enter. Then he would say: "Good morning, uncle, your Holiness. It is seven o'clock, and it is a fine day"; and the Pope would answer: "Thank you, my child, I know it, and God knows it, too."

One morning this scene took place once more: "Good morning, uncle, your Holiness. It is seven o'clock, and it is a fine day."

"Thank you, my child, I know it and God knows it, too."

"No, he doesn't, uncle, your Holiness, because it's nine o'clock and it's raining like hell."

The picture gallery of Parma is housed in one wing of the Pilotta. I have an introduction to the Signora Quintavalle, the keeper's wife. She is a small, dark woman with smouldering black eyes. She has an intense searching air, and it is an effort for her to smile. She is made of much better stuff than the owls of Cremona, and as we start on our tour through the gallery I know that she will not mind if I admire the right things for wrong reasons and *vice versa*, as long as she is satisfied that I am sincere. I shall struggle and she will redeem me.

We start with the early Emilian school.

Right opposite the entrance there is an Araldi which, so I am told, is a mystery picture. It is a St. Sebastian of great loveliness, naked, with a yellow sash tied round his middle, the ends fluttering against the background of a rocky wooded landscape. He has an arrow stuck through his forehead, but it does not seem to worry him. He takes his sufferings as a matter of course. Probably he has reached the stage described as desirable by Oscar Wilde, when "yellow satin consoles you for almost everything in life". He would have been approved by Oscar altogether because, though clad only with this sash, he manages to look a perfect dandy.

Lovely and lovable though he is, he is a source of worry to the Signora Quintavalle: he himself is painted in the Italian manner, but the landscape behind him is done in the German style. She is forced to conclude that Araldi knew Dürer and that he was something of a copy-cat. She also entreats me not to confuse this particular Araldi with all the other painters of that name, to whom he was in no way related. She need not have worried. Having never heard of them, how could I?

On the wall opposite, another handsome young man is being burnt with waffle-irons by two grey-clad soldiers. The marks on his body give the effect of batik on a scarf. He is not worried, either. Near the St. Sebastian there are three versions of the Madonna and saints, one beautiful, the other two good in parts, but on the whole clumsy and top-heavy. The beautiful one was done by Mazzola, and the two others by two other members of the Mazzola family. The Signora Quintavalle grows apologetic: "You see, I know they are not up to much. We are showing them only out of a sense of decency because these two were his uncles. They were very poor and they couldn't afford to study much and had to earn their living at an early age, and we are sorry for them."

As we walk from room to room I keep watching her eyes. They are smouldering all the time, but I know that sooner or later they will burst into fire. When will it be? It is like playing a guessing game with myself, getting warm, getting hot. Cima da Conegliano, Bassano, Schiavone, Beato Angelico, Paolo Veneziano – still cold. Now we enter the room where Correggio takes over. For a while we stand in silence in front of the Virgin and St. Jerome. Ah – hot, burning.

Here is none of the clarity of the early masters. Here everything is suffused and veiled by the golden glow peculiar to Correggio, in such a way that one cannot say whether the gold is spreading from without or within.

Also, the figures are not set out each on his own but there is an entrancing muddle of heads and limbs which takes up all the space so that the background barely gets a look in.

"Correggio, and after him Parmigianino, are the founders of the school of Parma," says the Signora Quintavalle.

"Of course," I say, "Correggio is one of the very great. But was the Parma school important as an influence?"

And now the flames are leaping into her eyes. "Tremendously important," she says; "you see, the Parma school is one of the two main branches of mannerism."

This is an occasion, where – unlike the case of palaeology – I want to know.

It appears that the first mannerist was – who would have thought it? – Michelangelo. Strictly speaking he himself did not know that he was a mannerist, but we know now. To be a mannerist you must be two things; first, a painter, second, tired.

Michelangelo was sick to death with the way most of his contemporaries painted. For instance, he could not stand the sight of landscapes any more. What was the good of painting landscape backgrounds when you could see landscapes a penny a dozen all over Italy in real life? And what was the good of painting hands like real hands and the stuff of gowns like real gowns, if one could see them all the time on real people? As life held for him no excitement any more he turned upon himself and painted what he chose to imagine and not what he saw. First of all he eliminated all landscape. This can be seen in the Capella Sistina, where he painted human figures only. Then, he made flesh look like marble, like stone, like iron. His composition, too, became forced, unnatural, and manufactured.

"For instance," says the Signora Quintavalle, "do you remember the Holy Family with angels, in the Uffizi?"

I do.

"There you are. It's done all in the round, with the cloak of the Virgin wrapped round her in a way you cannot wrap a cloak, and the angels also wrapped round her in a way no angels can be made to behave."

I do not know the way for angels to behave, but I am beginning to understand her.

She leads me into another room, to the marriage of St. Catherine, by Parmigianino. "Observe this. No hand ever looked like this. He painted a hand made of metal, in hues and texture. And look at this drapery. Again it is painted as though it were wrought of metal."

We return to the Correggios and then go back to the Parmigianinos. Some of these are frescoes, done in half-moon lunettes, ripped from God knows what walls. I don't care how important Parmigianino was – in those frescoes I loathe him. Here, the sun-kissed golden honey of Correggio has become spun sugar dyed yellow. Here, the veiling technique of the master has degenerated into curly-wurly soap-suds to cover up the lack of modelling.

What annoys me so much about the Parmigianino of those

lunettes is, that he was really such an outstandingly good painter when he wanted. The marriage of St. Catherine, for instance, is marvellous. So is the portrait called "The Turkish Slave". There is nothing Turkish about it except the turban and, considering that she is supposed to be a slave, the young girl looks very self-possessed, in the true meaning of the word.

With my eyes attuned to mannerism I can now see how Parmigianino fretted and strove to use the rounded twists of the turban as the key-note for the whole picture, and how he arranged everything else in rounded layers too, to follow suit.

I leave the Pilotta, still pondering all the Signora Quintavalle told me.

We talked French together, and in her beautifully correct French she kept referring to Parmigianino as "*le Parmesan*". Probably this is the name by which he is called in French art criticism, but it is not quite right. In Italian, Parmesan is *Parmigiano* whereas Parmigianino means the "little Parmesan". Up till now the word 'Parmesan' has meant only one thing: the cheese. I am sure the cheese was eaten long before Parmigianino's birth, and even to-day it is more famous than the painter. And so, as I have visited the little Parmesan, I feel I must now make a culinary pilgrimage to the great Parmesan. I should go and see Professor Lodi and Professor Castellani to whom I have been given letters of introduction. But I feel more inclined towards the cheese.

I return to the hotel, and tell the porter-grandson of my intention. "Nothing easier," he says.

In the evening he tells me that he has arranged everything. Signor Bianchi will call for me in the morning. And then, brutally, without any preparations, he delivers the blow: "Signor Bianchi will call for you at seven o'clock. You see, the cheese is always made early in the day."

"Damn the cheese," I say, and he replies with the beautiful Italian proverb which says that the early morning hour has gold in the mouth. I do not care for gold in the mouth. The Italians go in for gold fillings in their teeth, which I find atrocious. I prefer to be dazzled in other ways.

In the morning it is raining hard. Descending the stairs I recall Verlaine:

> *"Il pleure dans mon coeur*
> *Comme il pleut sur la ville;*
> *Quelle est cette langueur*
> *Qui pénètre dans mon coeur?"*

The langour does not penetrate my heart for long. The rain is nothing, because Signor Bianchi has a car. Also, he is tall, fair, charming, the typical ex-cavalry officer, and he kisses my hand. He is the director of the cheese factory, and manager of the milk-bottling centre of Parma. He says he likes it, because he can do what he wants. He is one of those people who possess that rare combination of openness and dignity which makes one feel that one can ask them anything one wants on the spur of the moment, and they will reply without being surprised or annoyed.

"Does this mean," I say, "that you can water the milk at liberty?"

"I could if I wanted to," he says. "But I don't. For one thing, milk is plentiful in Emilia. We are in the centre of dairy-farming. And secondly, I would have to bribe the people from the laboratory when they test the milk, and it would not be worth the trouble."

We drive out of the town and out of the suburbs till we are in the country, rain-sodden and slopping with mud. We turn into a small farmyard bordered by a modest dwelling-house and out-buildings. This is the factory.

Parmesan cheese factories are small because nobody ever gets enough milk for big-scale production. In one day two cheeses are made, sometimes less, according to the mood of the cows.

We enter an outbuilding. It has a stone-flagged floor traversed by a gutter filled with a steaming greenish liquid, and all the floor is swimming in this liquid too.

There are two men standing in front of vast copper vats filled with that same steaming green water, which they stir with an out-size wooden spoon. They wear rubber boots and white smocks, and look like a cross between sailors and hygienically garbed sorcerers. The vats are heated by pipes sprouted from stone-built baking-ovens, which serve as boilers or something of the kind, and look very old-fashioned.

"We have come at a good moment," says Signor Bianchi. "The cheese is nearly finished."

Nearly finished. Then it must be somewhere. But where? Where is the elusive cheese? I can nowhere see anything like a Parmesan. He draws me towards one of the cauldrons, where the brew looks sicklier than ever. There is a controlled excitement in the movements of the men, who now seem to be fishing for something which eludes them.

The cheese is formed, I am told. What I see is the rest of the milk. The sorcerers continue to grapple with the invisible and now, for an instant, there is a whitish moon bobbing to the surface and submerging again. If I were told it is the face of Moby Dick the White Whale I should believe it.

Slowly, gingerly, the white whale is caught once more and brought up. A great deal depends on this moment because, if the cheese breaks it is no good. They lug it out safe and whole.

It is of the size of a small cartwheel. It looks soft and rubbery and is of greenish pallor, like the face of a person who has fainted. It is put into a wooden mould on a table and covered with a board and weighed down with a stone.

The Parmesan is an antique cheese, and one cannot make it with modern methods. For instance, the milk has to be the milk of the night before, but it must not be sour and yet it must not be milk which has been kept on ice. It has to be stored overnight in a cool cellar. Up till now there is no way of imitating the temperature of a cool cellar.

Also, it cannot be warmed with steam heat or anything new-fangled; the coppers have to be heated from the bottom only, and the milk must be stirred continually with movements which no machine can imitate.

It pleases me to hear this. It also pleases me to see that the stone on top of the cheese is just a large stone picked up on a road.

We now go to the main building, which has been turned into a storeroom fitted with shelves. There, several hundred cheeses repose in various degrees of ripeness. The older they are the harder they look. It takes two years for them to reach maturity, and again, I am told, it is impossible to speed up this time by any modern method.

A ripe Parmesan when broken is greyish yellow, like weathered stone, and almost as hard as a rock. It breaks with an irregular, rugged surface. It forms a rind by itself from the effect of the air. There are people who give the rind a coat of black varnish, and I gather that those people are, as an Italian hairdresser would say, vile, irresponsible brutes fit to be cut into strips and fed to the pigs. And in this case there are pigs to whom one could feed them.

They are pink, with partly black faces which give them a debonair and raffish look. They get all the sickly whey left over from the cheese – they are welcome to it – and their ultimate end is *coppa* and ham. This is called planned economy.

We now have seen to what end the cheese can go, but we have not yet seen its beginnings. I am led to a byre, where I find a dozen cows. They are all of the same smooth, lovely fawn, and there is a bull of exactly matching shade. They are from Switzerland. They supply about a third of the milk needed. The country round Parma is the best dairy country in Italy, and there are many little farms which produce their own independent Parmesan. In summer, when milk is short, the Parma milk is sent to Rome.

We go back to the car. Signor Bianchi tells me that his men are good reliable men with great skill and heads free from Socialist rubbish. When he was new in his job he threw out nearly all the employees and picked new ones himself, ones whom he could like. "If I like them then they like me and we are all happy," he says. He is quite right. I am sure I would have done the same in his place.

We drive towards the town. We must now see the bottling centre. It is the most up-to-date of its kind in Europe.

I do not like seeing places which are the most up-to-date of their kind in Europe; there is nothing more depressing than to see so much efficiency concentrated in one spot. I am sorry to have to say this, but in the world of to-day, which is as it is, slackness and corruption are often the saving graces of humanity and take the place of kindness and charity, and mercifully counteract the horrors of efficiency.

I am sure that Hitler's gas chambers, too, were the "most up-to-date of their kind in Europe", and that the poor devils who escaped were helped only by the slackness and corruption of the guards.

I try to wriggle out of the bottling centre by saying that I have already taken up too much of Signor Bianchi's time. Always when I do not want people to waste my time I tell them that I am wasting theirs.

But it is no good. Signor Bianchi has set aside a whole morning for my instructive delectation, and the morning is, alas, still young. We halt in the suburbs in front of one of those beastly gates which open themselves by themselves, and drive into the factory yard. This time we enter a real factory, with wheels revolving and ribbons sliding and levers chugging up and down. There is the hissing of steam and the clanking of iron and the clinking of the bottles, and one cannot hear one's own words. Agony. I am always miserable in places where one cannot talk.

They seem to have got an awful lot of bottles. As far as I can make out they first get hold of the empty bottles and then they fill them. I cannot see anything marvellous in this, but I am told that it is truly marvellous because the milk flows into the bottles not in the ordinary way – that is to say by the force of gravity – but is compelled inside by suction.

We go outside for a while, and Signor Bianchi wants to explain to me something about a created vacuum in the bottles and asks me if I know physics. I don't.

This is not entirely my own fault, because my natural science

teacher was Monsieur Roche. His lessons were famous. He was
a great believer in experiments, and no experiment ever came off,
always owing to "the humidity in the air". His chemical experiments miscarried too, as well as stinking horribly and unaccount-
ably.

Once, while giving us a demonstration, he made the following
pronouncement: "During the course of this experiment you will
see small bubbles rising to the surface of the liquid, but you will not
see them because they are so small."

At the time we thought this screamingly funny, but I think there
is more to it than that. I think in a way this remark sums up one of
the plights of humanity. We are constantly told of things which we
cannot grasp and cannot verify, and yet we are expected to believe
in them and to act as though they were real to us.

Monsieur Roche also taught botany, and there, too, he tried to
make a demonstration out of everything. Thus he had huge models
made of wood and cardboard representing plant pollen and spores
and suchlike. One day these were brought out and we were told to
pass them to each other and to have a good look at them.

"They are not complete, though," he remarked morosely; "last
year I also had female reproductive organs, but I mislaid them."

Monsieur Roche often gave us to understand that he was not
impressed with our efforts, saying: "With me, you will never get
on to a green branch," or: "Edith drowns. Edith screams for help.
I happen to pass by on the shore. I see Edith drowning. I also see
a boat moored near by. It would be easy for me to get into the boat
and save Edith. But I pass on. I let Edith drown." And I nearly
did drown once, when I was so bad in mathematics that things
looked very black for me. The head of the school decreed that
I should have to pass a special examination if I wanted to get into
next year's class. Monsieur Roche was ominous too, repeating his
non-life-saving parable and varying it with another, where I was
screaming for help trapped in a blazing house.

The examination took place as follows: Monsieur Roche set me a problem and then worked it out himself with great speed. At the end, showing me the result, he said: "*Vous savez donc bien qu'une racine peut-être oubien positive oubien negative. Dans ce cas-là la racine est po- po- pos ——*"

And I said: "Positive."

He feigned surprise. "*Mais très bien, vous avez donc bien étudié*," and passed me. Yes, thank God, for inefficiency.

Anyway, in the end the bottles are capped with silver paper and on it they stamp the date, not to-day's date but a future date which shows till what time the milk will keep.

Signor Bianchi swears that the milk is in no way diluted. I have my doubts. My eyes tell me that English milk looks much more the way one likes milk to look.

Apparently the only way in which the milk is messed about, apart from being pasteurized, is that it passes through a filter. He shows me a filter which has filtered for two hours. It must have filtered like mad. It is filthy with straw, grass, grit, flakes of mud and other stuff of which he quite rightly remarks: "Better not to know." I agree with him. One must not know everything.

He takes me to his office, which is blissfully quiet and panelled with tropical wood and laid with a handsome Persian carpet.

We finish our drinks and drive back to the town, go into a café, and talk about horses till midday. Signor Bianchi, cavalier that he is, assures me that his car will be always at my command whenever I wish it.

He takes me back to the Button and, upon leave-taking, he hands the porter a parcel to be carried to my room. As soon as he has gone I throw myself on the parcel and tear it open. It contains a chunk of Parmesan weighing roughly four pounds.

"It is wonderful," I wail, "but what shall I do with it?"

"Take it with you on your journey and nibble at it each day like a little mouse," says the porter. I shall see.

In the afternoon, Professor Lodi comes to see me. He is youngish, round, and fair, and well on the way to becoming an owl. I am beginning to wonder where they all come from. Is there, perhaps, a labour exchange in Italy which trains people for university posts and accepts only those with a certain physique?

He has not got the light touch of Professor Gualazzini. For instance, when we come to the inevitable Guelfs and Ghibellines, he tells me that I could do worse than to make a study of them. It is a most rewarding subject.

I do not think that this Guelf and Ghibelline quarrel was ever a rewarding subject, except to historians. To me it seems terrible, because it is so complicated that I shall never be able to sort it out, and also because it shows the futility of quarrelling.

It was one of the greatest rows in history and, like all major rows, it started with a comparatively small difference of opinion and then it not only grew to unexpected proportions, but, as is always the case, overflowed its original bone of contention and in the end the row was about something quite different. And, of course, like all major rows, it remained undecided.

It started with a rivalry between two German families, each smallish local princes, who each wanted to become top dog. For reasons best known to themselves they carried their dispute out of Germany and into Italy, where each of them wanted to lord it as Holy Roman Emperor and, later on, in Dante's time for instance, it became a fight for power between the Pope and the Emperor. Lots of people, who were Ghibelline like Dante, said that the Pope should rule only spiritually over souls, and so far and no farther, and that the Emperor should rule politically and in the earthly way.

The Pope could not see why he should not unite spiritual and practical government, and the people who supported him, like Cavalcabò, for instance, were Guelf. It went on for hundreds of years, and not only tore Italy to shreds but even divided families.

In the time of Frederick II the original issue was already obscured. Really, as Frederick II had both Guelf and Ghibelline blood in him, the show might have come to an end, but they were by then too well away to stop.

Frederick II was red-haired, short, plump, and near-sighted. He certainly was an extraordinarily brilliant, colourful, and many-sided person, but he was cruel in a petty way which I do not like. I happen to know a few things about him, bits of sheer, unwarranted, personal, spiteful cruelty, which put me off him for good.

When I say cruelty I do not allude to the various murders which were committed at his command. Those were made purely for political reasons, and I have nothing against that. On the contrary, I do think it a pity that nowadays the fashion for political assasinations has ceased. The beliefs which really mean a lot to us are those for which we should be prepared to lay down our lives. The majority of people have no such beliefs. But I am naïve enough to expect a statesman to be serious about his profession – dead serious, in the literal meaning of the word. If someone wants to have a position of power where he can mess up the lives of millions of people, he should be prepared to pay with his life for this privilege. If he does not take his political convictions seriously enough to risk his life, then let him keep his hands off politics.

Anyway, the Guelf and Ghibelline fight is to me about as rewarding as it would be for me to get up at six every morning and to stop drinking.

The name 'Parma' comes from the word 'Palmia' or 'Palmal', which might be Etruscan. Even if it really is Etruscan nobody knows what it meant. In Roman times Parma lay on the Via Emilia, which was one of the great roads. It was a military bastion, but not as important as Cremona. Later it behaved very much like Cremona, was overrun by the barbarians, and got into a complete muddle and depression.

In the time of Frederick II it was Guelf, that is to say, it was against the Emperor. In principle it was really on the side of the Emperor, while in practice it was against him. This was because the Parmesans still had the Caesar tradition and were willing to recognize a Caesar in theory, but in practice they wanted to do what they liked. They were like bad servants who always say "Very well" to an order, and do not do anything.

Frederick II looked on for a while, and then he decided to conquer Parma.

He installed himself outside the town beneath the city walls in a military camp *de luxe*, with his court of poets and musicians and his harem, and he besieged them for ages. His men were housed in wooden shacks, and he gave this camping-place the name of "Vittoria", because he was so sure he would win.

This story is a butt for jokes among historians, but I think it is too easy for them to laugh now and I do not think that their 'merry-making' is of the 'greatest elegance'. There is an Italian proverb which says: "The ditches are full with the wisdom of after."

Also, I cannot see anything so funny about this "Vittoria". It was, in my opinion, a very clever morale-building gesture. Did not Churchill in the last war always make the V-sign for victory, even at times when he knew that things looked black?

So the siege went on till one day, on the 12th February, 1248, the Parmesans came out from behind their bastions and attacked the Emperor's troops. The Emperor was not there because he had gone hunting with his court. By the time he was called back a great number of his men had been killed and the rest put to flight. There was nothing for him but to make a quick exit and he went back to Cremona, where he had his residence at the time.

He was inconsiderate enough to leave his harem behind and at the mercy of the Parmesans. I do not know what became of the ladies, but I imagine some use was found for them.

On the morning after the battle a cobbler went for a walk beyond the ramparts of the town and there, in the mud, he found the Imperial crown.

At this point I begin to laugh, and am told: "Madam, this is not legend. This is history."

The crown in the mud became a symbol of the Emperor's fortunes. His defeat in Parma was the beginning of his downfall. For thirty years he had messed about in Italy, more or less victorious, but now his power was broken. I do not think that his power was really broken, but he thought it was and it comes to the same thing. This, together with Enzio's end, finished him, and he died two years later. I have never been able to keep up with all the times he was excommunicated, and I have a feeling that he did not see eye to eye with the Pope when he died, but I am glad to hear that the Bishop of Palermo behaved as though the Emperor had been a lamb and buried him in the cathedral in Palermo.

Then, for about two hundred years, Parma was ruled by the house of Anjou, and had its so-called golden period, and saddled itself with the cathedral; then it became a Farnese Duchy and the Pilotta was built.

Here I must say that the house of Anjou in those days had a finger in every pie and led a hectic life. First, they got thrown out of Sicily during the Sicilian Vespers, and when the population of Florence heard about this they liked the idea of the Sicilian Vespers so much that they started a sort of Florentine Vespers of their own and threw out the house of Anjou from their government too. As a consequence, either the Guelfs or the Ghibelline party made a come-back into power. Dante was in exile at that time and so he was not affected in any way. By then the Guelfs and Ghibellines had come and gone in Florence with such frequency that I cannot understand how anybody could take them seriously any more.

This is as far as we get. I am promised more at a later date and go to have dinner, reflecting that history in the hands of Professor Gualazzini was soufflé, whereas with Professor Lodi it has become a suet pudding.

To-night the Fontana has been transformed into a banqueting-hall. Two long tables have been put up, running the entire length of the dining-room, and the ordinary guests are treated like step-children, having to squeeze into odd corners.

The waiter tells me that the banqueteers are employees of the

Post Office, but he does not know what they are celebrating. I imagine that they are giving a farewell dinner to one of their superiors about to retire and, judging by their high good spirits, I feel sure that he must have been a swine. To-day there is less than an inch between my table and the one adjoining it, and the guest who occupies it is sitting practically at my side.

He is a handsome young ox of a man with large, blank eyes, wavy chestnut hair, and a well-rounded chin, which he tries to push out to make it look square and forceful. He also has a trick of hunching his shoulders forward in order to give himself an air of commanding virility.

He starts with the usual opening. Do I mind if he smokes? Then follows a conversation which is not new to me either, but I will give it in full because it is the prototype in cases like these and should be known, just as the Colosseum should be known as being the prototype of Victorian concert-halls, or Venetian campaniles, which are the models for Victorian water-towers.

First he holds forth on the merits of Italian cigarettes, and in what way they differ from English and American cigarettes, and so on. This cigarette lyric has two purposes: the performer establishes himself as a man of the world, and also he can thus impart to his audience all the countries he has visited, and draw exclamations like: "So you have been to Turkey? How interesting! Have you really?", and this gives him the chance of spending the rest of the time by entertaining you with the extraordinary experiences he had there.

As I do not act my part, Spain and Africa have been mentioned and passed by, unsung and unlamented. Now that he has established himself as a seasoned traveller, he can turn his attention to me.

"Will you be staying long in Parma?"

"No, I'm leaving to-morrow."

"Couldn't you stay longer? Is it not a pity to leave now that we have met?"

"I cannot stay on. I must go to Mantua."

"Will you allow me to drive you there in my car?"

"No, this is impossible," I say. "I have already booked my train ticket and I cannot disappoint the railways."

"Would you like it if I came to visit you in Mantua?"

I get so bored with this game of 'Would I? No, I would not', that I say to him: "Look here, why do you want to bother with me? There are plenty of women in Parma. You cannot seriously tell me that you haven't seen a white woman for two days."

He says, with a frankness which is almost revolting: "Ah, yes, but you are a foreigner."

I understand.

Here I must touch upon a point of travel in Italy which has not been mentioned by any of the famous travellers, like Goethe, Heine, Smollett, and Lord Byron in past centuries, or by D. H. Lawrence or Aldous Huxley in the present. They could not mention it because they did not know it, and they did not know it because they were men. The point is: What is it like for a foreign woman to travel through Italy?

I think I am very well suited to make a few observations on this subject because I am a woman, and neither young nor beautiful. Therefore my experiences are, so to speak, reduced to the lowest common denominator. If I had the face of a Garbo and the charm of a Marlene Dietrich I would never presume to generalize.

The foreign woman, be she fifteen or fifty, is highly prized as an acquisition by the Italian man. Often she is approached in the most harmless and impeccable manner but, whatever the opening, it is merely a short prelude. Very soon the Italian gets to the core of what is in his mind with a directness which some women find funny, some childish, some insulting, some disarmingly sincere, some flattering, some disgusting.

Furthermore, it is not only the speed and the directness of his approach, but also his perseverance, which the foreign woman finds astonishing.

It is quite a usual occurrence in, say, Florence and Venice, where the native men are specially foreigner-minded, that a man will follow a woman traveller through the streets for literally hours. Or, if he has found out where she lives, he will hang about in front of the house for literally days, hoping to find an occasion for catching sight of her and speaking to her. The traveller's hair will probably be wispy, her grey flannel skirt will be creased, and her blouse crumpled from frequent packing and unpacking. She will wear ugly and comfortable shoes because she has to walk miles a day through the heat, from one palace to another, and she will be aware of her dowdiness, as she observes the many young, pretty, well-groomed and well-dressed Italian women who move through the same town as the foreigner and who yet are never being followed in the streets, are never pestered when they visit museums, are never chased when they sit down on a bench in a park.

The Italian seems to be blind to these ravishing creatures and, the foreign woman is to him what the sun is to the sunflower. To her the Italian scene is peopled with men who try to make assignations. Even the policeman whom she has asked the way to Santa Croce regrets that as he is on duty he cannot accompany her now – but what about meeting in the evening? During my first stay in Italy I had experiences like these, and kept saying to myself: "This happens to me. But it does not happen to an Italian woman. Why? What is the matter with me? What have I done to make these men behave in such a forward manner?" and the whole time I felt I was playing a game of which I did not know the rules. "I travel alone. I like talking to people. Why am I not able to talk to Italians without giving them the idea that I am a tart who has reduced her fees?"

It took me several years to find the explanation, and what I offer here may not be the whole truth, but certainly is a great deal of it: The Italian behaviour springs from two main streams: calculation and vanity.

His common sense tells him that he cannot go wrong if he has an affair with a foreigner travelling by herself. If she is married, there is no husband on the spot who could be awkward. If she is a young girl, she cannot make him marry her because she has not got the hold over him which an Italian woman has. She cannot set her whole family to his heels and threaten to blacken his name in the whole town. She cannot make trouble for him if there should be any consequences to the affair because she would find it impossible to sue him for paternity across a thousand miles.

In other words, he can behave as irresponsibly as he wants to and he knows that no punishment will befall him.

With his own countrywomen, things are different. Hardly has he been seen promenading on the Corso with a young girl, than Mama will already want to know what his intentions are. And if, by a lucky chance, Mama does not get on to his scent, the girl herself will put in some good work and dissolve into tears and throw scenes in order to make him declare himself, and he will have to fight for every kiss. But most often he will not even get as far as this. Much as she might like to, a young Italian girl cannot afford to have a lover. Towns are small and life is narrow, and once she is known to have slipped, her chances of ever getting married are poor. No wonder that the realistic Italian thinks that a foreigner in the hand is better than two lovely Italian girls in the bush.

Add to this the fact that the young Italian has been brought up on brothels and is, therefore, not choosy. He is as sensitive to beauty in woman as any other man, but owing to his amatory upbringing he has learnt to compromise.

Now we come to the other mainspring, governed by vanity. This is maintained by a long tradition. For centuries Italy has been the education and playground of the young northerner of good family, English, German, and Scandinavian. This gave birth to the very understandable belief among Italians that every Englishman was a 'Milord', and monstrously rich into the bargain. A tradition like this does not die easily. Even to-day, when travel abroad is no longer a privilege of the ruling class, the Italian has not yet weaned himself of this prejudice. Also, since America has become a world Power there has been a steady industry of providing husbands of noble Italian birth for American heiresses. Considering all this is so natural that to the average Italian it is a matter of prestige to hook a foreign woman, no matter for how short a time. It is a conquest to be shown off on the Corso, to be bragged about in the café, to be boasted of not only to friends but to acquaintances.

But, you will say, surely it takes two to make a love affair. Of course it does.

Consider the ordinary English or German girl. Quite pretty, quite pleasant, but not very striking. In her own country she has had to work hard to find admirers. Her escorts to dances and parties did not grow on trees. In a discreet way she has had to chase the men and she has never been chased herself. Now she comes to Italy. She is told she is beautiful and that men swoon at her sight. She is told that her charms make a man's blood run hot. She is showered with attentions such as she never knew before, and I must admit that, when an Italian wants to be attentive and devoted, he is much better at it than other men. To him this is all routine; but the young girl does not stop to think, that, if he had not made the same identical protestations of love a hundred times before, he would not be so good at it.

And so, even if her admirer does not particularly appeal to her, her head will be turned and she will be an easy conquest.

Or take the other extreme, the wealthy woman of about fifty who has been a good wife and mother for the last thirty years, who finds herself widowed and wants to see the world. After having lived for so long with a bore she will fall even more easily than the young woman. Contrary to common belief, it is not the young who yearn for romance; it is the middle-aged.

And the harder she is on the surface, the softer she will be in her heart. The grimly efficient career woman who has looked after a business with all the ruses of a masculine brain, and who could see through a confidence-trickster in half a minute, will lose herself to the Italian who is nothing more than an amorous confidence-man. His job is easy. The well-worn clichés work well when nature does his wooing for him, with silky air, moonlight on ruins, and the lapping of waves against a distant shore.

The disintegration is quick. I remember once, in Taormina, a Swedish countess of about fifty who was cashing a cheque in front of me at the bank. She was got up like a widow of Royalty in ankle-length black draperies, and with a widow's cap with a heart-shaped peak pointing down the forehead, and a black veil. She was chatting with the cashier, and from her talk I gathered that she had just arrived in Taormina and intended to look for a house, to settle down in modest retirement.

I returned to Taormina half a year later. Like so many of her kind before her, she had become one of the sights of the village. Not only had she shed her weeds but she had been forced to take a short trip to Sweden in order to sell some securities because her Taorminese lover cost her very dear. So exuberant had she become that she used to enter shops, stop on the threshold, throw herself into a mock operatic attitude, and sing as though she were on the stage: "Be greeted, good people. My husband is dead."

My advice to the woman tourist who is pestered in the street by an Italian is: do not try to ignore him. If you do he may follow you for hours and spoil the whole afternoon for you. When he comes out with his usual request to be allowed to accompany you, say something like: "Alas, it is not possible."

"But why is it not possible?"

"Because I am on my way to meet my lover."

"Perhaps I am better than your lover. Is he nice?"

Put a hand on your heart, turn your eyes heavenward and say: "He is – I can't tell you how wonderful."

This will get rid of him. I guarantee the success.

In cases like these, Italians are like children. It is not enough to say no. "How no?" they will say. They must know why it is no. And they will go to great lengths to sway you.

Once in Naples I was pursued by one of the porters in my hotel. At first I said: "It's no use, you know. You will not get any money out of me."

"Ah, but I am not thinking of money."

"Sweet of you," I said, "but even so, forget about it."

"I am even prepared to spend money on you, madam. If it embarrasses you to see me in this hotel I will take a room in another hotel. Will you let me?"

"No," I said.

He made his last bid. "Look here, madam. I am a very good lover. Please try me. As you know, I am employed in this hotel. If you are not satisfied with me you can complain to the *padrone* about me and he will give me the sack."

If you are a stay-at-home do not be impressed by your friend who returns from Italy full of "adventures". My mother had a word for it. She would say: "What do you mean by 'adventures'? She just does not know how to say 'no'."

I am told by the porter that Professor Castellani has telephoned and would I please go and see him on the following day at two-thirty.

I am looking forward to this meeting. The professor is the head of the Istituto del'Arte, which was the first modern academy of painting in Europe. It was founded in the eighteenth century, and when the Royal Academy in London was established they modelled themselves on the Istituto del'Arte in Parma.

The Institute is just round the corner of the Pilotta, but I can say now from experience that, spiritually speaking, the kingdom of the Signora Quintavalle and that of Professor Castellani are a thousand leagues apart.

The door is locked. A porter comes out in answer to the bell and tells me that Professor Castellani is waiting for me. I follow him inside. On the head of the stairs I see a little old tramp dressed in a top-coat, on which he carries the filth of ages. He has wound a grey woollen scarf round his neck, probably given him by a charitable institution. He leers at me with black, broken teeth, and beckons to me.

"Up you go," says the porter, "don't keep the professor waiting."

The professor shakes hands with great liveliness, dancing about like an excited fox-terrier. He leads me up two flights of stairs, past landings with plaster copies of famous Greek statues. I am able to state that the thorn-puller has still not extracted the thorn from his foot, Laocoön and his sons still have not got rid of those beastly snakes, the disk-thrower has still not chucked his disk, and the garment of the Venus of Milo is still in the same place. I have never understood how she kept it there without losing it.

We enter a room with a worm-like secretary bent over ledgers, and pass into the professor's study. It has framed documents on the walls and busts of famous people everywhere, even on top of the stove.

Here I am introduced to an elderly man who reminds me very much of one of my uncles – not the leather merchant who was beaten up by his wife with an umbrella when he descended the stairs of an hotel arm-in-arm with an unknown lady – but Uncle Rudolf who was a spa doctor. He was a tall, distinguished-looking old man with gold-rimmed *pince-nez*, stubbly white hair and a knobbly, wine-coloured nose. He suffered from gout and was supposed to keep a rigid diet. When he was invited to lunch my grandmother always had special dishes prepared for him. He invariably waved them aside and applied himself to the ordinary food. My grandmother would say: "Rudolf, do my eyes deceive me?"

"Of course they don't deceive you. I wish I had your eyesight."

"In this case, I must be allowed to say that what you are eating is sheer poison."

"Oh, leave me alone," replied Uncle Rudolf, "I've got to die of something."

He had great accomplishments. He could tie a napkin into the shape of a mouse, settle it in the crook of his arm, and make it jump to the far corner of the room. As he had his practice in the spa of Marienbad, and an obsessive admiration for Goethe, he collected everything appertaining to Goethe's stay in Marienbad.

Resemblances are more than skin deep. I am told that this replica of Uncle Rudolf is a doctor, too, now retired. He too, is a collector. He lives in Rome and collects everything related to Goethe's stay in that city. Odd this, very. I dare not ask him about the mouse trick.

Meanwhile, Professor Castellani has gone into the next room. Now he comes dancing back, grabs his hat while executing half a pirouette, and leads us out of the study on to the landing.

This is a bit stiff, I think. He makes me come here and hardly have I arrived than he shows me out. We go downstairs, out of the house, and are invited to get into a car. As soon as we are settled the chauffeur drives off without being told where to go. I have no idea where we are going.

After twenty minutes' journey through flat, green country we get into a tiny town and stop in front of a small palace.

"This is my house," says the professor, "but I do not live here. I have made it into my museum. One must have one's own private museum, don't you think? What else is there in life?"

Both I and Uncle Rudolf hasten to agree.

"What is the name of this town?" I ask.

"Colorno, of course," says the professor. "Where else do you think would I take you?"

He unlocks the door and skips ahead of us. We follow him into a passage which cuts right across the whole width of the house and opens into an enchanting garden with crooked paths, peach trellises, magnolia trees, and long grass.

"That's only the garden," says the professor, "that's not interesting. You don't want to waste your time looking at it. It belonged to the Spanish Ambassador in Maria Luigia's time, when the Court was in Colorno."

We are beckoned to return to the hall, where a great unveiling is now taking place. That is to say, a very substantial unveiling, because it is boards which are shifted and put aside for our benefit. An easel is swivelled round and we behold him in life-size, with all the irritating mannerisms which his painters used to give him: lock fallen across the forehead, hand slid into waistcoat, scowling brow, masterfully squared jaw, and a short, pale finger laid on the military dispatch by his side.

And yet, the shoddy, melancholy, ill-starred symbols grip our heart, and we are singed by the spark of greatness.

Napoleon works on me hypnotically, like military brass bands. I can never get enough of him. But I am not allowed to sink into a trance. Another easel is turned round from shade into light. The picture is the pendant to that of Napoleon, and painted by the same execrable hand. And so they stand side by side, the self-created and self-crowned soldier-god, and the anaemic daughter of a bloodless father, the daughter of the Emperor by Divine right, the Habsburg, the archduchess Marie-Louise – a somewhat ridiculous pair.

She is a fairly tall, buxom young woman, with the thick wrists and the pink-tipped nose of the country wench, but her long head is narrow and overbred, and her tired blue eyes are those of her father the Emperor.

By my side the professor jumps excitedly from one foot to the other.

"How old was Napoleon at the time this was painted?" I ask.

"You see her here just after her marriage," replies the professor. "Look at her. Behold her. How dear she is. How lovely she is."

I would not call her lovely; quite handsome, I would say, and a bit stuck up and frigid. No sparkle and no imagination. His soldiers were right when they said after the wedding: "*Il aurait fait mieux de garder sa vieille.*"

I ask whether Napoleon ever stayed here in Colorno, and I get the reply that Marie-Louise resided in Parma during the winter and that Colorno was her summer palace.

Uncle Rudolf now takes over with a question about Napoleon's Italian campaign, and in reply he is given information about Marie-Louise's patronage of the arts.

It is a nightmarish conversation we are taking part in, reminiscent of those model phrases in simple grammars: "Have you seen my aunt taking the air in the garden?"

"No, but I am willing to lend you my pencil for the time being."

The oils are turned back into the oblivion of darkness and boarded up once more.

We are now led to long tables, their tops glazed over and shrouded in shirred green silk. The professor uncovers rows of medals, coins, and ribbons. By now, Uncle Rudolf and I know better than to ask questions. Silently we bend over the glittering miniature cavalcade of Napoleonic glory till the professor tugs at our sleeves and clatters impatient heels on the echoing parquet: "Come along," he squeaks, "this is not really interesting. This is only to do with Maria Luigia's first husband."

For a while I choke with silent rage, while Uncle Rudolf turns his back on us, ostensibly cleaning his glasses and holding them against the light.

It is Uncle Rudolf, who is older, wiser, and more self-possessed than I am, who walks up the stairs side by side with the professor, and he now takes care to ask questions only about the Austrian whose Italianised name rolls so easily off the professor's tongue. I lag a few steps behind them, just as I used to when, as a child, I was sulking and at the same time wanted to keep an ear on the conversation of the grown-ups.

We are made to stop on a landing where the walls are thickly hung with sketches, drawings, and water-colours. Considering the merits of these exhibits, it would be better to say that the walls are paved with them.

They are all early Victorian in date, and their subjects would lend themselves well for certain types of old-fashioned Christmas cards – the sort of cards one would send to one's old nanny.

Those posies of pansies and violets, those thatched cottages, those waterfalls and groups of kittens with bows, can evoke comments only like: "Look, dear, at the darling pussies. And that wee little cottage."

We are made to stand in front of these for a long time, and encouraged to contemplate them with loving care. And yet, downstairs, in front of some superbly well-cut cameos we were not allowed to dawdle. The professor dances about, giving one blacktoothed smile after another. It is really touching to see his pleasure. I am beginning to understand.

The framed excrescences in front of us are part of Marie-Louise's private art collection, acquired at a time when she had already left 'her first husband'.

This whole first-husband episode is tedious to the professor. He takes fire only after she had come to Parma and started a new life, so to speak, symbolized by the name of Maria Luigia, with which she signed all official documents.

"Every picture chosen by her own hand," squeaks the professor; "I shall now show you some more. You will see throughout that her taste was impeccable."

We enter a room filled with indifferent oils, which might be just as well described by their measurements as by their subjects. Mostly they are of a revoltingly cosy *genre*, some originals, some copies. More interesting are the objects arranged in glazed cabinets, which were dear and significant to her. Soon it is clear to me that the once ruler of Parma had the sentimentality of a seamstress and the taste of a maidservant.

From the cream-silk-lined wedding casket to her workbox, from blotting folders and thimble-holders to her combs and brushes, from her chocolate drinking-cups to her embroidery scissors, I piece together the cosy, homespun Odyssey of the Duchess of Parma who, during her travels incognito, chose the title of: "Countess of Colorno" and kept the incognito so badly that she was mentioned in the papers as "*Sa Majesté la Contesse de Colorno.*"

Marie-Louise stuck to Napoleon as long as all went well. But already, during the first *débâcle*, when he was put away on Elba, she thought that French soil was getting too hot for her and decided to go home to daddy. Napoleon's brothers Jerôme and Joseph tried to prevent her leaving in order to keep up some appearances of loyalty and fortitude, but there was no holding her. On her journey back to Vienna she was escorted by the Austrian general Count von Neipperk, an exceedingly handsome, florid soldier who wore the black patch over his eye with dash and distinction.

It is not known how soon their friendship ripened into love, but into love it did ripen, and there was no mistaking it.

Napoleon, while on Elba, asked her most pressingly to join him there, but she would not hear of it, being already well away with Neipperk. Also, during the Hundred Days when Napoleon made his come-back, she would not budge from Vienna, and showed no desire for Napoleon's success.

When Napoleon was exiled on St. Helena, Marie-Louise remembered her role as loving wife, and mentioned half-heartedly that she was willing to join him there. She probably knew quite well that he was not allowed to have any company of his choosing.

At that time Prince Metternich was getting his teeth sharpened for the Congress of Vienna. Marie-Louise, as a loving wife, did not suit him at all, because she was a Princess in her own right, and he was afraid that she might assume a position of power and upset his carefully planned apple-cart.

So, to put her off her husband once and for all, he first proceeded to give her a list of all Napoleon's past infidelities, rather in the manner of Leporello's 'Mille e Tré' aria in Don Giovanni, with the refrain: "Therefore, oh, donna, let him be, he is not worthy of your love."

This was a great relief to her. To cap it all, Metternich told her that, in any case, Napoleon had already consoled himself during her absence and that he was living on the island with Countess Walewska and their son. This was, of course, an utter lie. But it was a master-stroke on the part of Prince Metternich, because thus he gave Marie-Louise the chance of withdrawing from Napoleon in such a way that she could keep her self-respect. After this it was plain sailing. She disowned Napoleon officially. He was very generous about it and, as far as is known, held no grievance against her. Already before his death she was expecting a child by Neipperk, and as soon as Napoleon died she married the general with the full consent of the Emperor her father. No one can pretend that she was bowed with grief over Napoleon's misfortunes.

When Napoleon was at the height of his power and wanted to get married, Marie-Louise was not his first choice. He wanted one of the sisters of Alexander I of Russia. Alexander did not think this a good idea, and turned Napoleon down. After this relations between them turned from cold to icy.

It was, I think, Metternich who first put Marie-Louise forward as a possible wife. She was not popular in France for that role. The memory of the other '*Autrichienne*', also a Habsburg – Marie Antoinette – was not endearing to the French. They were sure that this Austrian would be as bad as the former.

It is obvious from her subsequent behaviour that Marie-Louise never cared for Napoleon. I do not blame her for not loving him, because she was forced into the marriage. Love cannot be ordered. Granted that he raped her in the travelling coach upon her arrival in France because he did not want to wait till after their wedding; granted that he was a bad lover, much too impatient and never taking his time, but even if she did not like him she could have shown some respect and loyalty. When one has a husband like Napoleon, the least one can do is to try to live up to him within one's own limitations. In my opinion she was a failure on every level.

Napoleon seems to have been fond of her, that is to say, at first he made himself believe he was in love with her. Certainly he showed much more good will than she did, right from the beginning, and was decent to the very end.

Judging by ordinary standards her marriage to Neipperk was a dreadful *mésalliance* for a Habsburg Princess, but Metternich was very keen to see her happily married because he knew that a woman in love has no head for political intrigues.

Also, to give her something to do and to create an appearance of establishing Napoleon's ex-wife, the Congress of Vienna made over to her the Duchy of Parma and Piacenza and in 1816 she took up residence in Parma in the Farnese Palace. She ruled for thirty years, and died in 1847. She was fifty-seven years old when she died. Officially she died of pneumonia, but it is thought that she was poisoned.

She had three children by Neipperk, and the boy and girl who survived took the name of Montenuovo, which is the Italianized version of Neipperk.

During most of this time the son of her first marriage, who had been born 'King of Rome', was kept in Vienna in the Imperial castle and in summer in Schoenbrunn, because Metternich was anxious to keep an eye on him. The Congress of Vienna, while creating her Duchess of Parma, did not make the Duchy hereditary, because there was no telling what Napoleon's son might get up to. They gave him the meaningless title of Duke of Reichstadt.

On rare occasions he was allowed to visit mama, and when this happened she did not let him play with her other children in the garden, and he had to play in a separate garden by himself.

Professor Castellani refuses to say why. Perhaps the Duke of Reichstadt had scabies at the time.

The Duke certainly did not inherit Napoleon's brain, but he had some of his fire. Prince Metternich was greatly relieved when he died of lung trouble in his 'teens, because he always presented a potential firebrand, all the more as the Napoleonic legend was gaining strength in the whole of Europe.

When Neipperk died, Marie-Louise's reputation in Parma became scandalous. There were tales that she mothered every bastard in the town, and that the walls of her bedroom were lined with secret passages, so that one lover could make an unseen get-away while the next one was admitted. I cannot say how much truth there was in this gossip. The professor, while telling it, dances about and wrings his hands and swears that it is all wicked calumny.

Some time later, in order to stop people's mouths, Marie-Louise took on her third husband, a Baron Werklein. The professor assures me that this marriage was a union in name only.

Marie-Louise took her job in Parma seriously. She did more for the town than any other ruler before or after her. She built roads, bridges, and public institutions, and founded the picture gallery in the Pilotta. She created orphanages and maternity homes, and was very keen on child welfare. In other words, she sounds a dreadful bore and busy-body. She was also the first person who modified the Code Napoleon, to include women's rights of inheritance and property.

We go from room to room. The professor brings out stacks of her diaries. Apparently she had the abominable habit of chewing over what she had been reading and making commentaries of her own. I am given one or two of her letters to read, couched in impeccable French. They are as conventional as I had expected, though less gracious and less condescending. Amiability was not her strong point. There are also the Marie-Louise sketching albums. He flips through the pages, giving us glimpses of thatched roof following waterfall, of moon-lit meadow following ruined castle. There is not a grain of talent, but a certain knack as copyist. To-day she might have earned her living by painting hunting scenes on cocktail mats and posies on lamp-shades.

From a cabinet the professor takes an empty crystal phial and lifts the stopper and I inhale a whiff of violets, a naïve, simple scent. "This was her favourite scent," he says, "the violets of Parma. The scent was so strong that it has clung to the bottle, which has long since been empty. I showed this phial some time ago to Lady Churchill, and she would not believe that what she could smell was the trace of the original scent, and she thinks that I put in a drop from time to time to keep up the illusion. Ah, but this is not the only way in which I am misunderstood."

Now that I have sampled Marie-Louise's favourite scent, I am sorry to say that I believe the professor entirely when he denies the truth of those scandalous rumours. No *grande amoureuse* would have used such an innocent perfume.

Still, if I told him that, on this issue at least, I join battle on his side, he would be offended. I begin to feel sorry for this little old learned monomaniac, so touchingly eager to make us share in his adoration, who, like all addicts, tries constantly to convert others, too, to his vice.

Professor Castellani is the greatest living authority on Marie-Louise. He owns practically all her letters and other personal documents, and his museum is unique in the world.

The finest piece in the whole collection, and the only one of good taste, is a magnificent china *bouillon* cup with its saucer, with two handles curved like swans' necks. It is painted with oval medallions in the Grecian Empire style, with heads which look like cameos.

There is an old Corsican custom that after the birth of a son the husband himself brings his wife a cup of broth to revive her. It is the first drink she receives after the ordeal.

It was this cup which Napoleon brought to Marie-Louise after the birth of the King of Rome. And to think that a woman who had been given a cup of soup by Napoleon's own hands should have – I cannot bear to say more. It chokes me.

The last exhibits we are shown are two oils of the King of Rome as a baby, one the original by Prud'hon, the other a copy. The King lies naked on a cushion of crimson velvet in a forest glade, two over-life-size butterflies winging archly over his head, and flowers nodding near his pudgy toes.

The professor goes into ecstasies over the accomplishment of the picture, while Uncle Rudolf murmurs into my ear "*Un gusto bestiale*", and I imagine that the painting would fall to cinders from one burning glance of Signora Quintavalle's eye.

One parting look at a miniature of Marie-Louise, done a year before her death. A faded woman with wrinkled lips. Only the hair has preserved some freshness. It has a golden chestnut sheen and

is done in tresses looped over the ears and partly hidden by the
wings of the homely lace cap. The tired blue Habsburg eyes are
red-rimmed. She wears a woollen scarf over her bowed shoulders.
She looks as though she were cold. And this is the creature who has
inspired the professor to call Napoleon "Marie-Louise's first
husband". We go downstairs and get into the car.

We shall now be driven to the Palazzo Ducale of Colorno. In
summer, Marie-Louise moved her court from Parma to Colorno,
and it was here that a Monsieur Henri Beyle stayed for some time
and observed the court atmosphere, from which he later took some
ideas for writing *La Chartreuse de Parme*.

Court life in those days was already tainted by early Victorian
cosiness and nicety, and must have seemed very tame to Stendhal.
It is clear in his book that he introduced figures of a stature of which
Marie-Louise could not have dreamt in her wildest nightmares.
I do not know what he thought of her. But I can deduce it from
the last sentence in his obituary which he wrote himself: "He
admired one man only—Napoleon."

We enter a vast courtyard, completely square, and faced on three
sides by grey stone wings of equal proportions.

The palace was built in 1700, after the designs of Bibbiena, for the
Bourbons, who then ruled Parma. It was meant to be a second
Versailles, and according to the ecstatic squeaks of the professor it
is the most wonderful palace of its kind after Versailles. True,
Bibbiena was the greatest architect of his day, but when he designed
Colorno he must have been constipated. The palace is large without
being grand, spacious without being dignified, massive without
being majestic. There is no ornament, no relief, to break up the
monotony of those uninspired rows of windows, which are all
surmounted by the same eyebrows of the same point and curl.

We pass through an archway to the front wing, which overlooks
the park. Here a measly double flight of stairs, thinly balustraded,
leads up to the main portal, and knowing most of Bibbiena's
fantastically grandiose drafts, I come to the conclusion that the fault

lay not with him. It is painfully obvious that the person who held the purse-strings was being very mean. Elegant economy is very well for ordinary people, but it ceases to be elegant when practised by the Bourbons of Parma.

The park is small, with a round pond and drooping willows, and some attempts at creating an up-hill and down-dale effect with rising and sinking lawns.

I am told that originally the park was spangled with statues and laid out in the rigidly symmetrical pattern of *Grand siècle* gardens with scrolled parterres, radiating avenues, topiary work, and fountains. The finest of these fountains, with a centre-piece of Proserpina's Rape by Giuliano Mozani, was uprooted and sold to England, where it is to this day. It was Marie-Louise who got the craze for the 'English style' park, who razed the Baroque pattern to the ground, and had it altered into a poor imitation of Nature's heaving bosom. In her days the idea was new no more, but no doubt she thought she was being revolutionary. She could not leave well alone.

We are led into two of the upstairs rooms, frescoed and empty. The windows on the ground floor are barred with iron and hung with poor people's washing. I am told that this part of the palace is now being used as a madhouse. The rest is uninhabited, and cannot even be thrown open to the public because there is nothing to show. In the eighteenth century the Palace of Colorno contained some of the finest tapestries and furniture of any palace in the country. When Italy was unified and became a kingdom, the new government ransacked the palace. Most of the furniture is now in Florence, in the Palazzo Pitti. Some of it has been put in the Quirinale, which is the seat of the President, and up to the last war, the throne used by the King of Italy was the throne taken from Colorno. The professor thinks that it is symbolical of our times that this palace of glory has now been transformed into a house of madness. Here is the Acrosticon which he has made on the subject, and to which he has given the title of: "Beheaded Versailles".

VERSAGLIA DECAPITATA

C *Città gloriosa d'arte ducale*
O *Ora rifugio manicomiale*
L *Libera patria ha vagheggiato:*
O *Oltraggioso schianto il resultato.*
R *Rovina et abandono regale*
N *Nella più deturpante agonia:*
O *Onesta vinta dalla ipocrisia.*

I have taken the liberty of rendering this in English, after my own way that is to say, not only in a different style but also in a different spirit:

VERSAILLES CRACKED IN MORE WAYS THAN ONE

C *City of glory and well-meaning inanity*
O *Outgrew the first on account of the latter;*
L *Leapt into insanity*
O *Out of the silver platter,*
R *Raving mad as a hatter.*
N *Now noblesse no more*
O *Obliges as it did (so I was told) before.*

During our drive back to Parma we are told that George Hayter, who was Court painter to Queen Victoria, stayed a long time at the court of Marie-Louise. He is practically unknown, and the professor is convinced that he deserves better. I am charged by him to do something to restore the memory of Hayter upon my return to England. I saw some of his stuff in the professor's museum, mostly feeble caricatures of hook-nosed women in outsize bonnets. England can well afford to by-pass Hayter. The professor can whistle for me. We each of us ride through life on our own hobby-horse, and hobby-horses are cranky animals, rarely inclined to become friendly with each other.

We return to the Institute and are taken upstairs, this time to the attic, which contains two rooms furnished with easels and benches. Here the budding Hayters of Parma are taught to draw and paint, and I am sorry to state that Marie-Louise's taste seems to have inspired most of the samples I am shown.

There is a fine portrait of Sir Thomas Lawrence by Canova. I should like to think that Sir Thomas never went to the Art Academy of Parma or, if he did, that it was worthier of that name than it is now.

The most interesting thing is a series of designs by a Frenchman called Petitot, who worked in Parma in the eighteenth century. They are designs for costumes for a fancy-dress ball 'à la Grècque', with the figures tricked out to look like pieces of playful architecture, garden urns, hermes, and little pyramids. This is an example of the theory that surrealism, like other art trends, was not evolved at a certain period but crops up over and over again whenever a suitable genius is born at a suitable age.

There is also Petitot's visiting-card designed by himself. It shows a cracked urn entwined by a serpent, and beneath it he has written the exquisite verse:

> "Il n'est point de serpent
> Point de monstre odieux
> Qui par l'art imité
> Ne puisse plaire aux yeux."

How true and how charmingly put.

At last, both Uncle Rudolf and I are dismissed. The car is downstairs to take us home. Uncle Rudolf wants to be driven to the station. He has come to Parma for the day only.

"Was your visit satisfactory?" I ask him; "was there anything special you wanted to see?"

"Yes. I was trying to find out whether Goethe made any contacts with the court of Parma during his Italian journey."

"And did you get anything?"

"No. All I got was Marie-Louise."

When I enter the Button the old lady with the wicked cigarette-holder and the porter-grandson are there to greet me.

"You are so enterprising, *signora*. What have you brought back this time?"

"I have nothing to show," I say, "but I carry the invisible weight of Marie-Louise."

"We could have told you this before you went. Marie-Louise's first husband was Napoleon. Her second husband was General Neipperk. Her third husband was Baron Werklein. Her fourth husband is Professor Castellani."

"I smelt her scent," I say. "Is it still made to-day?"

The old lady makes a face. And well she might. To judge by her cigarette-holder, her taste in perfumes will be sultry.

"I know," she says; "it is a nasty, cheap perfume. Yes, they still make it from the violets which grow in the spring tra-la on the banks of the rivers. I don't think you would fancy it, *signora*. It is mainly exported to South America."

"I think I will leave to-morrow," I say, "and I wanted to ask you if I could leave my Parmesan cheese."

"Certainly. We shall be very glad to have it."

While I wait at the desk for the cheese to be brought down, a man comes up to me. He has overheard our conversation and he wants to know more about the cheese.

As soon as he is told he begins to be abusive: "That's not a good cheese, that's old-fashioned stuff. It has a crust which means a piece of waste, and it takes years till it is ready for use. You should try my own modern Parmesan cheese, without a crust, every morsel fit to be eaten, no waste and no waiting." And he pulls from his coat pocket a round carton-box, whips the lid off, and reveals six triangular segments wrapped in silver paper and brightly labelled. I do not like the look of it, and I say so.

"But it is ridiculous, *signora*," he says. "Would you ride in a horse-drawn carriage when you could go by motor-car?"

"I certainly would," I say.

He smiles with contempt, thinking that I am trying to be funny.

"But, seriously now, why do you want to bother with the old type of cheese with all its disadvantages? Look at mine, so neat, so handy, so – "

By now I am really annoyed and tell him to leave me alone and, if he cannot respect my Parmesan cheese, will he please sweep the doorstep of his own Parmesan.

There are no short cuts in life. You cannot acquire true learning in a year, nor can you expect true Parmesan to ripen in a day.

Now the cheese of contention is brought, and I want to place it on the counter and go. But the old lady will not hear of it. One of her sons is summoned and we troop, procession-like, into the hotel kitchen. There the cheese is tasted by the whole family and pronounced to be about eighteen months old. Then it is put on the scales. Then I am given a glass of Strega, shake hands all round, and leave.

At night, as I return from dinner, I am told that Professor Castellani has come to see me.

He has wanted to salute me, he says, giving me a winsome leer with his dusky ruins of teeth. We sit down in the lounge. After the first minute I realize that he has really come to break his heart to me. I listen to tale after tale of how other scholars during the past forty years have misrepresented Marie-Louise's character. Also, how they slipped up in their learning, and gave wrong dates or connected incidents which were never related to each other. The professor's memory is brighter than his teeth: "On the first of January, in 1912, there appeared an article in the *Revue des deux Mondes* in which –"

I feel sorry for him. I agree with him that it was not Marie-Louise's fault that she was not present when her son died in Vienna. It is sad to think that a man with so much learning has become such a figure of ridicule that he is forced to go to passing strangers like me when he wants to find an audience for his grievance. I imagine that even his charwoman is no longer willing to lend Marie-Louise a sympathetic ear.

On the following day, when I want to leave, my bill is made out and half of it is written off, this being the value of the Parmesan. I protest. I had never thought of anything like it. But the old lady is adamant. "We know the value of our products, *signora*," she says, "don't worry. It was a pleasure. And come again."

This, to me, is the ultimate proof that my cheese, Signor Bianchi's cheese, the great classical cheese of Parma, is still ruling supreme in our speed-ridden world. Payment is the greatest flattery.

MANTUA

It is a fine day, not warm but sunny, and I decide to travel to Mantua by motor coach. The porter has promised to get my ticket and to meet me at the coach stop in front of the Pilotta with my luggage. Now I am sitting for the last time in the Piazza Garibaldi, which looks more than ever like an old print of itself.

I am just on the point of offering myself a second farewell drink when my eye is caught by the most hideous top-coat I have ever seen on a man. It is of dirty mustard colour with pink stripes. I try to imagine the mentality of the man who chose it, when the top-coat turns and comes towards me with pink-striped arms out-stretched.

"Dearest Edith."

It is the Pal.

"My friend had to go to Parma for the day and so I went with him, in the hope of seeing you. I went to your hotel and they told me you had left."

"How did you know where I stayed?"

"I telephoned to Professor Lodi and he told me. Is it really true you are leaving?"

I assure him that it is really true.

"I knew that if you were still here you would be in the piazza. How fortunate that Parma is such a small town."

How fortunate indeed.

"They told me at your hotel that you are going to Mantua. Is that really so?"

And, although I have not asked him anything of the kind he promises to come to see me in Mantua if I will let him know my address. He walks with me to the Pilotta, where the porter-grandson and the luggage-man welcome us with great cheerfulness.

The porter, beast that he is and expanding in the old lady's absence, asks me if the *signor professore* is also going to Mantua. It will be no trouble at all to get a ticket for him. And then, as I say no, he exclaims: "Do not be sad, *signora*. Partings are not for ever."

The Pal cannot see me into the coach because he has to rejoin his bald friend.

After his departure, both the porter and the luggageer burst out laughing.

"He left a note for you at the hotel," says the porter: "shall we send it on to you? I could have brought it with me but somehow I had the idea that you would not be interested," and once more they go into fits of laughter.

On the way to Mantua we cross the strangest bridge I have ever seen. Rough planks bordered with a rough wooden railing, resting on a row of boats which are set in the water at even intervals, ranged from one bank to the other. The stream must be very shallow.

The country-side is dull and messy, as before. We stop in villages which have names like: Buscolo, Boscoli, Bosoli, and so on. They sound like a lesson in etymology, showing the various stages by which a word is altered during the passage of centuries.

I consult my guide-book. On the principle that among the blind the one-eyed is kind, the third-rate hotel Romagna is the best in Mantua.

The approach to Mantua is very pretty. No drab suburbs, but a juicy green park, and in the distance a blue expanse of water. This is one of the three lakes which girdle the town. They are formed by the river Mincio.

I hate the Romagna at first sight. It has a modern façade stuck on to an old building. I dislike hypocrisy in all forms. Inside there are a fat, bald, thin-lipped mercenary-looking manager and a large-eyed youth swaying like a reed. There is no sitting- or reading-room of any kind, only a dining-room out of use, where an accountant sits at a bare table, driving his finger down a column of figures.

My room, on the first floor, is all flash and no comfort. It has an expensive wash-basin with rounded corners and gleaming taps, but there is no running hot water. The hot water has to be rung for and is brought after a longish wait. And then it turns out to be cooler than my temper.

In the basin there is a tricky knob which, when twisted, raises and lowers a hidden plug. After I have finished washing I work the dazzling knob and find that the waste is very slow. The basin seems to go to sleep when it is expected to empty itself.

There are several bright metal rods for towels, which can be swivelled forwards and backwards, but there are not enough towels to swivel, and those provided are as thin as crêpe paper.

There is a reading-lamp, very flashily encased in a tube mounted in chrome and set into a panel of pink mirror squares; it is placed not above the bed, but beside it. The old-fashioned type of lamp which stands on the bedside table can at least be turned towards the bed. This one is immovable because it is built into the wall, and is therefore useless.

Cursing all this modern eyewash I go downstairs, where I find out that, to make up for the lack of comfort, they are charging a first-class price. I am too tired and hungry to look for another hotel.

The manager speaks English: "Here is your passport, Mrs."

Damn his English. I would much rather have Italian-speaking hot water.

By the time I have installed myself in the nasty Romagna it is past three o'clock. I go out to eat and find a *trattoria* off the Piazza Mantegna. It is agreeably filthy. There is the right sort of filth and the wrong sort of filth. In Italy most filth is of the right sort.

By now it is half-past three. There is never a "Sorry, we are closed", in an Italian restaurant, and "Sorry, we can't help you". They are open and they are happy to help you.

I get a *zuppa Pavese*, which is clear broth floating a fried egg and slices of toast, then grilled ribs of beef, a green salad, and half a *Provolone*, which is a softly crumbling white cream cheese sold in little muslin bags. It has a faint milky flavour, and has a dewy fresh charm of its own which is enhanced by rough red wine. When it is put on my plate it still bears the imprint of the weave of the muslin and the creases where the cloth was folded and tied at the top.

The bread rolls of Mantua are quite simple in shape, rounded and with a dent down the middle, and they taste as bad as those of Cremona.

At one table there is a party of labourers playing cards and drinking wine.

The kitchen door is open, and I can hear a row going on. It is the small daughter of the *padrone* ; she complains about her schoolteacher, and her father says that the schoolteacher is right and that she shouldn't be so lazy; the mother says the daughter is not lazy, and that the teacher is sitting on her. The daughter says that the teacher has favourites and that it isn't fair. I have never yet heard anyone complain when favouritism worked in his own way. String-pulling is an agreeable practice when there are strings that can be pulled – though sometimes it has the opposite effect from the one desired.

I once knew a man who wanted to get a very high position in an international concern. Three people pulled strings for him: a Cabinet Minister, a Cardinal, and the vice-President of an American oil company. He did not get the job. The reply was something like this: "Your qualifications are perfect, but a man who has such influential friends as you has no need to take this job."

The row in the kitchen has calmed down.

The daughter is doing a solo whine on the theme: "And find what wind serves to advance an honest mind." Only she does not put it so well. This is one of the reasons why children should learn poetry, lots of it and by heart; they can then express their predicaments much more tersely and more agreeably by quotation.

I ponder about Mantua. Apart from Virgil's *"Mantua me genuit"*, which is part of his epitaph, I know only one more thing about Mantua.

I learnt about it in a horrible song, when I was four years old. Even then I knew that the song was horrible. It is about a man called Andreas Hofer, who was an Austrian. What business he had in Mantua I do not know. He was captured in Mantua and put in front of a firing squad. If one is to believe the song, the hearts of Germany and Austria bled for him. Being a finicky person he demanded to be allowed to take the bandage off his eyes. Also, he wanted to give the command "Fire" himself. This was granted. And then there comes the passage which has always puzzled me:

"Und von dem Haupt die Binde nimmt ihm der Korporal,
Andreas Hofer betet allhier zum letzten mal.
   Dann ruft er, ach, nun ist mir's recht,
Gebt Feuer! Ach, wie schiesst Ihr schlecht!
Adee mein Land Tyrol. Adee mein Land Tyrol."

The corporal takes the bandage from his face. All right. Andreas Hofer says his last prayers. All right. Then he cried: "Now I am ready. Fire! My God, how ill you shoot. Good-bye, my land Tyrol."

It seems incredible to me that he had so much time for making comments on their marksmanship, and that he was able to indulge in such long-drawn farewells to his fatherland Tyrol – it is almost coloratura singing, before he finishes. I must find out about him.

Now that I have eaten I am ready for some food for the soul. Plato says: "You feed your body which is mortal. How much more should you feed your soul which is immortal." I have never yet disagreed with anything of Plato's. The only trouble about this body and soul business is that the body can make itself much more unpleasant than the soul when hungry, and in a much shorter time. The soul can always wait. Perhaps the soul is so patient because it knows that it has all eternity before it.

Mantua is delicious. The *corso* leading past my hotel is a long, unbroken, double chain of arcades, all old, of various hues and various ages. From one end of the *corso*, where the Teatro Sociale protrudes in a triangle like an arrow head, to the other end, where it leads into the Piazza Mantegna, one can walk sheltered and at leisure, lingering in front of shops, listening to the song coming from a hidden courtyard, and if it rains not one drop will bespatter you, and if it is fine not even the tip of your nose will get burned.

On one corner of the Piazza Mantegna stands Sant 'Andrea, which is a felicitous mess. It started life as a basilica, and from some angles one can still see the old red walls. The façade is just for once Renaissance, with fluted pillars and sheltering arches, so that it shall not be said that people can do their shopping with dry feet and get wet when they go to church. And the eighteenth century, which did not want to pass unnoticed either, crowned it with a tall, elegantly narrow dome. More arcades are running right and left from the church, and half-way round the corner to the Piazza dell 'Erbe, which is still used to-day as vegetable market.

The stands are shaded by square baldachins of grey-and-white-striped linen. In the foreground, like a gigantic peach washed ashore by the tides of a fruit-filled sea and forgotten since, lies San Lorenzo, pink and completely round. I love those round early churches. They are always a pleasure to look at. One cannot go wrong with them.

The profusion of fresh fruit and plants is framed by old houses painted green and pink and yellow, all faded. It seems as though they have stood for so many centuries looking on the juicy green, the luscious red, the glowing gold of those fruits below, ever new, ever fresh, that they have become imbued with their tints. Farther down the square the vegetables give way to brushes and cords, shoes and hats, nets and velvets, and behind them rises a medley of old arcades, old bells, old clocks, old towers.

I pass beneath two ancient archways which, too, have got their share of arcades; but they bear them on the top, above the arch and, because they are useless up there, they have been walled in. These two archways enclose a tiny square of their own, the Broletto, a sort of ante-room. The arches form the doors and the towers flanking them are the door curtains : they open into a large square, with yet more arcades. If there seems to be a lot of arcades in my description this is not my fault.

Really, these three squares, each leading into the other, each built on a rising slope, remind me of the seventeen Plitvitz lakes in Croatia, where each lake situated on a level slightly higher than the preceding one, spills its water in a splendid cascade into the brim of the lake beneath it. It is obvious that for hundreds of years Mantua was so enamoured with arcades that one square alone could not hold them all and they had to spill forth into the adjoining squares, and from there they trickled down the streets. This third square is called the Sordello. As I sort out the buildings I see that the main arcade generator is the modest-sized Palazzo Ducale, the Gonzaga Palace.

But this time the arcades are not of pale water-colour hues and roundly arched and feminine: they are dark red brick and pointed, their virile outlines seamed with square white stones. The *motif* of the pointed arches is repeated in the pointed and arched windows of the palace, set like twins and united under yet another pointed arch, whereas the white stones are repeated in the white pillars separating the twin windows.

I walk nearer. Although from the distance dark red in colour, when approached the palace fades into a delicately and unevenly blushing grey – a most nostalgic hue. It reminds me very much of the colour of raw goose liver. I mean, of course, the special goose liver, gained from geese who have to live an existence of boredom and fatty degeneration, and who give their lives solely for the purpose of *pâté de foie gras*.

Moreover, the white stones pointing the arcades remind me of the peeled, gleaming white almonds which are stuck into the goose liver before it is fried. A well-prepared goose liver should be so richly spiked with almonds as to bristle like a hedgehog. All this goes to say that the Gonzaga Palace is beautiful. One beautiful thing makes me think of another, I am full of human frailty, and, to my mind, this is the worthiest description one can produce.

Opposite the Gonzaga Palace there are two more fine chunks of goose liver, very similar, only smaller, and one of them without arcades, built at the same time, between the thirteenth and fourteenth centuries. Here I have reached the marrow of Mantua, full of grim efficiency, culminating in the tower with an iron cage attached. Here people who were in disgrace used to be exhibited to make them feel ashamed of themselves.

The Sordello narrows towards the top and it is closed by the cathedral, which is quite pleasant, with a triangular pediment supported by pillars, designed by Giulio Romano; he spread himself in late Renaissance Mantua for all he was worth, having a finger in every artistic pie, probably on account of having been one of Raphael's pupils.

To one side of the cathedral is a fine white palace, seventeenth century in all its glory, the triumph of whipped cream. It is bursting with bulging wrought-iron grilles in front of the windows, with bulging balustrades in front of the balconies, with bulging statues on its roof, and bulging caryatides beneath its portals – in short, it has everything it should have and has it plentifully. But it is no use. It happens to face the Gonzaga Palace, and therefore it has not got a chance. The simple majesty of *foie gras* wins over whipped cream hands down.

I return through side streets filled with more flowers and vegetables, the backwash of the stream of nature's riches which has overflowed from the main market square. Here the stands are humbler, sheltered by grey umbrellas and placed against the backs of buildings I have already passed, so that I have the feeling of wandering amidst the props and wings at the back of a stage. I catch glimpses of towers and flying buttresses and windows giving into courtyards, stepped up in a rising line like a flight of stairs. I turn the corner of the Palazzo della Ragione; it is another fine example of goose liver, identical down to the almonds, only in this case the windows are triplets as opposed to the twins of the Gonzaga Palace.

It is getting dusk. I watch the flower-sellers fold their umbrellas till they droop like moths' wings, and buy the last handful of gentians that has remained in the baskets.

The people of Mantua are a handsome breed, much better to look at than those of Parma and Cremona, who are neither fair nor dark, with no distinction and with pinched, irregular features as though God, being forced to give them the usual eyes, mouths, and noses, had grudged every inch he gave them.

The Mantuans are tall and well made, strong and robust, with brown-black hair, round brown eyes, thick level eyebrows, straight strong noses, and full lips. They look like a cross between Alpine people and Romans, and they give you straight, smiling glances, whereas the Cremonese and Parmesans are inclined to be surly.

I do not know why there are such masses of gentians for sale but it seems to me that the sturdy gentian, with its strongly burning blue flame, its short, straight stem, and its plain, robustly sculptured chalice, is the perfect flowery emblem of the Mantuans.

I take a street branching off the Broletto and emerge on the Piazza Virgiliana. An ugly modern garden has been laid out in the midst of slummy houses and rubble heaps. A few sickly young fir-trees are planted along the paths, and at the top, above two fountains, stands the monument which the town of Mantua put up in honour of Virgil in 1927, which seems a bit late in the day.

Considering that Virgil is Mantua's crowning glory they have been very restrained, to say the least of it.

Two mourning figures in white stone are flanking a white stone balustrade. In the centre rises a pedestal of stone on which they have placed the poet in what, I am sorry to say, looks like cast iron.

He seems a frigid gentleman in flowing garments, one arm raised – about as inspired as though he were addressing a meeting of shareholders of a firm manufacturing underwear.

Behind the garden lies one of the three lakes which embrace the town in their mild blue arms; but to make sure that no element of beauty should reach out to the poet, the view has been cut off with a wall.

I climb on top of the coping and look at the water banded by poplars. It is a prospect of sweet Virgilian melancholy, but empty and expiring, as though this were not the gloaming of the day but the gloaming of poetry itself. The sweetness has gone flat and cloying. It is not the true Virgilian sweetness, but the sweetness to be found in the works of his imitators. I am so disappointed I could weep.

I turn back.

Making my way past the monument I see that, while one of the fountains is playing, the other is dry; and in the middle of the basin there sits a handsome young man in a boiler suit as blue as a gentian flower. He could have come straight out of the *Eclogues*. He who would have been a shepherd in the days long past is now a garage-hand, and the fingers which clasped the flute now hold the spanner. I will refrain from quoting, but – oh, Tityre, albeit thou dost not recline beneath the shelter of the spreading beech, slender reed in hand, musing upon a woodland tune, you have given me the living breath of Virgil. You are my own Virgilian monument which will last as long as I shall.

On the following morning I could make out a list of instructions of how not to furnish a hotel bedroom. The wardrobe, for instance, garishly veneered with some tropical fancy wood, is so high that whenever I want to hang up a dress I have to stand on a chair. This arrangement might be of some use if all my dresses were evening gowns. I am so annoyed that I decide to take my breakfast in a café in the town. They shall not get a penny out of me beyond the price they charge for their streamlined uncomfortable nights.

In the *corso* the arcades are choked with another incipient revolution but, thanks to the presence of sponge-sellers, I am not seized by panic and know that this is a day for 'merry-making'. I think that one can always tell a revolution from market-day by the absence of those sponge-sellers: during a revolution people are so busy that they have no time to think of washing.

In the Piazza dell'Erbe I look at the spinach. It is quite different from ours. The leaves are smaller, a lighter green, and have frayed edges. But who would look for long at the spinach when there are piles of artichokes to behold, of two kinds, some with bluish-purple tips, others shot with fawn. The main colour is a blunted green reminiscent of the patina of antique copper domes and spires.

There is nothing clear-cut in the colouring of the artichoke. There is nothing straightforward in its taste, either. It has a melancholy flavour suggestive of mould and dust and of old books rotting away unread in the damp baronial libraries of old country manors.

Because of its nostalgic complexity, and for many other reasons which I will try to render, the artichoke is my favourite vegetable.

To start with, it is a thing of beauty. In Florence there is the celebrated artichoke fountain, and if I had money I would get myself a copy of it. But nobody in their senses would want a fountain of the carrot or of the turnip.

Now, the artichoke is not a suitable meal for the businessman or the salesgirl. It is by nature inaccessible to him who is used to cutting up his greens, shovelling them on to the fork together with meat and potatoes and swallowing in haste. To eat an artichoke you must have time and space. On your table there must be room not only for the dish containing this subtle and rewarding plant, but also for a sauceboat or a platter with the ingredients from which you can make your own sauce. Then, apart from your plate, there must be a large dish for the discarded leaves and, lastly, a finger-bowl with water floating a slice of lemon. In this case, to have water scented with rose petals would be a frippery in bad taste.

Like so many excellent dishes the artichoke must be eaten with the fingers. It has to be approached at leisure and with reverence, leaf by leaf, and it yields its succulence in such frail measure that each morsel makes one long for the next.

In serving it there are different schools of thought. I think that it should be eaten cold, preferably iced, and be accompanied by a sauce based on oil or butter.

The fashion of doing away with the leaves and serving only the heart fills me with horror. Nothing will excuse this practice, not even in the case of the 'artichaut à l'Aurore', in which instance the plant is hollowed out and serves as a vehicle for a ragoût of mushrooms. This is a degradation fit only for low vegetables, like the marrow or the cucumber. He who does not take the time to conquer the artichoke by stages does not deserve to penetrate to its heart. There are no short cuts in life to anything: least of all to the artichoke.

And, surely, no right-thinking person would forgo willingly the excitement of deflowering the artichoke. As leaf after leaf is stripped away, the texture becomes more tender and the flavour changes. Slowly, as the innermost leaves are reached, one finds that their fleshy part is creamy and pale, with a melting taste which is exquisite. Eating an artichoke is like watching a dance of the seven veils. When the last wreath is peeled off from its base there is the last obstacle to overcome; the centre full of strawy threads which must be scraped away carefully so as not to injure the tender heart underneath.

Most people eat the heart with a fork. I think this is wrong. In any case, if a fork is used, it must be of silver. But better still is to eat it by hand.

After lunch I decide to go and see the Gonzaga Palace. It is quite nice as thirteenth-century palaces go, I say to myself, but rather on the small side and nothing to write home about. But then, what can you expect in a town of the size of Mantua?

And so I walk inside into a dark room and get my ticket of admission. I have to wait for a while, because I have to be accompanied by one of the guards and he has not yet returned from his meal. This annoys me because I hate sightseeing with a guide. It is ridiculous, I think. I have found my way in much larger places than this. But I must submit. It is one of their rules. Probably they are afraid that people might steal or damage some of the stuff.

The guard turns out to be a nice comfortable old man, a bit stiff in the knees. And we set off.

We pass through several rooms with good pictures and not so good pictures and copies of marvellous pictures. Mainly Gonzaga family portraits and the portraits of their courtiers, their philosophers, their musicians, and their dwarfs. There are so many copies of paintings because the originals are in collections in other towns, all over the world. There exist about four hundred and fifty Gonzaga family portraits, done by people like Leonardo, Tintoretto, Titian, Van Dyck, Rubens, El Greco, Clouet, the best that money could buy at various ages. The Gonzaga did not believe in stinting themselves.

There is a Rubens, large as paintings go in general but modest as far as Rubens goes. It shows the then reigning Gonzaga with his wife, and the courtiers crowding on the steps leading to the throne, and above their heads Rubens has worked up a lather of clouds which promise a build-up of a celestial army and a mêlée of allegorical figures. If I know my Rubens, one of them should float down and crown the ruler with laurels. But they are not there. Instead, there is a black streak cutting through the soap-suds. Then the painting goes on with a battle-scene. This, too, stops half-way, and there is something else. And on the side there are two or three Rubenesque fragments separately framed. What is it all about? Did Rubens paint a jigsaw puzzle?

He did not. He painted a huge picture, in his grandest and most successful manner. When Napoleon came to Mantua he wanted to steal the picture and take it with him to Paris. But the thing was so large. Napoleon cut up the canvas. And there was still so much of it that Napoleon lost heart. He took some bits and pieces with him, what he fancied most, and left the rest behind. It is this scum and backwash left in the Napoleonic wake which has been pieced together and put back on the wall.

Now, here for once there arises the curious situation that we behold an original work of art chopped up already into what is known as 'details'. Details are the invention of art books. Art books are a pest. A well-meaning pest but still a pest.

Opening an art book we might come across a colour-plate with the following text: "Winged dachshund with Vienna sausage and garland, detail from an allegorical painting by Mrs. Edith Templeton. On the extreme left can be seen the nostril of Mrs. Templeton's aunt Alice, the donor of the picture."

Owing to publications such as this, thousands of people are familiar with a detail, say the arm of a prophet or the head of an angel, seen with a clarity and thoroughness with which they were never meant to be seen. Also, the posture of arm or head loses its meaning because one cannot tell what they are balancing in the rest of the picture.

Whether you like it or not – I myself love it – the greatest paintings ever done were aristocratic in character. They were not meant to be placed in cosy little rooms in cosy little houses. They were composed to fill the entire ceiling of a church or the halls of palaces or the vaults of tombs. They were not meant for human ants to climb up close to them, train electric flash-lights on them, and click a camera for reproductions in art books.

If you know Giotto or Michelangelo from art books you never know them at all, because you cannot get the extreme ecstasy which I call 'the plunge'. The plunge is like all plunges – in the nature of a shock. It is an overwhelming feeling of such strength that it affects you bodily. It is the finished sum and harmony of, say, Giotto's art which rushes at you in an instant and drowns you. It is only when you have come up once more to the surface that you begin to sort yourself out and, with it, the picture.

The very fact that painting can make you plunge is, to me, the proof that painting is the highest of arts. Even with a statue you have to walk round, till you can take it in completely. With music and letters the process is slower still, and you have to listen and read for a long time till you can follow the gradual unfolding of the theme.

And it is just these infernal details which prevent your ever taking the plunge. There is a saying beloved by literary editors when they return a manuscript practically unread: "I don't have to eat the whole ox to know that the meat is tough."

For the only possible enjoyment of the master painters the opposite is true. You must take them whole or leave them alone.

When it comes to painting, eat the whole ox and you will thrive. Eat a *filet mignon* and it will give you indigestion.

"It's a pity," I say to my guide, and we leave the butchered Rubens and enter the next room. I look out of the window. Now, I know full well that every self-respecting palace is built round a courtyard, and as I look out I see the usual stately pillared square, with green shrubs and urns and a statue in the middle. All very proper and just as it should be.

We enter the dining-hall, where the walls and ceiling are painted all over with *trompe-d'oeil* trelliswork entwined with vines and behind the lattices there are glimpses of landscapes, so that it seems as though we were walking through a garden.

Once more I look out of the window. We should by now have done the round. But there is a different courtyard this time, also framed with a pillared colonnade, but in the sixteenth-century style, whereas the former was early Renaissance. Here there are no statues but wisteria has drawn its grey stems up and down the pillars and unfurled its melancholy flags of amethyst. "The palace is bigger than I thought," I say to myself.

More rooms. Some have ceilings worked in geometrical patterns embossed and encrusted, mostly blue and gilt, some have frescoes by Giulio Romano and his school. I do not know how many rooms we are traversing but I have the impression that everything that ever existed, or was believed to have existed, is painted in these halls – everything that is good and expensive, from the episode of the wooden horse in Troy down to scenes of Renaissance duck shooting.

I glance out of the window and behind a wall I see a church with a square tower. I try to place it in the city.

"What is this church?" I ask. "Where exactly in Mantua is it? I thought I had seen all the main churches, but I have not come across this one yet."

"Of course not, *signora*. This church is within the Gonzaga Palace."

We pass on, and each time I look out of the window there is a different courtyard. I am beginning to lose feeling of time and space, walking beneath these ever-changing frescoes, moving past those ever-changing views outside.

Meanwhile there is a profusion of the beautiful and the curious to distract me from my bewilderment, and sometimes it is difficult to separate the two. One of the ceilings had a medallion with a picture of Amor and Psyche kissing, and the painter has given them only one nose between them. I must say, they do very well as it is. He must have felt already what our present-day photographers always preach: "For photography, your nose cannot be too small. A nose is a nuisance, it always gets in the way of other more interesting features."

Another ceiling is worked in the lines of a labyrinth. I like this idea. I imagine a Gonzaga, tired of reading and talking philosophy, lying down in his bedroom and solving the meanders of the labyrinth instead of doing a crossword puzzle.

In one of the ballrooms there is a fresco of a female Victory, stretching out an arm which holds a laurel wreath. It is a piece of trick painting. Wherever you may stand, the arm with the wreath is pointing at you. I should have liked to give this room with this fresco as a present to the Iron Duke. I think he would have been more amused with such flattery than with all those unimaginative Field-marshal's batons which the sovereigns of his time presented to him. Fortunate Wellington. Wherever you stood, Victory stood facing you.

How very different from him whom you defeated, and whose spectral bust in white plaster now comes before my eyes.

We are now in the room where Napoleon slept during his

conqueror's visit to Mantua. Napoleon's bedroom is not large and is quite square. It is furnished with simple mahogany and jade-green hangings. I touch one of the tattered curtains which drape the four-poster bed and feel the threads of the coarse silk slipping between my fingers. Not a desirable bedroom, rather dark. And no settee or soft chair of any kind. Still, I would rather have it than my room at the Romagna. And now I must look out and see what view Napoleon had when he got up in the morning. I go to the window and this time I see a fortress, built in the fourteenth century. It is the Castel San Giorgio and, needless to say, it also is contained within the grounds of the Gonzaga Palace. I begin to wonder what isn't. I hope Napoleon liked it. I like it very much. It has those crenella-tions, particular to that period, which run close beneath the top of the roof and the top of the tower, curving outwards like the petals of a blossom half in bud and ready to burst open.

We move on, and pass the Castel from another side, and now I see that the moat is still filled with water and beyond it spreads one of the Mantuan lakes. To put me out of my agony the guide tells me that the palace contains the mere trifle of fifteen courtyards. I feel like reeling.

We come to another wing, and now we have to climb up a spiral staircase which is not a staircase at all but merely a spirally mounting slope, set at intervals with flat stone ridges. This was made for horses, to prevent their slipping: the Gonzaga at one time used to ride on horseback into their banqueting-halls. There is a completely self-contained palace built for the ten court dwarfs, with tiny rooms, tiny alcoves, and tiny stairs, and there is a special suite of rooms for the two favourite dwarfs.

In another wing there is the chair on which Virgil sat, a throne-shaped seat carved out of a single stone, the curved back made in one piece with the arms. Of course, Virgil never sat on it, this is sheer tourists' delight, but perhaps the chair dates from Virgilian days, and when the guide invites me to sit down on it I do so like a shot.

"Don't be shy. Make yourself comfortable," he says. I lean back. Yes, it is very comfortable, though chilly.

"Now you will become very clever, because you have sat on Virgil's chair."

I tell him what I think of such irresponsible statements. My mother used to make me eat brains by telling me that they would make me clever, and when one day I pointed out to her that the brains in question were calf's and sheep brains and that, really, she should give me human brains if she wanted to get results, she got huffy and told me never to mention brains to her again.

Before this, when my logic was not yet as advanced, my mother used to tell me that if I ate up my rice-pudding supper instead of spitting it on to Nanny and the walls, I should grow up into a lovely, blonde, blue-eyed woman. I always wanted to have blonde hair and blue eyes, and so I ate the pudding night after night. I should have known better than to barter present joys for future achievements. Now I have no nanny and no nursery walls to spit upon and I still have dark hair and dark eyes. The guide is sympathetic, he says he is sorry for me, but on the other hand he is also sorry for my mother and cannot really blame her.

We climb up a gallery above another courtyard. The arches, framed by thick twisted pillars, are open on both sides. One side looks down on the lake; the other, jutting with balconies, on to a long stretched lawn. This space was reserved for jousts and tournaments. The ladies were seated on the balconies, and when they were tired of throwing their gloves to the knights below, to give them something to tilt about, they could turn round and watch the regattas held on the lake.

We descend and come into the part of the palace called the "*gabinetti Isabelliani*", after Isabella d'Este, who was the most famous of the Gonzaga wives. Her husband, the Duke Francesco di Gonzaga, was the most important of the Gonzaga but he was not a good soldier. He was better at diplomacy.

Earlier in the afternoon I had passed several of Isabella's portraits, among them a copy of the best-known one, by Titian, which is now in the museum in Vienna. She is a fair, pale, round-faced lady with shaved-off eyebrows which was fashionable at that time, though on the Titian she still has them. She was one of the greatest patrons of the arts that ever lived. After her husband's death she went into life-long mourning, and had these chambers specially built for the purpose of retirement. For reasons best known to herself they are situated very low and one has to descend some stairs into a sort of semi-basement. The rooms are tiny and have low ceilings – it is obvious that she wanted something cosy and intimate by then and was tired of grandeur. Also, she wanted to be sorry for herself and to be able to complain to her friends how cramped she was: "No room at all. I couldn't swing a dwarf round."

One chamber has door frames and cornices carved of a semi-precious stone, veined and mottled in colours of autumnal foliage, and the walls are hung with crimson satin embossed with Isabella's emblem – a bundle of flames. On one wall there is the inscription of her motto: "*Nec spera, nec time.*" It is a vile motto, I think, "Fear not, hope not." One might just as well not be alive.

Another motto, the favourite one of Francesco, to be found written round the ceiling of the labyrinth room, is the famous: "*Forse che si, forse che no.*" Apparently the labyrinth is the visual representation of this "Perhaps yes, perhaps no".

The guide shows me another of her portraits, done after her husband's death. He shows it with a leer, saying: "It is not a nice painting, but I think the painter must have been a nice man."

It seems that Isabella was consoled by art in more ways than one. When d'Annunzio visited the Gonzaga Palace with some friends, one of them asked him whether he thought that Isabella's seclusion had been really – so to speak – watertight, and he replied: "*Forse che si, forse che no.*"

In another room there is a draft of Mantegna's painting of the *Madonna of the Victory*, done by a seventeenth-century painter. It is very strange. Thin white lines drawn on a black board. It is only the skeleton of a picture and one looks at it with a deep shudder, the same shudder one feels when looking at someone's bones in an X-ray photograph. One feels one has really no right to see it at all. The lines are so faint that from some angles they are barely visible, as though a long-dead spider had spun its web centuries ago.

The story about the picture is stranger still: Francesco Gonzaga fought a battle at Fornovo against the King of France. When the battle was over, each of them rode away, claiming that he had gained the victory. This was not one of the occasions when Francesco said to himself: perhaps yes, perhaps no. And in order to celebrate the victory of which he was so sure, he commissioned Mantegna to paint the *Madonna of the Victory*. The picture is now in the Louvre.

Now we enter the Castel San Giorgio, and come to the room which is the pearl of this town known as the Palazzo Gonzaga. It is a small, square room with a high ceiling, and is called the *Camera degli Sposi*. Heaven knows why it is called bridal chamber, because no groom and bride, or anybody else, ever lived here. Of course, the guide does not tell me this – that sort of chill fact is not beloved by tourists.

I was told so later. But already now, while I am contemplating it, I feel that there is nothing about this chamber which strikes one as the least bit wedding-like. Unless, of course, one might say that it symbolizes the fact that marriage is built on deceit. For in this room, which in the guide's words is "*tutto Mantegna*," Mantegna has celebrated an orgy of faking.

Looking up, one sees a cupola rising from the middle of the ceiling encircled by a balustrade with delicious cherubs peeping over it. My common sense tells me, of course, that the cherubs are not real and that they are painted, but what my common sense does not tell me at once is that there is no cupola and no balustrade. The ceiling is completely flat.

Surrounding this central fake the ceiling space is divided into stuccoed reliefs in the shape of oval medallions, with the sculptured heads of men and women popping out from the beading and looking down. There are no stucco reliefs and no sculptured heads. It is only paint on flat surface.

One wall is covered with a yellowish paper patterned in black, hung so carelessly that the corners have come unstuck and curled up. There is no wallpaper. It is paint.

We turn to the two other walls.

Here Mantegna has dropped his disguises of builder, stone mason, stucco worker, and paper-hanger. He has reverted to painting. I behold the two greatest pictures in the world. This is rot, of course, there is no such thing. But while I am here this is what I feel. No, it is much more than that. I know it with the certainty of illumination. It is an ecstasy like falling in love or being forgiven one's sins and, like all ecstasies, it does not last. Like a crocodile one comes to the surface, sees the sun, and sinks back into the mire. Now I will try to describe my glimpse of the sun.

There are two gentlemen hunters, seen talking to each other in a wood. One of them is leaning against his horse, his fist resting on his hip, while the other, listening to him, holds his hound on a leash. This hound, a white bull-terrier, is also provided with a friend of his own kind, the other hunter's hound, and communes with him in his own way.

It is not only that the two couples, human and canine, are facing each other in a similar manner, but the masters' faces bear a great resemblance to those of their animals. All four of them look noble, sober, decent, stupid, lazy, and reliable. The two hunters could be English country squires, and they are clearly barking in mono-syllables, saying something like:

"Had a good day?"

"Not bad."

"Same here."

"Fair kill?"

"Middling."

"Same here."

The hounds say exactly the same. Only the horse seems to be an outsider.

In the background there are crazily shaped rocks which look very unsafe. They hang over and form a natural tunnel. It is not clear what keeps them from toppling over and, as though to show his conviction that they are quite safe, Mantegna has put a fortress on each of them. The whole is rendered in clear, clean colours with each line well defined and no messy shadows. In the lower right-hand corner Mantegna got playful again and faked a stone balustrade which seems to protrude into the room and made one of the hounds step over it and out of the picture, with one front paw.

On the second wall is the other of the two best pictures in the world. It is given over entirely to a huge Gonzaga family, all queueing up to get into the picture, and here Mantegna has faked again, to make us believe that they are crowded together in a room with sloping walls and under a sloping roof; the place is so crammed with Gonzagas that the last two or three members of the family, young men who have not yet proved their worth, have been pushed out of the room and, because they are eager to be in the picture nevertheless, they have squeezed themselves on to a flight of stairs leading down from the place. The effect is overwhelming.

I am too dazed to pay much attention to the sights on our way back. And then, God knows how many hours after I started, I stand once more outside on the Sordello. I suppose I have only seen a tenth of that 'modest-sized' Gonzaga Palace, which "is quite nice as palaces go, . . . but nothing to write home about. But then, what can you expect in a town of the size of Mantua?"

I have found a good restaurant off the Piazza Mantegna. It is called Vesuvio. Like most small restaurants it has a bar where one can drink coffee, wine, and *apéritifs*, served by the *padrone*. From the bar one enters the dining-room, where one is received by Virgilio, the waiter. Virgilio has a sweet nature and he needs it, because the Italian is a difficult customer when he goes to eat. He has to be cosseted by the waiter, coaxed and talked into ordering.

Through the raised transom of the service hatch one can see straight into the kitchen, and if one has forgotten to order something from Virgilio one can yell one's afterthought to the cook.

If one is unlucky, she will come out and make a personal appearance, brandishing a carving-knife and treating one to a résumé of one's character and the character of one's ancestors. Being human, she assumes the worst. Her favourite word on such occasions is "*Mal educata*". For instance, one is 'ill educated' when one demands brains on a day when the butcher has not sent any. But this does not mean that she does not like you. If you are lucky, she will make a peaceful and harmonious entry, bearing a token of her goodwill. She will carry a whole joint on a trencher – raw, of course – for your approval. You will inspect the meat and indicate which part shall be sliced and cooked for you. This is what I call being served. As my mother would have said, ironically: "*Tout comme chez nous.*" Virgilio always keeps an artichoke for me, even if he has to deny other guests for my sake. This has nothing to do with his tip. It is typically Italian. When an Italian likes you, he will do anything to please.

I remember once, in Florence, when I went to Santo Spirito, there were about five other people in the church, sightseeing. A friar entered from the vestry, came up to me and asked me if I wanted to see the sacristy. Of course I said yes. It was a lovely octagonal room, covered with paintings by Sangallo, and because it was so precious it was kept under lock and key by the monk. When we came out I asked him why he did not show the sacristy to the other people, too. "Because I didn't like them," he said.

Virgilio serves a sweet dish called the "*coppa Vesuvio*". As the name says, it is an edifice served in a silver cup. A foundation of melted chocolate and Marsala rises to pinnacles of whipped cream. When I do not feel like a pudding there is a fine choice of cheeses, some of them local. The *panettone* is pale, like old ivory, with a faintly bitter flavour of almonds, a cheese of ineffable melancholy, of truly Virgilian elegy. The *stracchino* is a full-cream cheese, soft and supple. It arrives brick-shaped and wrapped in waxed paper. If one could eat marble and creamy alabaster this is what it would taste like. Who would dare to describe it?

Eating cheese in Mantua is a thoughtful business, made for pondering over Virgil. Virgil was not born in Mantua, but in a village near it, called Andes. Now it is called Pietole. There are some beastly scholars who deny this and say that he was born on the shores of Lake Garda. They are in a minority and nobody believes them. One has only to look at the Mantuan countryside, marshy, reedy, with elms, beeches, and willows, and one can see Virgil written all over it. Water and soil intermingle constantly, there are no clear, well-defined outlines. Here nature is truly flooded with tears. It is this which creates the charming sadness of the Virgilian landscape, together with the colouring. Even on a bright day the blue of sky and water are dulled, as though reflected in a pewter mirror.

All that is known about Virgil's person is that he was dark, tall, with an awkward slouching bearing, exceedingly pale and that he suffered from stomach trouble. The stomach trouble is known from *The Journey to Brindisi*, which is one of Horace's satires, although it is not a satire at all but a humorously chatty account of a junket in which Horace took part, written in the rather slovenly, comfortable Horatian hexameters. The excuse for this journey was a mission, in which Maecenas had to go to Brindisi from Rome. Maecenas was not just a lover of the arts, he was a dictator of the arts and a very important person in the service of Octavian, who later became the Emperor Augustus. To-day we might say that Maecenas was the Minister of Information and that he was to the Roman Empire what the Arts Council and the BBC are to us to-day. The writers who conformed to the official policy were highly rewarded, like Horace and Virgil. Those who did not, were exiled, like Ovid, and their works were banned from the Public Libraries.

At that time, after Caesar's death, the power of Rome was split between Octavian and Mark Antony. Although Octavian's sister was Mark Antony's wife, there was no love lost between the two. Octavian was jealous of Mark Antony, who was older, more experienced, and more popular with Caesar's legions, whereas Mark Antony was constantly egged on by Cleopatra to go to war against the young Octavian and to finish him off once for all. And so, although these two would have liked to eat each other for breakfast, they had to make a pact of alliance and mutual assistance, because they were threatened by other enemies. Octavian was worried about Pompey, and Mark Antony was not comfortable on account of a Berber King in Africa. They agreed to meet at Brindisi and, in order to prepare this conference, they sent out their ambassadors to arrange matters in advance.

Now Maecenas did not feel like making such a long and boring journey on his own, and therefore some of the literary *élite* were asked to join him during his trip.

To start with, Horace set out from Rome with a Greek scholar, who was also a member of the Maecenas clique. He chose the Appian route, because it was less strenuous and he was lazy. He got ill from some water he drank on the way and was huffy when he could not eat and had to watch his friends making a good dinner. At Anxus he met Maecenas and his party, which included some of those wretched creatures, found at every official and private court, who are tolerated merely because they lend themselves as the butt for other people's jokes and whose natural element is shame and derision. There was also Fonteinus Capito, who was so polished that "you could pass a nail across him without detecting a flaw".

They were welcomed by the town clerk of Anxus, who, to do them honour had put on his best uniform of purple and was preceded by a boy carrying burning incense; the sophisticated gentlemen from Rome nearly died with laughter at the sight of this provincial fop.

They continued their journey, and on the following day they

were joined by Virgil, and by his friends, Plotius and Varius, who were also poets. Horace's pleasure at seeing them is touching: "Souls more candid than they the earth never bore. Oh, what embraces, what rejoicings. There is nothing better on earth than to have good friends."

They stopped in a cottage at midday. Some of the party went off to play tennis, but Horace and Virgil both went to rest indoors: Horace because the strong light hurt his inflamed eyes, and Virgil, because he could not indulge in games owing to his weak digestion. "To play goes Maecenas. To sleep myself and Virgil. The sport is bad for blear eyes and a weak stomach."

During the whole journey Horace had to put salve on his eyes. They continued, and stopped for dinner at a country inn in Beneventum, where the host, overcome by the honour of receiving such grand company, lost his head and set the kitchen range on fire. This incident, too, was welcomed with great hilarity. The gentlemen from Rome had the time of their lives rescuing some of the charred dinner from the flames, whereas their slaves looked on with scared faces.

The following night they spent in a cottage, where the smoke of damp logs annoyed Horace. But there was worse to come. He had made an assignation with one of the local girls – Virgil was not up to such sport, owing to his stomach trouble – and waited for "the lying wench" half the night. She did not turn up. "At last I fell asleep and the sacrifice I had prepared for Venus was taken from me during a dream." I am certain she had summed up the situation. Horace was young then, and appetizing, but, like most poets, he had nothing to offer, apart from his natural charm. From the girl's point of view Maecenas must have been much more rewarding.

After this they proceeded by carriage through Apulia, and stopped in Aquatia, and again there was great merriment – this time over the local superstition, which was the belief that on a certain stone incense would burst into flame without being lit. It was a miracle of the gods. Horace and his party, enlightened as they were and as contemptuous of folksy lore as any of their counterparts would be to-day, refused even to be given a demonstration of the miracle. "The gods live their own selfish lives and do not care for the mortals. Let Apelles the Jew believe this – not I." In other words, Horace's attitude is, "Tell it to the marines". And yet, what a pity he was so enlightened. Because the superstition was true. Frankincense did take fire on the sacred stone owing to a phenomenon which to-day would have delighted the world. It was burning petrol, which seeped through a crack in the soil.

The next day they reached their destination: "In Brindisi I have reached the end of my paper and journey." This is the most charming ending of a traveller's account I have ever read.

So, really, what with his bad health, his native landscape, and the sorrow over his confiscated estates, it is not astonishing that Virgil's poetry was infused with sadness.

Although Virgil seems conventional to us to-day because we are used to him, he was, in his youth, in the literary *avant-garde*. In his day Epicureanism was fashionable among the intellectual set because it was considered daring and a menace against the existing order. Virgil was influenced by it. That he was a proper Epicurean, which means that he was all for austerity, is obvious in the *Georgics*. It is a silly popular misconception to think that Epicureanism advocates the chasing of pleasures, regardless of consequences. Epicurus divides the pleasures into those which are necessary and those which are not, and by the time he has finished one finds that the necessary pleasures, of which he approves, are precious few. Where the teaching became revolutionary was in its conviction that the gods are indifferent to men, that there is no heaven and no hell, and that therefore it would be idiotic to regulate one's life in order to please the gods. The Roman authorities did not like this idea, because fear of the gods was a great help in governing the masses.

Virgil was not only beloved by his contemporaries as a person – which is a great merit, considering how malicious literary cliques always are – but even as a poet he was of a modesty which is admirable. Thus, after he had finished the *Aeneid* he was quite depressed about it, and did not want to have it published. He set out for a three years' journey to Greece, in order to get authentic local copy for the parts which take place in Greece, and he wanted to rewrite the poem afterwards. In Athens he met the Emperor, who asked him to accompany him back to Rome. Virgil could not refuse the august invitation. During the journey, in North Africa, he 'got a sunstroke', fell ill, and died shortly afterwards when they reached Brindisi. He was only fifty-one. I think he must have died from a stomach ulcer which perforated his inside.

Before he set out for Greece he had given instructions to a friend that the *Aeneid* should be burned, in case he died before rewriting it. Fortunately Augustus forbade it, and the poem was published in its unfinished state.

This is so unlike his cocky, tippling friend Horace, who had no doubts about his own merit and who assured the world that in his poems he had built himself a monument higher than the pyramids, more lasting than bronze, and so on. What is now so amusing about it is, that Horace believed he would last as long as the Roman Empire lasted, which, in his opinion, was for ever. Here, Horace, conceited as he was, was not conceited enough. The Vestal Virgin descends no more the temple steps with the *pontifex maximus*, the Roman Empire is no more. But Horace is still read.

During the Middle Ages, Virgil was the most famous poet in the world. Not because of the beauty of his work, but because people had got it into their heads that he had predicted the advent of Christ and the foundation of the Church. This is complete nonsense, of course, but it is picturesque nonsense and it persists to this day.

In that particular poem, the fourth Eclogue, Virgil prophesies the birth of a boy who will rule the world and inaugurate an age of universal peace. Most probably he referred to the child which Augustus was expecting to be born at the time, and the poem was nothing but political flattery. Christ never ruled the world, as child or otherwise, and he made it clear that he didn't want to. And as to the political record of Christianity and the spreading of universal peace under its influence, the least said about it the better.

Because of this prophetic poem Virgil was made into a mystic and magic figure, a chief witch doctor, and had shrines built to him and was adored. In Dante's days there was a flourishing industry of idiotic tales about Virgil and his sorcery. One of them sounds very much like television: Virgil built a mirror in which one could see and hear the armies advancing to besiege Rome, when they were still a hundred miles away. Most of them were set in Naples, probably because he was buried there. These legends are so crude and cruel that they do not bear repeating, and are a sad example of the fact that great men are rarely popular for what they really achieved.

It takes mental acrobatics to read anything smacking of Christianity into Virgil's works. He was a pagan in the finest sense of the word. His God was impersonal, and he saw him all over the place in nature, in the pantheistic way. Virgil's philosophy is Indian in origin and came to Rome through Greece.

In Mantua, too, Virgil became a local deity, and they put up the first Virgilian monument in 1200, stuck on the wall of a palace in the Broletto. It is still there. It is small, and so worn that one cannot see much except that he seems to be seated on a throne and looks uncomfortable. And he would have felt most uncomfortable, had he known that the Mantuans worshipped him as the patron saint of their commune. It is one of the ironies of life that Virgil, of all people, who made the finest propaganda for the Roman Empire, should have been chosen as symbol for the independence of a little city-state like Mantua.

I think that it is very unfair when people say that Virgil was pandering to Augustus when he wrote the *Aeneid*, and that he was glorifying the Roman Empire only in order to please Augustus. I am convinced that by the time he wrote the *Aeneid*, when Octavian had already become Emperor, Virgil had shed all youthful political fancies and had become sincerely conservative and firmly believed that Rome was a guarantee of peace and stability. People also think that they are very nasty about him by saying that he imitated the Greeks. Of course he did, he had to start with something. Nobody ever dropped ready-made from the sky. But being Virgil, he soon found his own blue-grey, watery, twilit charm which flows through every line: even the goddess of love appears to Aeneas wrapped in a grey-blue cloak. I don't care what anybody says, he is one of the greatest poets.

When people abuse him I always want to say: "If you don't like him don't read him." Unfortunately I cannot make this remark, because so many had to read him at school, whether they wanted to or not, and this is probably one of the reasons why he is not universally liked. Bad teaching creates dislike where it should have bred admiration.

This does not mean that I like the whole of the *Aeneid*. The *Aeneid* is an epic plum-pudding and one must pick out the fruit and leave the suet on one's plate. Yet, Virgil is my darling among poets, and I will talk now about the largest plum. It is Dido.

The creation of Dido is revolutionary because Dido is the first ill-used woman in literature. A woman who has lived for thirty years and has never been ill-used, has not lived at all. Therefore Dido is as universally important as Hamlet, Faust and Don Juan.

Superficially speaking, Dido is not the first legendary woman who was made use of and left high and dry by her lover. To name a few only, there was Medea and Ariadne and Circe and Calypso and Nausicaa. In all these cases the lover-hero behaved shabbily, with a similar sort of shabbiness as Aeneas towards Dido.

Yet, there is a vast difference. In all those cases previous to Dido, the deserted women found some balm which soothed their wounds, something to fall back on, something which enabled them to snap their fingers and say: "He has made his exit most disgracefully; there will never be anyone like him, and if I ever come across anybody like him, again, I will run for dear life. To hell with him."

Ill-starred Dido is the only one among them who is truly tragic;

when Aeneas left her, she had to demolish herself, because she had lost all her life-preserving forces.

Let us take the others one by one to see the difference.

Medea, when Jason left her could get her own back on him. She killed him and his new bride and her own children and left the country in a magic chariot and spent the rest of her long life as guest at a king's court.

Both Circe and Calypso were the *demi-mondaines* of the antique world. We are told they were immortal. This means that they were women of indeterminate age who did not have to possess youth in order to fascinate. Being immortal they were as hard-boiled as they come; they knew perfectly well that the affair with Odysseus could not last for ever. They could not complain when he left them, because they were not young girls whom he had seduced: they had done the seducing themselves and very efficiently too. We are told that they lived on lonely islands. This was no hardship for them because an attractive woman will find a lover even in the desert. The lonely island means that socially they lived in isolation and independence. They had private means and no family ties. They could do what they wanted and were responsible to no one. Circe is the woman who has a string of lovers whom she has degraded to such depth that one could say she has turned them into swine. Calypso on the other hand concentrates on one man at the time. Yet, fundamentally they are the same, and, whatever a man does to them, they will not be mortally wounded.

Ariadne, it is true, must have had a very nasty awakening on Naxos, when she found in the early light of the morning that Theseus had disappeared. But her shock was not a deep or lasting one, because there was Bacchus all ready to pounce on her as soon as Theseus was out of the way. It was a case of good riddance to bad rubbish: any woman in her senses, given the choice, would rather have a God than a soldier of fortune.

Now we come to the most difficult case, that of Nausicaa. Here we have a warm-hearted, sensitive, impulsive young girl of good

family, who has led a sheltered life and who cannot tell a gig-
olo when she sees one. By the time she has fallen in love with
Odysseus and planned the trousseau and seen herself already
married to him, it becomes clear that he is a married man and has
no intention even of making love to her. This is bitter. This means
suffering. But Nausicaa is the type of girl with whose sufferings
one cannot feel pity—one only feels impatient. She is over-sensitive,
intelligent and foolish at the same time. A bad mixture. It is a
mixture which makes her fall in love invariably with the most
unsuitable men. I am sure that, before Odysseus, Nausicaa had
already fallen in love with her father's driver and with her drawing
teacher. Odysseus was merely the most glamorous of all the partners
in her one-sided love affairs. Though she was more vulnerable
than the immortal nymphs, she had no intention of committing
suicide. When Odysseus bade her farewell, she found nothing better
to say than: "When you get home safely, do think of me sometimes. After all, I did save your life, you know." And he, polite as
ever, assured her that he would pray to her like to a goddess. It
did not mean a thing and he could not have said less in the circumstances. The thing to do with the Nausicaas of this world is to hit
them over the head and to force them into an arranged marriage.

But Dido? Poor Dido. She was neither a man-eater like the
immortal nymphs, nor an extremely clever and capable intellectual
like Medea, nor an insipid young goose like Nausicaa, nor an
accommodating scatter-brain like Ariadne. Dido is an ordinary
woman, but built on a scale of such magnitude that she becomes
heroic. She is fine, beautiful, not particularly distinguished and not
particularly clever. Whereas the women who fell for Odysseus
were outside of life owing to their circumstances, like the nymphs,
or because they had not yet entered into life, like Nausicaa, Dido
is in the middle of life. She has a decent past of which she need not
be ashamed. She has been happily married. When we meet her
she is a widow. She is a ruling Queen and as such is responsible to
her people, not only in official matters but also in her private life.

She cannot do what she wants because every one of her actions will be criticized. As soon as she becomes Aeneas's mistress, gossip sweeps through the town of Carthage, with hundred eyes, hundred ears and hundred tongues. She has no magic to fall back on like the nymphs and like Medea. She has not got the shelter of her family like Nausicaa. If she were of smaller stature, Aeneas's behaviour would leave her deeply hurt; as she is heroic, she has to behave like the ordinary woman pushed to the extreme of magnitude: she has to demolish herself.

She is a woman in the fullest meaning of the word. Even in her greatest moment of shame and grief she behaves like a complete woman. She says: "You are going to leave me. I cannot bear it. If at least I had a child by you, to remind me of you always."

But the heart of Dido's tragedy does not lie in the fact that Aeneas left her. It lies in his unworthiness.

That he is a low adventurer is clear already in the beginning, when he first meets Dido: would a decent man tell of his woes in public and regale a large number of guests at an official banquet – all strangers to him – with a long string of hard luck stories? You may say that Odysseus did the same during his travels. But then, Odysseus was not a decent man either.

Yet, Odysseus, being the accomplished soldier of fortune that he is, wins all our hearts. The world does not bear Odysseus a grudge because he left so many women. But no one has ever forgiven Aeneas for having deserted Dido. Aeneas is shown up as the utterly conventional bore that he is, a tailor's dummy with a mission, a pompous dunce, a cold fish.

When the Gods tell him that he must leave Carthage and get busy founding the Roman Empire, he has not even got the guts to tell Dido about it. And when at last she confronts him and tells him that she saw his men building his new fleet, he has nothing more inspiring to say than: "Yes, that's quite true, but you know, I never did promise you marriage, did I?" It was the knowledge that she had given herself to this creature that made her end her life. And

Aeneas, mean and suburban to the end, tried to get Dido's forgiveness when he met her shade in the underworld. Not for her sake, of course, but because he wanted to console himself that he had not behaved so badly after all. I am glad to say that her spectre, still bleeding from her mortal wound, turned speechlessly away from him, despite his entreaties. Aeneas is the man who uses words like: "frankly, honestly, as a matter of fact," at the beginning of his utterances, in order to lend more weight to his platitudinous opinions.

"Frankly, I've got to go, the Gods are getting short tempered with me. Actually, it's all about this business of founding the Roman Empire. Incidentally, there'll be a lot of fighting before I'm through." What can one do with a creature like this? For me, the *Aeneid* is finished after Dido's death. But is she dead?

I will now put her on the scales and see what happens. On this plate of the scales I put Dido on her funeral pyre, with the sword in her breast, bleeding to death. And just when she sinks into the mists of antiquity and has become invisible, I see her rising up again, in the bright light of our own times. Again she is of exalted rank. Again she is a fine beautiful woman, not very clever, not very distinguished. Again Aeneas has forsaken her. Although this time he has not left her side to set out for the Italian shore, she knows just as surely that his love for her has died. Again she is mortally wounded and again she is driven to demolish herself. I see her placing her red bag by her side and laying herself on the rails and I hear the roar of the approaching train: I have witnessed the end of Anna Karenina.

In the beginning of the eighteenth century the Mantuans founded the Academia Virgiliana as an institute for culture and science. It is still going strong to-day, and stands in the Piazza Dante. Needless to say, Dante also came to Mantua during his exile, but he did not stay for long. It is not known with whom he quarrelled there.

Apart from that shrine to Virgil, the Mantuans did nothing about him. When the French came to Mantua during the wars of the revolution, in 1789, their general, who was a lover of Virgil, commanded that something should be done about the poet. And so they built the Piazza Virgiliana, in very good taste, in the neo-classic style of that time, discreetly sumptuous, rather like the Place Vendôme in Paris, but without the Ritz. In the middle of this oval piazza, in the place where in Paris Napoleon stands on a column, they put up a column with Virgil's bust in bronze, in restrained and impeccable taste.

This was a very good thing, because the less there is of a statue the less chances there are that it will look foolish. A head with only a neck attached can never get itself into all the innumerable silly attitudes of which the whole body is capable. What I saw the other evening was the ground of this original Piazza Virgiliana, destroyed by bombs during the war. But partly it had been pulled down already, before that, and made resplendent with the new garden and the new monument. If they had to do something they should have had the sense to rebuild the old square as it was.

Now that I have seen the Gonzaga Palace I am not surprised to learn that this little place of theirs was not sufficient for their needs. When the Gonzaga had to have country air, and wanted to get right away from things, they could retire to Sabbioneta, which is twenty miles away from the town. But on the outskirts of Mantua they built the Palazzo del Te and put their mistresses inside it, to have them close at hand. The Palazzo del Te is only ten minutes' walk from the *corso*. It lies at the end of an avenue of poplars which look good against the sky of Virgilian blue.

A quick-eyed, sharp-featured old woman meets me at the gate. "Isn't it dreadful to think of it, *signora*?"

"Too dreadful for words," I say, "but, you know, it is the way of the world."

"I suppose so," she says, with a sigh, and goes to fetch her keys. It does not take a very long time to find out about the 'dreadfulness' from the old woman.

Like so many Italians, she has a vivid sense of the past, and in order to do her justice I have to follow her into the past, too. The trouble with ancient Mantua was that it was an exceptionally strong city, fortified up to the hilt. Part of the fortifications were her walls, but her trump card was provided by nature, as she was entirely surrounded by bog.

Dante gives quite a long write-up to Mantua in the *Inferno*, when Virgil, who acts as his guide, breaks into a description of his native land apropos of nothing in particular. Virgil is made to start with the river Mincio and, working down its course, he arrives at Mantua. He says: "She was strong owing to the mud she had in all parts."

This is a very good example of one of the reasons why Dante is so wonderful. He is not a high-falutin poet, swollen with grand words, but has a precision which is non-heroic and, if I may say so, journalistic. It takes some courage to call mud 'mud' in a poem.

The lakes which exist to-day are the left-overs of that unbroken girdle of water which circled Mantua in medieval times. A song of those days says:

> *You, Venice, are the most lovely,*
> *But you, Mantua, are the strongest.*
> *Water spreads round you right up to your gates:*
> *It would be hard to sack you.*

Of course, this song alone was asking for trouble. Nothing excites people so much to action as when they are told that it cannot be done. Because Mantua was a hard nut to crack she was cracked many times, in many ages, and by many nations.

"Some time ago," as the old woman says, I think it was in the eighteenth century, Mantua was besieged and taken by the French, and the 'dreadfulness' dates from that time. That is to say, the bronze gates outside the palace, the bronze doors inside the palace, and the bronze statues which used to line the grand avenue in the garden, were carried away. And though it happened 'some time ago' it irks the old woman very much when she has to open the wrought-iron gates and walk with visitors past empty niches and through an unadorned park.

The Palazzo del Te was built in the early sixteenth century by Giulio Romano, who seems to have dug himself well in with the Gonzaga, and it has nothing to do with tea. It is designed like a long sausage bent into a square, that is to say, it consists of one floor only which is built round the central courtyard. It is a beautifully proportioned and dignified sausage, and in the front, where the sausage returns into itself, it has a magnificent entrance made by a two-fold crescent of arches.

The sharp old woman takes me into the hall, and every time she mentions the Gonzaga she speaks with a special hushed voice, raises her eyes to the ceiling, and crosses herself. This particular ceiling is painted with "The Sun setting and the Moon rising". Both sun and moon are human figures, standing in horse-drawn chariots, one going up-hill, the other going down-hill. They are an odd sight because the painter, clearly very keen on showing his mastery of foreshortening, has given us nothing but the hind quarters of the steeds and the buttocks of Sun and Moon – in both instances almost naked, because their cloaks are a-flutter. All the frescoes are done by Giulio Romano and his school, and it seems to me that he threw in everything which he thought he had left out in the town residence.

For instance, there is a room called the *sala dei cavalli*. On each wall there is the life-size portrait of a favourite Gonzaga horse, framed in painted pillars and with a strip of melancholy Mantuan landscape showing in the background, somewhere beneath the horse's belly.

In another room there is a banquet going full swing right round the walls, with exceedingly abandoned ladies draped round the tables and satyrs handing the bread and pouring the wine. The fact that there are some angels above, beating drums and cymbals, does not make it any more respectable.

The ceilings are richly worked, and what is so remarkable is that the mosaic patterns on the floor repeat the design of the ceilings above. On one of these is the motif of a lizard and Mount Olympus, coupled together. Both were Gonzaga emblems.

The most famous room is the Hall of the Giants. It is overwhelming in a nasty way. It shows the battle between Gods and Titans and the manner in which Giulio Romano conceived the Titans gets on my nerves. They are red-nosed, clumsy, crafty old dodderers who hide under crags and rocks. They seem to be the models from which Walt Disney created his dwarfs in his abominable version of *Snow White and the Seven Dwarfs*. It hurts me to see fine myths and legends made ridiculous for the sake of amusing people – even if the people in this case were the Gonzaga.

Of course, it was very well to pull the Titan's legs, but when it came to their own persons the Gonzaga lost their sense of the ridiculous. In one room there is a frieze of white reliefs on apple-green ground, all Gonzaga portraits, and every one of them is beautiful and dignified.

If one adds the Palazzo del Te to the Palazzo Ducale one gets the sum total of a continuous bragging which did not express itself in words but in buildings. But the bragging is on such a grand scale that it is admirable.

We now leave the palace and visit a pavilion in the garden. This pavilion is a little mansion on its own, built round its own tiny courtyard. Its whole purpose was to provide a bathroom of suitable proportions for the Gonzaga.

The floors are inlaid with coloured pebbles and pierced with holes. In the old days the space below the floors was flooded with perfume and when the baths were used the scent would rise from the floor and fill the steam-warmed air.

There is an artificial waterfall coursing down an artificial grotto and constructed in such a way that its sprays dripped on to wire strings and produced music. It is clear that the Gonzaga did not know any more what to do with themselves.

"What gay times they must have had," says the old woman, crossing herself complacently, and she goes on to insinuate that the Gonzaga did not take their baths in loneliness and that the Duke could muster a whole regiment of court ladies to keep him company and scrub his back.

Gay? Not at all. The incredible luxury of this bath pavilion does not reveal the gaiety of the Gonzaga, but their gloom. It is here, in the heart of Renaissance riches and Renaissance flamboyance, that I, for the first time in my life, can lay a finger on the racing Renaissance pulse and feel its elusive flicker against my own flesh. This bathroom, once shrouded in scented steam, was built for pleasure by a panic-stricken breed. It is only now that I understand the horror and fright which lies behind the creed so often and so beautifully expressed: "Enjoy yourselves while you can."

This, of course, was nothing new. But when, for instance, Horace says: "Pluck the day," he says it calmly, jovially, and he is not out of breath while he says it. It was only during the Renaissance that this theme was taken up with a new feverish fervour, that it became a hysterical preoccupation, that it was shrieked and sighed and panted.

The trouble with the Renaissance was, that this day, these rose-buds, these cherry lips, which they tried to pluck so forcefully, eluded their grasp. They had not any more the nerves for pleasure. And how could they? How could they be pleasured when they were unable to come to terms with death? Their fear of death had grown to such an extent that instead of giving to life a healthy glow by contrast, it overshadowed it and swallowed it up.

The best example I can find for this is in a poem by Lorenzo de Medici, who was not among the best poets of that time but perhaps the most typical one. On this occasion Lorenzo had all the goodwill in the world to praise youth and gaiety, because he was composing a carnival song. But almost at once he slithered off his set theme and, instead of dwelling on youth, he lamented its passing. The anxiety of his age could not be hidden, not even during the refrain of a song:

> *"Fair is youth and free of sorrow*
> *Yet how soon its joys we bury.*
> *Let who would be, now be merry:*
> *Sure is no one of to-morrow."**

The telling phrase is: "Let who would be, now be merry." Obviously Lorenzo cannot.

No one is sure of to-morrow. But other generations have been able to say: "And so what?" They were fortified by all sorts of things: Stoicism, a belief in universal justice, a belief in reason, smugness and righteousness, a belief in progress, a belief in a cruel God, a belief in a merciful God.

The Renaissance had none of these comforts. Most of its rulers were a bunch of *parvenus, nouveau-riche* bankers like the Medici in Florence or captains of gangsters like the Scaligeri in Verona and the Gonzaga in Mantua. They trailed their newly tailored purple through mud and blood and glory, and when at the end of their journey they found that their gowns were not only encrusted with jewels but also caked with mud, not only embroidered with gold thread but also clinging with torn entrails, they felt queasy. They wriggled and squirmed in their uneasiness, and they wriggled and squirmed so beautifully and flashily, constantly spot-lighting new masks of themselves, that even to-day we are puzzled and enthralled by their glitter.

And now all the Gonzaga emblems and the Gonzaga portraits crowd upon me with a new, insistent power. One moment steadfast and imperishable like Mount Olympus, one moment sliding with furtive speed into a hiding-place like the lizard, one moment blazing openly and splendidly like a bundle of flames, one moment invisible, chasing round and round in the secret of their self-made mazes.

---

* Translation by Jefferson Butler Fletcher, Macmillan, New York, 1934.

One moment Greek gods, one moment country squires, one moment brutal heroes, one moment contrite sinners.

What were they really? How were they really? Like this? Like that? And from all around me I get the Renaissance answer, given with the famous Renaissance smile, the crooked, one-sided, unsatisfying smile of the *Mona Lisa:* "Perhaps yes, perhaps no."

The sharp old woman takes me back to the palace and points out to me all the niches, all the galleries, which in Gonzaga times were filled with bronzes.

She tells me that there are about twenty-five empty rooms in the palace.

"I wish you'd let me have a flat here," I say.

She does not like the thought, which to her is as sacrilegious as wanting to install oneself domestically in the nave of a cathedral. As she is too polite to tell me her real feelings, she tries to discourage me 'for my own sake'.

"You would not be happy here, *signora*. It would get on your nerves," she exclaims. "Imagine living for ever under painted ceilings and within frescoed walls. You would feel suffocated."

I would not feel suffocated at all. I would wallow in it. My sharp old woman is a deplorable victim of our modern taste in interior decoration. Nowadays it is thought that, to start with, opulence is sinful. The interior decorator has no 'sin' in his dictionary, but he has the expression 'bad taste'. Opulence is in bad taste. He believes in contrasts. He believes that if one puts one fine work of art in a room the rest of the room must be bare in order to give breathing-space to the one work of art. This, of course, is aesthetic nonsense and artistic cowardice. It is also immoral. By doing what he does the interior decorator denies the parable of the loaves and fishes. This parable tells us about the nature of love. It means that our love is not rationed, and that it can grow larger and larger according to our needs. If we love one person it does not mean that in order to love another we have to chop our existing love in half and deprive the first person of the love which we want to give to the other person.

In the same way, we can love ten paintings in one room. We do not have to limit ourselves to one single painting.

The solitary picture stranded in the bare, whitewashed room of to-day freezes and shrinks like a flower cast on a naked rock. How I loathe the bare rooms of to-day. What is one vase? What is one water-colour? And what has the ceiling done to deserve to be so naked? And why must the floor be covered with fitted, uniformly coloured stuff, preferably 'mushroom', which to me is just plain desolating mud colour.

When one looks at the masterpieces of interior decoration, like the Gothic Rathaus chambers in Lüneburg, the saracen Capella Palatina in Palermo, the Renaissance dining-room of the Gonzaga Palace or the Rococo drawing-rooms of Sans Souci in Potsdam, one finds that every inch of wall and ceiling has been covered with ornament, every door, every architrave, every door knob and key plate, every latch, every sconce.

The Platonic saying that only the like can understand the like also holds true in interior decoration. Only riches can enhance riches. Only sumptuousness can be coupled with sumptuousness. Only splendour can underline splendour.

No one piece of art is crushed. On the contrary, each is enriched by the added glow of its neighbours.

I cannot imagine Raphael saying, when he was commissioned to decorate the Vatican chambers: "Please, let me paint one picture on one wall only and leave the rest bare. Otherwise my picture will not stand out sufficiently." Nothing of the kind. He slapped it on all over, just as masters before and after him have slapped it on.

Nowadays people are lacking in self-assurance for that sort of thing, and by disliking it they write their own certificate of mediocrity. They feel uncomfortable by massed splendour because they are poor in themselves. Our poor in the spirit are the brigade of the Scandinavian wooden bowl, of the rush mats, of the inbuilt cabinet, of the concealed lighting. They spurn the spirit which shaped Lyons Corner Houses, and they smile indulgently at the taste that furnished the Ritz. On the other hand they admire the basilica of San Marco in Venice. They would be horrified if one told them that Lyons Corner House and San Marco are sisters under the skin, because they both are suffused with warmth, life, and exuberance.

And so, I still say: "I wish I could have an apartment here."

Now I want to see the third instalment of Gonzaga bragging, Sabbioneta. But during lunch I decide to give the Gonzaga a rest when Virgilio tells me that I should go to Santa Maria delle Grazie. It is a sanctuary, and it is not in my guide-book. This is sufficient recommendation.

After lunch I take my coffee in the smartest café in Mantua, which is situated in front of the theatre.

The full name of the theatre is Teatro Sociale. This in another town would seem an oddly superfluous name for a theatre, but here in Mantua it is right that it should be called thus. For here we are in the stronghold of the Gonzaga, who used to have anti-social theatres, for their private use only.

The cafés in the *corso* are more lovable: so narrow, so shadowy, so intimate, set beneath the dark arcades.

Here, the tables are put in front of the elephantine columns of the theatre entrance, and an awning spreads its wings overhead. When it rains one can sit in the very portico, and when it rains hard, the tables are moved into the *foyer* of the theatre. This gives an agreeable sense of trespassing.

To one side of the theatre is the terminus of the tram, the only tram-line in Mantua. The buses which roll through Mantua's streets are new and long, and painted Virgilian blue.

The tram is a battered old rattle-box, frail and noisy, like a village ancient, and it is painted dark green. It consists of three cars, linked by rusty chains.

I get in, and we set off on our shaking, rattling way. I try to tell myself that we are in the hands of God, but feel that we are somewhat too much in the hands of God for my liking.

We drive out of the town and through marshy country. Half-way, we suddenly stop in front of a villa and the driver gets out.

A young Alsatian leaps up behind the garden fence, and each of his leaps is countered by a leap of the driver outside. Then the dog lies low and waits for his human partner to give the lead in this un-equal ballet. After some time they manage to time and anticipate each other's movements, and execute a *pas de deux*, chasing up and down, each on his side of the fence. This is an incident after my own heart. Here is no nonsense about having to run to a time-table.

After the driver has had his fill he mounts, and we move on our way.

I get out in le Grazie, in front of two taverns where old men drink and play cards. The sanctuary is at the end of the village street.

I walk past a few booths displaying religious junk. Hens are scratching in the dust, and the drivers of three motor-coaches, parked near the church, are scratching their heads and throwing stones at stray cats.

The church itself looks more like a barn than a sanctuary, with a dirty yellow front of wide-flung arches, large enough for the passage of laden hay-carts.

I step inside. A service is in full swing.

There are things which one knows without being told. I will go even further, and say that there are things one remembers though one has never experienced them before. And as soon as I find myself inside, before I have had even time for a perfunctory look round, I know that I am standing on miracle-working ground. I offer no explanation. It is like that.

Quite apart from this, I find that the church has the strongest personality I have ever come across in churches. Here, for once, is a church which went its own way, pig-headed and without caring for the advantages of refined architecture. It is just like a big room. The walls have been transformed into two-tiered galleries with rows of pilasters, short and thick, like out-size sausages, and of the colour of dried blood, entwined with carvings which look like tarnished gilt ropes. The niches between the pilasters are filled with figures. These are carved of wood, ancient, dry, and brittle, like old corn stalks. Add to this the enormous green and black flowers on the ceiling, which might be copied from a peasant quilt, and you realize that you do not stand in a church but in a rustic store-room in which, instead of vats and apples and hams and grain, there have been stored scores of solid and inexplicable miracles.

In front of the altar bathed in candle-light stands a young priest talking into a microphone. And he needs it; the congregation is made up entirely of little boys.

Here and there a banner sticks out above their restless heads, bearing the name of the village from which they have come to do homage to the sanctuary of delle Grazie.

Here and there, too, one can see a seminarist or a woman schoolteacher, grimacing threateningly under the lace of her black mantilla and making gestures symbolic of the thrashing which she will deal out to her charges once they are outside the sacred ground. These grown-ups have a hard time.

I happen to stand near a seminarist, and while he conducts with one hand the singing of his little flock he delves with the other hand into the hair of two of the worst offenders, pulls them apart and slaps them gently.

The boys, even while yelling hymns, even while roaring prayers, swivel round constantly like spinning tops, kick, pinch, shove, and throw their caps into the air.

After the stormy service is over there is a rush to the altar, where the officiating priest twines an exhausted hand round the stem of the microphone. He is now required to bless every object which the children offer him. Between blessings he raises a scarf or a scrip and shouts into the microphone in order to trace the owner of the lost property.

One schoolteacher leads her party to the altar rail. It is clear that she has not been quite satisfied with the service and that she is now going to improve the devotional exercises. The poor little devils have to say one *Ave Maria* after the other at her command. I stand by and listen and count. All in all seven rounds. "One for all dead children" and "Now one for all sick children". The last being "For the fatherland and to make sure it will always be a Christian country". If she goes on like this it won't.

By now it has dawned on me that the big attraction in the church is a Madonna, a hideous head-and-shoulder painting hung behind the altar, mercifully hidden in the shadow.

Meanwhile the hardworking priest distributes little sacks of grain which he has blessed. By now the boys, too, seem to be worn out. They retreat with a minimum of scuffling, rally round the various banners and stream out of the church, happy children, with their fertility rites happily enacted.

The priest, after a weary genuflexion, deserts the altar and microphone and disappears into the vestry. He has finished. But I have only started.

I stroll down the central gangway, determined not to leave till I have got answers to all the questions I want to ask.

On one side the nave opens into a small room, which in turn leads into a hall where prayer books and rosaries are offered for sale. It is there that I see a man of about thirty-five, dressed in the black soutane of a priest. He comes up to me, smooth, well brushed, well tailored. He has ravishingly heavy eyelids and looks like a cross between a reception clerk at the Ritz and Lucifer, always bearing in mind that Lucifer was the most beautiful of all the angels.

"Would you like me to bless anything for you, madame?" he asks, with an enticing discreet voice, as though saying: "Bathroom and dressing-room, of course. But would you perhaps care for a private drawing-room?"

"I have brought with me no object worthy to be blessed," I say and he bows. The preliminaries are over.

"I want to ask you a lot of questions, monsignore," I say.

He crosses his white hands and slides them into his sleeves.

"It is part of my calling to listen to questions, madame."

"And to answer them?" I ask.

"Not necessarily," he remarks, "and I must warn you now, that when you will be putting your last question to me, I shall fail you."

"But I only want to ask you things about the church and when it was founded, monsignore. And who built it. And that sort of thing."

"I know. We shall see."

He tells me readily enough that the children came here for a pilgrimage to the wonder-working Madonna. These pilgrimages are organized for boys and girls separately and according to age-groups, in order to give them the service most suited to their understanding.

The church was built in the fourteenth century by Ludovico – needless to say – Gonzaga, and it was looked after by Franciscans. When Napoleon conquered Mantua he threw out the Franciscans and they have been fretting ever since, trying to get back and plaguing the Pope about it. There are Dominicans now in charge of the sanctuary.

"And the Madonna?" I ask.

He raises his eyes to me for a moment as though trying to determine whether I deserve the yellow suite after all, the one giving on to the park.

"Well, yes," he says, "she – works wonders."

"What is her story?"

Now he has lowered his lids and caresses the sleeves of his soutane with fastidious fingers.

"Well – you know – "

He seems at once pained and relieved when we are joined by another, younger man, a Dominican with glasses, who at once charges head-long into the story.

"The Madonna walked over the river Mincio and across the three lakes and revealed herself to a shepherd while he was asleep and commanded him to make it known to the people that a sanctuary was to be built for her."

The priest looks at me with the knowing eyes of the man of the world and gives me a smile, partly resigned, partly vicious, as though to say: "There you are. If you will ask foolish questions you will get foolish answers."

He dismisses the monk and takes me back to the small room, to show me the votive offerings to the Madonna delle Grazie. They are mostly pictures, illustrating the disease or accident where the Madonna intervened and saved the lives of the faithful. They are all ghastly, drawn, wrought, and embroidered with sincerity and bad taste. But it is impossible to laugh them off because of their bad taste. The sincerity is stronger. It is undeniable that something in this place exerts some kind of power. Not the Madonna, but something else. Who shall ever say what it is? It was probably already at work in Virgilian times. And before then.

We walk back to the nave to look at the carved figures. They are folksy art, a complete human encyclopedia of the Middle Ages, with every type and every class, all done with unpleasant realism. King and beggar, peasant and wandering minstrel, court lady and merchant's wife. There is a man hanged and another man about to be hanged, saying his prayers in front of the gibbet with the noose round his neck. They are made with wrinkles and warts and irregular features, with that medieval insistence on the ugliness of the flesh and on its frailty, which some people mistake for truth in art. I do not care for it no matter how well it is done.

"Do you notice the empty niches?" asks the priest.

It is only now that I perceive that between every two figures there are pilasters which frame an empty space.

"I suppose," I say, "the niches were meant for, say, sixty figures and the money ran out and so they carved only thirty of them."

He smiles, and this time the reception clerk has vanished and Lucifer has taken over.

"Come and have a drink with me," he says and, as I follow him out of the sanctuary I know that, whatever he is going to tell me should not be told at all and that, furthermore, he will tell it without entreating me to keep it quiet as the grave. Whatever vices Lucifer may have had he was never provincial.

It is late afternoon by now. The coaches have gone and so have the hens and the stray cats. The owners of the booths are packing up for the night their manifold renderings of the wonder-working Madonna. The old men are still in front of the taverns with their cards and their wine.

The man dressed like a priest parts the bead curtains for me and we sit down in the bar room filled with chill and mustiness, where packets of washing-powder and *pasta* are stacked side by side with dusty oil-jars and wine-flasks.

He asks for a bottle of Martini, sends the *padrona* away, and pours the wine himself.

"The figures you saw," he says, "are all genuine fourteenth-century carvings. They always stood where they are now. And the niches between them were filled with statues of knights in armour. The friars in charge of the place used to make a great fuss about the wooden figures because, even to their imbecile eyes, they looked old. But the knights in armour they despised because they were made of cardboard.

"This state of affairs went on for centuries. Archaeologists came from all parts of the world, looked at the wooden stuff and admired it and said what a pity it was that the church was spoilt by those imitation knights in armour. Just a year before the war, in 1938, there came an Englishman to Santa Maria delle Grazie, I think it was Lord North.

"Probably he was already irritated by the story about the Madonna, but this story, like so many other stories, is a thing you cannot prove and you cannot disprove either. But the knights were there for him to see, cardboard and all. He examined them. They were made of fine steel and they were finer than any known examples of fourteenth-century mail in Italy.

"As soon as this had been established there was an outcry in the art world; those knights were far too precious to be left in the sanctuary and they should be placed in one of the great museums."

"Oh, I see," I say. "Now I understand why the niches are empty. Where are the knights? In Rome?"

The heavy eyelids flicker. "No."

"In Florence?"

"No."

"I know, of course. In Mantua, in the Gonzaga palace."

"No."

"Well," I say, "where are they? Were they stolen and sold to America?"

"No. That at least would have been profitable to somebody."

"What happened?"

"The monks were offended," he replies. "When one has been proved to be an ass one is always offended. The monks promptly took the knights out of their niches and stored them in an underground vault. This has two great advantages. First, they have now made quite sure that nobody can have a look at the priceless knights. Secondly, since they have been put away, the knights have started to get rotten with rust. Whereas all the time before, while they were openly exposed in the church, they remained well preserved."

"But isn't anybody going to do something about it?" I ask.

"It is very difficult. One cannot get at the monks in the same way as one could get at a private citizen. Some archaeologists are now trying to put pressure on them, by working on the Pope. If he interceded, they would have to let go."

"And do you think the Pope will intercede?"

The eyelids flutter, and so does his hand. "He might in the end." I know I cannot ask any further. For a while we drink in silence.

"And what do you think about the miracles?" I say.

His smile deepens. "I will make a prediction," he says. "Let me see. We are now at the end of April. On the ninth of June there will be the general political elections for the whole of the country. I predict that between now and the ninth of June there will be a fine crop of miracles. The last time two little girls had visions of the holy Virgin and the sun was dancing for them. Perhaps this time it will be

two little boys and the moon will dance. People show little imagination, even when it comes to miracles. It is always like this, before
elections. The church party is very strong, you know."

"I can see that," I say, "but I mean the miracles here, of Santa
Maria delle Grazie."

As I watch his hands slide back into his sleeves I reflect that, really,
there is nothing like black to enhance human dignity. It is not
for nothing that all the best-dressed women wear black year in year
out. And now the pale hands move out of their shadowy retreat
with a fresh, startling grace.

"Man has great powers," he says, "and the riches of the human
soul are immense. Man can, by intense worship, call into being a
sort of – an independent minor deity. This demon will get the
stronger, the more it is worshipped. In the end it will get so strong
that it will make itself felt to almost everyone who enters its sanctuary. But this is about all it can achieve. Faith cannot move mountains because mountains are made of earthy matter and faith is made
of spiritual stuff. Only mountains can move mountains and only
faith can move faith. The demon, nourished by faith, can increase
faith in its turn. If faith declines and the demon goes hungry of worship, it will wither away and die, like all man-made things."

"So you don't think it has anything to do with real religion?"
I ask.

"It has nothing to do with religion," he says. "When I was younger
I was so exasperated by people clamouring for miracles that I told
my congregation that each time they produced a so-called miracle
they were creating a wart on the face of God. As I say, I was young,
then."

"You don't believe this any more?"

"I do not. How could I dare to talk about the face of God when
I do not know it? God is infinitely great. How can I presume to
know the will of God when I cannot even tell what goes on in the
mind of my bishop? We cannot know the unknowable. If I told
you I did, I would be insane. Would you care for another glass?"

For an instant the fallen angel and the reception clerk mingle in his smile. Would madame care for a private suite with a view on the park or would madame care for the Kingdom of God? They are both to be had for the asking, madame. Yes, certainly. That is, if madame can pay. Each at a price.

"But the price, the price," I want to scream, "show me how I can find the money."

"There have been many books written about the way to find the money. Would you care to look through them? The Bible, perhaps? The *Imitation of Christ*? The *Exercitiae* by Loyola? We have a good selection of guide-books."

"I have no trust in guide-books," I say, "they always let me down. But can't you tell me yourself how I could find the money?"

"The money, madame? I am afraid that is entirely your own problem. I am only the reception clerk in this establishment."

My head is reeling. Is it the Martini or this unspoken conversation between us? Who is he, that he could foresee my last question even though I never said it aloud? What is he, this man of disturbing beauty who wears the priest's uniform like fancy dress?

I continue to ponder this question till my tram arrives.

"Mind you," I say to myself, as I climb inside, "whoever he was, he could not have been the devil. Because if he had been the devil, he would have known all the answers."

If the most influential man of a provincial town asked me to visit him in his country house, what would I expect to find, apart from the house itself? Perhaps a couple of tennis-courts and a swimming-pool. Riding-stables. Gardens, park land, and a model farm. I can think of little else.

Sabbioneta is the sixteenth-century version of that sort of retreat. I will imagine that a Gonzaga has invited me to come and see him in the country. What shall I find?

First of all there will be the house. Probably a palace, which would be just right and proper for a person of his consequence. Then, let us say, a week-end picture gallery, to house some of his pictures, which are only a fraction of the collection he has in Mantua, in his town house. These would be the equivalent of to-day's private cinema. Then, the gardens, flower parterres and pleasure grounds, courts for ball games and courts for tournaments, which would take the place of our modern tennis-courts and golf-course. In other words, I shall probably find that he was no more extravagant than a present-day millionaire.

I go to Sabbioneta by bus. I would advise anybody who can, to go there by car because the bus service is bad. Once you have been put down in Sabbioneta you must wait for six hours for the bus which will take you back to Mantua.

I descend in front of a miserable inn right in the country. On the road there are two little steam-rollers, looking ridiculously inefficient and bizarre, as though they had been designed by Emett for the pages of *Punch*. The men who should be repairing the road are sitting in the shade in front of the house and drinking wine.

The old woman who serves, places a table for me in the back garden, beneath lines of washing, and brings a meal of greasy sausage, unwashed lettuce, and red wine with black bits in it which I prefer not to investigate. Afterwards I ask the way to the palace of Sabbioneta. The old woman is shocked: "It is not a palace. Whatever made you think so?"

I apologize. "Well, the house, you know, the villa – anyway – the Gonzaga place, you know."

Once more I am rebuked. "Sabbioneta is not a house. It is a town."

"Sorry," I say, "I did not know. But where is the town and where in the town is the place? Can you tell me how to get there?"

It appears that it took more than a palace to satisfy Vespasiano Gonzaga. Before he built his residence, he created a complete town for no other purpose than to house his staff of servants and officials. The town was walled in and guarded by gates at each end, and whoever wanted to enter had to show a written passport.

Other homely touches were provided by a theatre in a building on its own, by a church or two, and by the absolute necessity of a mint which coined currency valid in Sabbioneta only. All this was provided by Vespasiano by himself, for himself, and as, after his death, the succeeding Gonzaga did not fancy the air of Sabbioneta, the town fell into ruin and was never enjoyed again. Only a few villagers live within the gates of this Renaissance pleasure-ground.

I walk about two miles on the road, through flat fields and patches of sand and stones. And suddenly, without anything spectacular leading up to it, I find myself in front of the stone walls and the gaping archway.

Whatever made Vespasiano choose this dreary stretch of land for his enterprise? He admitted that he had built on sand because he called it Sabbioneta, after the Italian *sabbia* which means sand. Sabbioneta means something like "Little Sandy". How could he? I imagine it was another of those grand, arrogant, protesting Gonzaga gestures, made to prove that he did not have to rely on the beauties of nature in order to create a pleasure-ground. The whole show had to be Gonzaga, dyed in the wool. Very well.

I enter what is now the main village street, lined by fairly tall houses, whitewashed and begrimed, with every crack in the plaster showing in the bright sun, and I come to a square and walk into the café called the *Bar Ducale*.

It is kept by two young people, I think brother and sister. A man with a bicycle is dispatched to the town hall and by the time I have drunk a black coffee he has returned with the message that the one and only official guide, who has all the keys, has gone to Mantua for the day.

At that the young girl behind the counter throws down the dish-cloth and puts away the glass which she has been polishing, takes her apron off, crawls out beneath the flap and hooks her arm into mine.

"Let's go," she says; "if you are going to have a good time, why shouldn't I?"

We walk round the corner and come to the town hall and go inside. I do not really understand why we should enter the town hall but later on I see that, behind the façade, which is of a more recent date, there is still a chunk of an odd Gonzaga palace inside it. The girl knocks up the caretaker's wife, who at once forsakes her saucepans on the stove, although I beg her not to do so, and joins us, as she is, in apron and slippers.

Now the three of us mount the stairs and are shown some of the rooms where the town clerk works under carved wooden ceilings, amidst statues of Gonzaga on horseback, and under the glaring eyes of high-relief portraits of more Gonzaga.

Once out in the street, we now enter the hospital and, through a passage inside the courtyard, we gain the entrance to a remarkable church. Why this church has to be so intimately mixed up with the civic hospital I do not understand.

The church has a high, narrow dome set with a mixture of real windows and faked windows, and apart from the real light coming inside and casting real shadows, there is also painted faked light and faked shadows which make the dome appear wonderfully high. There is some sort of effigy of the Madonna and Child in the centre, to keep up appearances, but the true centre of the church, the real spiritual centre so to speak, is on the left where Vespasiano Gonzaga sits on a throne, in black and gold and horribly frowning, and in much greater splendour than the Virgin.

It would be surprising if it were otherwise. Dear Vespasiano. I imagine he was rather like my grandmother: wherever he happened to sit, he was sitting at the head of the table.

Vespasiano began life as a Duke of Mantua, but he was Emperor by the time he built himself Sabbioneta, Emperor of Mantua, self-created. It sounds ridiculous. And yet, it was a cheap pleasure to invest oneself with the title of Emperor, as compared with the building of this cosy little summer residence.

We leave the church and pass the Imperial mint, which is half in ruins. So is the theatre, which was, in Gonzaga days, one of the three theatres in Europe. The first and also the best was certainly the

Teatro Olympico in Vicenza, built by Palladio. It was wisely named, because, at least in my opinion, it was fit for the gods. The second best, also built by Palladio and his pupils, was the Farnese theatre in the Pilotta in Parma. To describe this theatre it is necessary to be as good a writer as Schiller when he wrote *Wilhelm Tell*: Schiller, who had never been to Switzerland, wrote descriptions of Switzerland which are better than anybody else's. What I mean by all this is, that the Teatro Farnese does not exist any more.

I cannot tear myself away from this subject of describing what one does not know and has never experienced without telling a story about – I will not say who or I would spoil it.

It was like this: In the beginning of this century there was a professor at the university of Berlin who had in his classes quite a number of Chinese students. He was interested in Chinese literature himself, and one day he assembled these students and told them that he was going to read to them ten German renderings of Chinese poems. Some of these, he said, were translations by eminent scholars, and after the reading he would require the students to tell him which of these poems was most Chinese in manner and feeling.

After he had finished, all the students declared themselves for one particular poem, which, they said, was outstandingly true to Chinese feeling. It was not a translation at all. It was a poem by Goethe, who had put it together one day, to amuse himself, in what he imagined might be the Chinese manner.

And this reminds me of Mérimée, the author of *Carmen*, who always wanted to visit Greece and could not afford the journey. He wrote a travel-book on Greece and went to Greece on the proceeds.

We enter the theatre. The auditorium is still fairly intact, but the stage and the wings have gone to the devil. The theatre is being rebuilt and the place is filled with planks and the air is heavy with the dust of wood shavings.

The auditorium is crescent-shaped and rising in tiers, and the curving walls are decorated with the statues of a great number of Gonzaga, dressed up as Greek gods and Greek heroes, but not very convincingly. Still, I will not hold it against them. If to-day, in London, one of the theatres were to blossom out with statues of H. M. Tennent and the backers of his productions, they would not cut better figures either.

On the ceiling there are traces of a blue sky strewn with stars and seamed with pink clouds. And when the stage is rebuilt I imagine it will have a permanent set with a town square with streets radiating away from it, giving an impression of far greater depth than there really is.

After this we take ourselves to the main palace, which has one jutting wing which was built for the picture gallery. This is the first time that I was right in my guess.

The palace, too, has partly fallen to bits and is filled with masons in white pointed paper caps, bright-eyed, and whistling like thrushes.

More frescoes by the inevitable Giulio Romano. I like best a small landing painted with a filigree of green leaves on a white ground, which could have been designed by William Morris. At the back of the palace there used to be the Imperial garden and it represents another task for Schiller and Goethe. Let other pens . . .

Our aproned and slippered guide takes her leave and tells me that now she will have to make the sauce from tinned tomato purée because there is no time to stew fresh tomatoes. I am touched by her kindness. Would I have done the same, in her place?

Now the young girl is in sole charge of me. She takes me to yet another church.

"Was this also built by Gonzaga?" I ask.

She is shocked by my question. How could there exist anything worth while which was not created by Vespasiano?

In a side chapel there is a bit of faking I have not come across yet: a ceiling painted to look like an open grille of wrought iron with a troubled blue sky showing behind it. Very well done. But, really, Vespasiano, are you not ashamed of yourself? Masquerades, pretence, and make-believe as far as the eye can see. Was there nothing that could make you blush? And were you ever able to blush without the aid of rouge?

By now the young girl is impatient. Never mind the *trompe-d'oeil* of this chapel. I must come and see the martyrs.

Where are they?

Over there. She leaves me to contemplate what looks like a couple of gilt-framed shop windows of a Mayfair hairdresser, curtained with red silk.

She comes back accompanied by the verger's daughter, who disappears behind those shop windows and raises the curtain from inside. There they lie revealed, three lots of martyrs, on three bunks, one above the other as in a sleeping-car. Each martyr is enclosed in a glass coffin and is no more than an under-life-size wax doll, rigged out in a fantasy medieval costume of provincial pantomime standard.

The young girl is rapt in admiration. "Aren't they dear? Aren't they lovely? Look, how beautiful they are."

I am at a loss for what to say. "Why are they so small?"

"Oh, because they were child martyrs."

In vain I try to guess whether this makes them better or worse as martyrs go.

"Look, this one is Saint Dorothea."

I have never heard of Saint Dorothea. I have a feeling she was one of those rash young girls who repulsed the advances of a Roman nobleman and chose a career of martyrdom instead. One must not condemn her out of hand, of course. The nobleman may have been frightful.

The verger's daughter sees that I still do not show enough enthusiasm. She says: "All the real skeletons are inside, you know. Every bit of every bone. But here are some bits left over which we could not put together and so they are here, on their own."

Another curtain is raised and I behold a handful of bones, in a glass case, bedded on red damask.

"And here," and she picks up a glass tube, "are the martyrs'

teeth." So they are. Lots of teeth. She gives them a good shaking
and rattles them up and down in their container as though she were
mixing a cocktail.

I propose that we return to the Ducal Bar.

"Tired?"

"No," I say, "but I can do with a strong coffee."

We get an affectionate good-bye from the verger's daughter:
"Ah, yes, our martyrs are lovely. Everybody who visits Sabbioneta
goes away satisfied."

As far as I am concerned this is true. My desire for martyrs' teeth
has been satisfied for life.

At the café the young girl steps behind the counter and continues
polishing the glass where she left off. We have been away for about
three hours.

I buy an illustrated paper in the main street, which is called, of
course, Via Vespasiano, and go back to the inn and sit down with
the roadmenders and drink some of their wine.

"Why did you come to Sabbioneta? Have you relatives living
here?"

"No."

"Friends?"

"No."

"Why, then?"

I say: "To see the Gonzaga town."

"Ah, that."

They barely hide their contempt. I think I could still save my
standing with them if I told them that I saw the martyrs' teeth. But
I am too lazy.

I have now followed the entire track left by the Gonzaga and
here, in Sabbioneta, I feel more than ever the insecurity of that age
pressing all round me, squandering its riches, shedding its life blood,
in an ever-renewed attempt to prove its power and its glory.

That they could not cope with life is certain. But, anxiety-ridden
though they were, I have no right to draw a parallel and to pretend

that they were our psychological cousins just because we, too, feel insecure and afraid of life to-day.

Their attitude was quite different from ours. They protested against the shortness of human life and against the instability of all things by being as alive as they possibly could be. They ate sensations by the spoonful and turned themselves into a salad of all sorts of contradictory human qualities. Lots of instances are known about the men and women of the Renaissance where one and the same person could be cruel and kind, coarse and refined, worldly and other-worldly in turn, to a degree which would be quite impossible to-day. Each man wanted to be himself and as different as could be from his fellows.

We to-day behave in the opposite manner. We imagine that the less different and the less conspicuous we are, the less we shall be noticed by the forces of life and the safer we shall be.

If I, now, sitting with the roadmenders, borrow from them a copy of the *Mantua Mail*, I shall find on page 2 the personal column written by "Mantua Maligner". I read:

"Duke Vespasiano (Goggles to his friends) Gonzaga tells me that he is going to spend the next fortnight quietly in his cottage on his estate in Sabbioneta. Vivacious dark-eyed daughter Elisabetta, who keeps house for him, prefers to live in the country because 'it is grand to put a new-laid egg on Daddy's breakfast-plate. Besides, being away from Court I find more time to iron Daddy's shirts.' "

Thus, we are told that the great administrator has a funny nick-name, just like an ordinary man. His staff of servants has been sup-pressed for the readers' benefit, and we are made to believe that he is being looked after by his daughter, just like any other ordinary widower, that new-laid eggs are as much a treat to him as to ordin-ary people, and so on. Heaven forbid that anyone should get the impression that Vespasiano has a genius for statesmanship, that he lives in the luxury which he deserves, and that his recreational acti-vities are beyond the pale of ordinary mortals. Virtues and vices alike have been compressed and ironed out. He is ordinary, after all, thank God, we say, and breathe more freely.

On the following evening I go to visit Professor Mirelli and am shown into his study. The bookshelves and furniture are all made of the same chestnut-brown wood, and the books look too well behaved for my liking, bound in matching leather and neatly ranged along the walls. They are neither crammed together nor piled on top of each other, nor do they overflow on to the floor and tables.

Even before he enters I know that the professor does not smoke because there is an array of ash-trays in unlikely places, where no one ever could reach them, and also because these ash-trays are made of precious stuffs, alabaster, cornelian, and beaten silver: it would need true Gonzaga arrogance to place the end of a burning cigarette inside them and to crush it out.

The professor is as well behaved and neat as his study but, though he has the owl physique, being plump and fair, mild voiced and youngish, he just escapes being an owl, probably because he carries his erudition lightly. He is not flippant either, but he tends to deprecate his vast knowledge.

As an hors-d'œuvre I tackle him about the Andreas Hofer of that song who parted from life with a coloratura farewell.

I am grieved to learn that Andreas Hofer never stirred a ripple in the Mantuan lakes, and that his fate would have drawn no sigh from a Virgilian shepherd's reed.

Andreas Hofer was an inn-keeper, a political amateur and a minor thorn in the Napoleonic flesh. He was one of the first nails in Napoleon's coffin.

He was Tyrolean by birth and he did not want his country to be under Napoleon's rule. If I were to write a book on history I should call him 'misguided'. He was bitten by the liberty bug and stirred up the peasants with bad and patriotic speeches, and he worked them up for the independence of his land Tyrol. Hence in the song, the tremolo insistence on *"mein Land Tyrol"*. He had to flee from the Imperial police and was finally tracked down in Mantua, which in those days was an Austrian garrison town under French rule. Because he was caught there, he was executed there. He was not worth the transport to Vienna. The Mantuans had no sympathy for him because they were not interested in Tyrol and they liked Napoleon.

And now let us talk about the Gonzaga.

They did not drop from the sky. They were a family of big-estate owners and, as was the very necessary custom of those days, they kept a private army of their own. In the Middle Ages, about a hundred years before Dante's time, the Gonzaga were not tops but they were up and coming. In the thirteenth century the most powerful family with the greatest military influence were the Casalodi. They had no particular title, but they were the lords of Mantua.

And here the professor tells me a lovely little piece of medieval statesmanship which is also mentioned by Dante, in Virgil's account of the origins of Mantua: the Bonascolsi were runners-up in power to the Casalodi. Pinamonte Bonascolsi went to see Alberto, who was the head of the Casalodi family, and suggested to him that it would be a good idea if he, Alberto, were to kill off all the other patricians of Mantua. Alberto saw the point at once and acted on the advice. After he had finished with the massacre, Pinamonte killed Alberto and thus, with very little effort, became ruler of Mantua.

The Bonascolsi reigned for a hundred years, and their palace on the Sordello is one of the minor chunks of *pâté de foie gras*.

In 1328 Luigi Gonzaga got together his private army, marched with them from his estates to Mantua and made the guard open the city gates by pretending that a girl was waiting for him in the town. Thus he entered during the night and grabbed the power by killing Rinaldo Bonascolsi, who was his brother-in-law, and thus he became the founder of the Gonzaga dynasty. He conquered quite a bit of the country-side round Mantua and sent his ships down the Mincio to the Po and into the Adriatic. Mantua became more and more important and in 1407 the Emperor Sigismund created the Gonzaga

Marquesses and gave them a coat of arms with a black eagle and a
red cross on a white ground. They were created Dukes by Charles V
in 1530. Nobody cares about the black eagle and the red cross. But
they are important because they mean that from now on the
Gonzaga gangsters became respectable in the eyes of the world, and
that they were allowed officially to keep all they had stolen from
others.

Mantua was an enormous town in those days; it had fifty thousand
inhabitants, which is as many as it has to-day, but which meant
much more in those times. The amazing thing is that half of the
town was inhabited by the Gonzaga court and the other half by the
people.

The most important Gonzaga was Francesco, who married Isabella d'Este, and this marriage was something to be proud of because
the Este of Ferrara were one of the very few families in Italy who
were not *parvenus*. But this achievement was not enough. The Gonzaga, driven on by this terrible insecurity inside themselves, became
grander and grander.

At this point I interrupt.

"It was not grandeur any more," I say, "it was *folie de grandeur*.
Sheer megalomania, if you ask me."

"No," says the professor, "it was not *folie de grandeur*. What you
have seen, the palaces and Sabbioneta and so on, were not an expression of madness. They were an economic necessity."

"Why?" I say. "There is no economic necessity for me to buy
myself an ermine coat."

"Not for you," he says; "if you have the money to buy an ermine
coat you need not buy it. You can, for instance, invest the money
in shares. But try to imagine life in those days: the Gonzaga owned
tremendous funds derived from military campaigns and loot. There
was no industry in those days. They could not, for instance, build
factories, nor could they spend their money on the development of
mines and oil-wells. Yet, the money had to be put into circulation
otherwise the people would have starved. The only outlet for money

was to create palaces and to commission the most expensive artists to decorate them."

"I don't believe it," I say. "Look, for instance, at Venice. In Gonzaga times Venice was the greatest sea power in the world. Compared with it Mantua was a flash in the pan. And in the whole of Venice there is nothing to compare in size with the Gonzaga Palace. The Venetian palaces are lovely, but small and dainty. And no Venetian ever built himself a town when he wanted to spend a week in the country."

"Of course," says the professor. "But you have overlooked the Venetian economy. The Venetians could well afford to build small palaces because they had other outlets for their riches. They had colonies which they could develop, and they had to find money for the upkeep of their enormous fleet for military and merchant expeditions. It is the same to-day. Rich people can invest their money."

But he admits that in the end the Gonzaga overstepped themselves badly, and he agrees with me that the cause for this was entirely neurotic.

Here is a beauty: in 1608 the marriage took place between Francesco di Gonzaga and Marguerite of Savoy. Monteverdi composed his *Ariadne*, which was performed on that occasion. The festivities for this marriage cost so much money that the State of Mantua became bankrupt. There were artifices of fire and water produced on the lakes. One knows exactly what went on because the engineer who designed the machines for the display wrote a book about it afterwards with technical illustrations. Because they were so utterly broke, the Gonzagas were forced to sell most of their picture collection, which was perhaps the largest of that age. They sold them to Charles I of England. Among them were the nine Mantegna cartoons of the Triumph of Caesar which are now in the orangery in Hampton Court. What was left of the pictures was stolen by the later rulers of Mantua, like Maria Theresia of Austria and Napoleon, and this is why there are practically no pictures to-day in the Gonzaga Palace.

This expensive Gonzaga marriage was the beginning of the end. They never recovered from their bankruptcy and they managed to stay on for another hundred years, till Lombardy was occupied by Austria in the early eighteenth century and Mantua became one of the four corner-stones of the Austrian fortress square, made up of Parma, Cremona, Mantua, and Modena.

The Gonzaga still exist to-day. They live in Rome. They are not to be pitied. There are few people in the world who can live out their obsessions as completely as the Gonzaga have done.

In the history of Mantua there is the record of what is one of the earliest-known strikes. In the eleventh century there was a monastery near the town called San Benedetto Po. The monks did nothing you could lay your hands on – I imagine they did a lot of meditating – and with the peasants who worked for them this did not cut any ice. The peasants had to look after the monastic estates, and they were allowed to till their own fields only one day out of ten.

The peasants did not think this was a good idea and they went on strike. The monks hanged some of the strike-leaders with truly Christian mercy, and established the old order. Later on they relaxed the routine a bit and were slightly more charitable.

Then we talk about Virgil and his friendship with Horace. This reminds me of Mrs. Krasnopolski, one of my grandmother's friends who was devoted to the classics and whose husband was called Horace. My grandmother used to say of her: "What a life this woman leads. She goes to bed with Virgil and rises with Horace."

"The Mantuans are very proud of Virgil," says the professor, "and even those who don't know Latin, know some of his most famous lines by heart."

"That's nice," I say.

"It is nice, when you are an ordinary Mantuan," he says, "but when you are a Mantuan and a poet yourself, you find that the shadow of Virgil gets in your way all the time. Have you ever heard of Folengo and Macaronic literature?"

Folengo was a monk who left the monastery and led an adventurous life and had many love affairs. He was a contemporary of Luther's and had great sympathies with protestantism but never went over to the new faith. In his youth he used to write Latin poetry and everybody said to him: "Extraordinarily good, you know. But of course, not a patch on Virgil." Folengo got so tired of hearing it that he decided it would be better to get a *succès de scandale* than a *succès de mérite*. He started to write parodies in the grand epic Virgilian manner and not only this, he wrote them in a Latin of his own – rather like an Italian schoolboy who, in his distress, puts Italian endings on to Latin words. For instance, he invoked the aid of the muses, like Homer and Virgil, but instead of giving them the classical names, he called them by the names of the sluts of his local village. The result was so funny that his fame spread over the whole of Europe. At the end of his life, Folengo got faith once more and went back to his monastery. Like so many other people he regretted the literary follies of his youth and wrote learned Latin treatises about religious matters and tried to live down his Macaronic writings. But it was no use. The world was bored with the treatises and still shook with laughter about his mock epics. He certainly is the precursor of Rabelais and, in Professor Mirelli's opinion he is the precursor of James Joyce, with his invention of a new language, like in *Finnegans Wake*. I don't agree with this. Because the droolings in *Finnegans Wake* are rancid and turn your stomach, whereas Folengo is wholesome and still reads like butter. Why, then, is Folengo so little known in general? The reason is sad and simple. He is only for those who know both Latin and Italian fairly well.

The best-known Mantuan apart from Virgil is Baldassare Castiglione. Charles V of Spain called him the first cavalier of Europe, which did not prevent Charles V from double-crossing him when Castiglione was sent to him on a diplomatic mission. Lots of people at the time said that Castiglione had not been double-crossed but had turned traitor on his own accord, and they tried to prove it by

the fact that Castiglione, after the miscarriage of his mission, did not
return to Italy but stayed on in Spain and allowed himself to be
made Bishop of Seville. I don't believe this. But one will never know.

Castiglione is called "one of those extraordinary versatile Renaissance figures", but I think this is rot. He was soldier, courtier, diplo-
mat, and writer, and I do not find this so typically Renaissance at
all. I can think of quite a few soldiers right down to our own age,
who also engaged in diplomacy and wrote books as well.

The book he wrote is the book of the High Renaissance. It is
called *The Courtier*, and in it he lays down his ideal of what a gentleman should be; it was the greatest best-seller of that time.

Castiglione did not stay in Mantua, but went to Urbino where he
served the reigning family of Montefeltro. He must have been mad
to go there, when you think that just at that time the court in Mantua was kept by Francesco and Isabella and they had such illustrious
hangers-on as Pietro Pomponazzo, who was the greatest Aristotelian of his day, and Pico della Mirandola, one of the best Platonists,
who had such a phenomenal memory that he could, after reading a
book, recite it by heart backward.

Pico, freakishly brilliant as he was, had a typical Renaissance bee
in his bonnet and was obsessed with mystifications, secret codes, and
hidden meanings. I imagine it was he who egged on the Gonzaga
to spread their lizards and labyrinths everywhere. He was the type of
man who will discover a secret message in anything, always bearing
in mind that the secret message is an expression of his own beliefs.

Thus, Pico 'discovered' the mystery of the Holy Trinity in Judaic
texts. He also 'discovered' the same sort of thing in practically every
Greek manuscript he could lay hands on, and when he came across
a pagan myth he fancied he 'discovered' that it contained a hidden
Christian allegory, prophetic, of course. If he were alive to-day
Pico would turn his brilliance on to psychoanalysis, and contort his
wonderful hair-splitting mind to prove that his patients' dreams,
interpreted on all levels, were always making sense according to
Freudian doctrine.

Now that I come to think of it, perhaps it was not so mad, after all, for Castiglione to go to Urbino. Perhaps Pico got on his nerves. And I imagine that a continuous bickering must have been going on between Pomponazzo the Aristotelian and Pico the Platonist.

Also, the wife of the then reigning prince in Urbino was Elisabetta Gonzaga, and I suppose she pulled strings for him. His book is set in the court in Urbino, as a conversation among the lords- and ladies-in-waiting, and all the characters are the real courtiers of Urbino.

Castiglione did much more thoroughly for his age what Lord Chesterfield did in the eighteenth century in his letters to his son and, like Lord Chesterfield, he harps on 'the graces'. What I like best in the book is the end; after having talked their heads off all night about what goes to the making of the perfect courtier, they draw aside the heavy curtains and behold the dawn spreading over the sleeping town. They go to bed without candles because there is already the light of the new day.

I don't like Castiglione because I don't approve of his "ideal lady". She is to be alluring and seducing, but as soon as she has hooked a man, she must turn his love for her to the love of heavenly beauty and the contemplation of the eternal ideas. In other words, she is nothing more than a bait for the study of philosophy and as such must be part Circe, part governess and part police-woman. The ideal courtier, if she be successful, turns his glance away from her and upwards, to the Heavens. But what becomes of her? Her predicament reminds me of the children who were promised an outing. In the last minute their father could not keep his promise. The children screamed: "And now we are left standing, with our washed necks!"

When I get back to the Romagna, the swaying reed who does night duty at the reception hands me a letter from England. As I tear it open he asks me if he could have the stamp. With pleasure. He might as well have it. It is all he will get from me.

While I read the letter a young man who has been lingering in the back of the hall detaches himself from the wallpaper and comes forward.

"Excuse me, but do you come from England?"

"But yes," I say.

"And excuse me, but what is England like?"

"Very English," I say.

"Excuse me that I am asking you, but, you see, I have always wanted to go to England. I am a journalist. I was supposed to go there last year to a congress, and then, in the last moment someone else was sent in my place."

"I see."

"I am from Rome," he says. "I have been sent here to cover the floods in the neighbourhood."

"And are there any floods?" I ask.

He looks aghast at my question. I don't understand why. One journalist does not make a flood.

"I am still very young," he remarks, "but I have dreams of fame. One day my political column will be syndicated in all the papers in the world. The only thing which worries me is, how will they translate my writings? My style is intensely personal and incisive, you know. I feel sure it will lose its effect by translation."

"Like Goethe's German," I suggest. "Goethe is practically unreadable in translations."

"Yes, just like that," he says gravely. After an instant he revives: "From political journalism I shall pass on to active politics. I shall become a statesman. I shall be so famous one day that they will put up my monument in public parks. And by that time I shall be married and have a little girl. And I shall take her for walks through the park and show her my statue."

"How do you know you will have a little girl?" I say. "What if you have three boys instead? Sure is no one of to-morrow. Good night."

As I walk up the stairs I have the feeling that, behind my back, the journalist is touching his forehead and murmuring: "She is crazy";

while I, in my turn, reflect that the spirit of the Gonzaga must have got on his brain.

On the following day the English-speaking manager and the swaying reed are nowhere to be seen. The chambermaid thinks that they have gone off together on a lovers' jaunt.

My bill is given me by an elderly woman and in it there is an entry for a hundred lire which I do not understand. Neither does she. I have never yet kicked up a fuss over a hotel bill in Italy. But this time I am thirsting for a fuss because I dislike the hotel so much. The woman says she will ask the accountant when he comes and he might be able to give an explanation.

I go off to the café in front of the theatre and am soothed by a white vermouth and the sight of Virgilian shepherds masquerading as waiters, hairdressers, and messenger-boys. A man at the table next to mine is telling a dream he had last night to a couple of friends. Something about alighting on an island and being met by a skeleton. Really. He must have been reading Baudelaire on an empty stomach.

I get back to the Romagna, and by now I am too lazy to ask for explanations. The road to Heaven is paved with bad intentions.

I am told that the national monument called on me while I was out. He wanted to salute me. The idiot. And yet, who can tell? Perhaps he really will succeed in some way. Perhaps it is only men with simple minds and strong wills who succeed in politics. But what a dream to conceive. To be turned into a monument, in the park, on the greensward, surrounded by prams and nursery-maids. This, quite appropriately, is the fate of bores.

Only people like Ressel, the inventor of the ship's screw, ever get monuments in a park. The charmers never do. Who would dream of setting up a statue to Don Juan? Or to Oscar Wilde? And yet he was the greatest conversationalist of all times.

My taxi has been ordered and I go outside with the boy who carries my cases. While we are waiting, a big expensive car drives up and an ugly and expensive-looking man gets out.

Am I waiting for a taxi? Could he be of any use to me? He is staying at the hotel. Am I, too, staying at the hotel? And if so, why has he not met me till now? Is it not a pity that he never met me till now?

I am non-committal about the 'pity'. The rest of the answers have been supplied by the luggage-boy, who informs him that my stay in the hotel is by now a thing of the past, and that I am on my way to the station.

Could he not take me to the station?

I decline on the grounds that the taxi has already been ordered.

And now the taxi arrives. I get in.

I have hardly settled in the waiting-room in the station, and the porter has hardly finished swearing that he will put me in the right train at the right time and that God will strike him dead on the spot if he won't, when the ugly and expensive-looking man comes in, with a winning smile.

"Are you, too, catching a train?" I ask.

He kisses my hand. No, nothing of the kind. He has only come to see me on to the train, out of the goodness of his heart. But very soon it becomes clear that this is exactly what he is trying to prevent. He does not want me to catch the train at all, he wants me to come with him to Milan instead, on the following day. And then to Venice.

I tell him that I am all set for Ravenna.

He implores me to come to Milan. He would set great store by my company, he tells me, because with me he can talka the English and he needa plenty of exercise. And if I am really determined on Ravenna he will follow me to Ravenna. Though, in this case, I must tell him my name. How can he find me in Ravenna, if he does not know for whom to inquire?

I am tempted to tell him that my name is Smith, Poppy Smith – but decide against it. For one thing, he would not appreciate the beauty of the name. You needa knowa plenty of the English for that. And secondly, the name Poppy would require endless explanations. Though I know the Italian for poppy, honestly, I do.

Here I must admit that the conceit of 'Poppy Smith' did not jump out of my brain like Pallas Athene jumped out of Jove's forehead, in full armour. It is not my idea at all. It is like this: Years ago I saw a wonderful film called *Shanghai Gesture*. There was a scene in it where girls were auctioned and sold in cages. But although the film made an awful fuss about the cruelty of this type of auctioning, it never said how much the girls fetched.

Now, in one scene, the heroine and the hero were sitting in a night club and the owneress of the night club, very vicious too, came along and stopped by their table. She said to the heroine: "Who are you and who is this man you are with?"

And the heroine replied: "My name is Smith – Poppy Smith, and he is my brother."

The owneress said: "Your name is not Poppy Smith. And he is not your brother." Just like that. Coldly.

I never forgot this bit of dialogue. Brilliant script writing. Ever since, I have dreamt of finding myself one day in a situation where I could say: "My name is Smith – Poppy Smith. And he's my brother."

Now, perhaps, if there had been another man with me in the waiting-room I could have said it. But, as it is, I could only have said: "My name is Smith – Poppy Smith", and no more. And that would not be the same thing.

I decide to skip it altogether, and I say instead that we in England have a fearful prejudice about telling our names to strangers.

The ugly and expensive-looking man switches over to Locke, Hume, and Berkeley. And well may he switch, because I know nothing about these philosophers.

"What is the truth?" he asks. "Did they not all try to find it?"

"Philosophers generally do," I say.

"And what about Einstein?" he adds, "and the theory of relativity?"

There are two theories of relativity, but he does not say which one he means. And from that theory – whichever it is – he gets back to his original request for my name.

It appears that we are two tiny bits swirling about in the infinite. And how can we ever meet again, if he does not know my name?

I once understood both theories of relativity, for half an hour, and once for two days. But there was nothing in them about giving your name when you don't want to. From what I remember I can only make the following application to my present predicament:

To me, travelling through space at a certain speed, the man who pesters me at this moment looks as ugly and as rich as Hephaistos. But to a girl friend of mine, standing on a different planet and travelling at a different speed, he may seem as poor and as beautiful as Endymion. I am right and so is my girl friend. And the sum total of this is, that two girls in the right do not make one man in the wrong, but that, relatively speaking, he is a sorry man indeed who has to drag in Einstein when he wants to get off with a woman.

And now that I think of it, Einstein's general theory can even be applied further. Say, for instance, I were having an affair with this man. To me, standing in the waiting-room, which is my here-now, I am in the present. Whereas my girl friend, who stands on another planet, in another here-now, looking down on me, will see me in this waiting-room with this man as already in the past. But for this I do not need Einstein. My friends can always see an affair of mine already finished when I still think it is going strong.

And now my porter comes to fetch me, the man kisses my hand, I get into the train, and roll away to Ravenna.

Or perhaps I remain in the stationary train while the station of Mantua is rolling away from me, bearing the ugly and expensive man with it. I shall not quarrel over it. Farewell, sweet Mantua.

RAVENNA

Ravenna is the first touristy town on this journey.

This is evident at once by the fact that the Roma, which is the newest and best hotel in the place, is full. I have to go next door to the equally new but humbler hotel Touring, where I am given a room after having been told to praise my stars for my luck.

The room is on the second floor. There is no lift but otherwise I can find no fault.

I unpack while praising my stars and go out in search of dinner. The first restaurant I pass is the one belonging to the Roma. I stop outside and look at the menu.

It is written in English. This is always a bad sign. It means rotten food and high prices.

I walk past a leaning tower, turn into a side street, and arrive at a place called Regina. I enter one of those hotel dining-rooms which are utterly silent, though fully occupied. All the guests are travelling couples, French and Americans, in their fifties, and by the look of them they have been married so long that there is nothing left to talk about.

The women are grey-haired, well curled, with long ear-rings, uncrushable hats specially bought for travelling, and long, well-bred faces, like elderly greyhounds. The husbands are short, red-faced, and vulgar. Certainly a come-down. Why have all these women married beneath themselves?

The service is beautiful. I order tongue, green sauce, and spinach. The red wine, called San Giovannese, is better than the one in Mantua, which was young and prickly. The bread is bad and varied in shape. My own particular roll at the moment looks as though three lobsters had a fight, ran off, and left their claws behind, all entwined.

The tongue arrives. The ox who carried it in his mouth must have been an anaemic beast. The spinach tastes of soap. For a minute I

197

waver between yellow kitchen soap, Oxydol, and Persil. After a few more mouthfuls I award the palm to Persil. I order crême caramel. The Persil has got into that, too. This paragraph is not written as an advertisement for Persil and I was not offered any money for mentioning this product.

Vale, Regina, thou shalt never see me again. I always had a dread of good honest soap and water.

I find that the international news is sold in a stand beneath the leaning tower – is this symbolical? – and I buy the Continental *Daily Mail*, which I take with me to a café. Straight away I solve half of the crossword puzzle. I think that the clues have grown less warped and perverted. Or perhaps I have grown more warped and perverted.

Then I talk to a girl at the next table. She is an art student and has come to Ravenna to study the mosaics. There is a college for that purpose. She also tells me that she comes from Wisconsin. Why tell me? Though sorry to hear it, there is nothing I can do to help.

On the next morning I take my breakfast in the main square. In order to understand the main square of an Italian town one must think of the town as a house, with a hall, kitchen, bedrooms, and drawing-room. The square is the drawing-room. All the activities which take place in a drawing-room are enacted in this square. People dress up and go there to see and be seen. They meet their friends and flirt and gossip. They take refreshments and play cards. They stay for hours. The square is not a glorified street, it is a vast room, but instead of settees and chandeliers and vases and china figures, it is furnished with palaces, churches, clock towers, columns, and statues, and has the sky for ceiling. People enter and leave through narrow archways and openings in the arcades, as through doors.

The finest drawing-room in Italy is the Piazza San Marco in Venice. It is the drawing-room of Europe.

Ravenna has a pretty little reception room, well furnished with a medieval palace, a Baroque palace or two, a church with a clock that lights up at night, arcades along two walls, and two Renaissance columns with saints on them. Behind their heads one can just see the tip of the leaning tower.

The waiters in the best café on the square are very elegant, in fawn coats with silver buttons, black trousers, and white waistcoats.

I refuse myself a second coffee and walk through mean little streets till I get to San Vitale. It is a red-brick basilica with bulging apses and some flying buttresses clad in ivy. It looks old and dirty and undistinguished, and could easily be taken for the annexe of a London hospital or railway station.

Inside it is one of the marvels of the world.

To start with, the stage management is wonderful. It is a round room. That is to say, when one steps inside it looks round, although it is really eight-sided, and when one looks again one is not sure any more that it is eight-sided and one looks up, for relief and to collect oneself. There are three rows of windows encircling the walls and instead of glass they have panes of dull gold alabaster, so that everything one sees is dipped into a cloud of golden light, but unevenly golden, because the alabaster is veined and streaked.

Then, as I walk into the choir, there is more gold and more and more. I move beneath a tempest of gold, I stand amidst golden showers, I pass from rains of gold, and cascades of gold, into torrents of gold, and slowly I perceive that there are people looking down on me, with only their heads visible, as though having parted golden curtains; that there are pillars dividing those draperies of gold, and that there are patterns weaving over the manifold arches, all bathed in the streaming shimmer of gold.

I realize that the whole choir is clad with mosaics and that this golden-rain effect has been achieved by putting the colours against a golden background and, according to how much gold there can be seen, the golden rain changes from drops to torrents. There are strange plants and animals which have grown in this golden climate. The pillars are crowned by baskets carved in openwork, like stony lace, and the small arches spanning them have grown chains of doves and fish-scales and peacock fans, and in the centre of the ceiling there stands a white horse with a halo of gold.

Every one of these patterns has a meaning. The horse is Christ and the doves are the souls of the faithful. It is a religious shorthand written in mosaics on the walls.

Yet, the dominating part is the people.

When I say people I do not mean only the heads of the Apostles which gaze down from the ribs of the arches – they play only the part of onlookers, like stage crowds. And I do not mean only the star performers, which is to say, the Emperor and his court on one side of the choir and the Empress and her ladies on the other side. I also mean Christ with the angels, who holds the centre. They are all human beings, exceedingly elegant and exceedingly polished. Christ is merely another Emperor, and a minor Emperor at that – and the angels are his courtiers.

What would be called side parts or character parts of the stage, are here supplied by mosaics of biblical figures, flanking the two star turns. There are Moses, Abraham and Isaac, mountains, and a lot of sheep. They are done in a different style, with more *naïveté*, rather like modern strip cartoons, with flags curling above their heads with their names written on them, all neatly labelled so that there shall be no misunderstanding.

I return to the Emperor and his court. How urbane it all is, how sophisticated, how truly grown-up. There is not a breath of divinity anywhere.

I do another round. It is not a church. It might have been the Ritz of the West Roman Empire, or the sixth-century Harrods.

I walk back once more to the Imperial portraits. There is no doubt about it, they are the reason for the whole show. Why bother to bring in Christ and the others, really? I take a good look at the Empress Theodora, the ex-chorus girl. A remarkable career. And still I look.

"Well, you see, darling, Moses and Abraham were all dear good people. Not quite our sort, of course, but we could not very well leave them out, considering they were the founder members. And Christ – well – I don't mind that he was a carpenter, really, what I always feel is, that it is the personal effort that matters – don't you? And then, he is the chairman of the show – he does deserve the place in the centre, don't you think? After all, we are all people of the world, aren't we? You do understand, don't you?"

Yes, I understand.

The Emperor and the Empress are dressed in long, white, draped gowns, and their attendants in coloured, shorter garments. They are small well-made people, with delicate bones, pale narrow faces, and large black eyes, and they all look uncomfortably intelligent.

There is no doubt about it, the Empress is the most striking person of the lot. She is known to have been a beauty, but I am convinced that this beauty of hers was the least of her outstanding qualities.

The Empress Theodora was by birth the lowest of the low. Her father was employed in the circus in Constantinople as keeper of the trained bears, to feed them and to clean their kennels. Any reasonably pretty and intelligent girl born into Theodora's background would have followed the calling which she took up. While still a child she became a performer in cabaret and, as most of their kind, she merely used this profession for picking up men.

She rose to the ranks of the *grande cocotte*, went to Africa with the governor of a province, learnt good manners from him, threw him over and returned to Constantinople where she managed to catch the eye of Justinian, who, at that time was an Imperial apprentice, being the nephew of his uncle the Emperor, who himself was childless.

Justinian's infatuation with Theodora was the scandal of the East Roman Empire. He wanted to marry her, but his aunt Euphemia put her foot down, which is quite understandable.

After Euphemia's death Justinian kept pestering his uncle to be allowed to marry till the uncle gave way. But it was not easy, because in those days men of noble birth were forbidden by law to marry 'actresses'. The law had to be abolished by Imperial decree and the marriage took place. Even during the old Emperor's lifetime, Theodora was given a hand in the government, and afterwards, when Justinian became Emperor, she was made Empress – reigning in her own right.

She must have been outstandingly capable. This is already proven by the fact that she became a great courtesan. It takes as much intelligence and determination to become a great courtesan as it takes to become prominent in any other calling.

Her nerves must have been of iron: courtesans cannot afford to be squeamish.

I think that she was altogether a greater person than Justinian. He is, it is true, the most famous of Byzantine Emperors, but he was by no means a great ruler.

He did not have the calm, far-seeing eye, nor the unswerving determination, nor the psychology, nor the sense for timing, which are necessary to be great.

He muffed one venture after another, spent the public money in silly campaigns and exhausted everybody's patience by engaging in long-drawn-out religious controversies and persecutions of heretics.

Even when he was successful in his military campaigns they were really failures, because the effort was not worth the result. His last idiotic conquest was that of Italy, which he wrested out of the grasp of the barbarians. He got Italy all right and had it round his neck, including all the financial messes the country was in. It was after this conquest that he built San Vitale and had his portrait put up in the choir. Ravenna, which up till then had been the capital of the West Roman Empire, became the leading colonial town of the East Roman Empire.

Justinian and Theodora disagreed in most things, beginning with religion. Theodora believed in a heresy which Justinian was busily persecuting.

It was she who saved his crown when, during an uprising, he wanted to run away from the mob and she insisted that they remain in the palace.

Theodora was not a nice person, but then, outstanding people rarely are. As to her faithfulness to Justinian, opinions are divided. Many historians believe that she betrayed him right and left. I am convinced that she was completely faithful to her husband. Real courtesans, as opposed to ladies of adventure, make invariably faithful wives, because they are frigid by nature. They have to be, otherwise they could not pursue their profession. An excellent example of this can be found in Moll Flanders, who never gets any pleasure out of her lovers and husbands and who will stay with any man as long as he pays. Defoe knew his business better than most modern writers.

Theodora also had all the traits which one might expect her type to possess. She was inordinately cruel and implacable, whereas her husband was easy-going and could be influenced by anyone who knew how to flatter him. She also was the greatest stickler for court etiquette, and no ceremonial was too stiff for her. This is quite natural. Upstarts are always keener when they get to the top of the tree than those who were born already at the top. People who approached her had to humble themselves before her. In other words, she revenged herself for her hard early life and for all the humiliations she must have suffered.

She was not capable of religious feelings, but, true to form, she was bigoted. One has only to think of Madame de Maintenon for a parallel.

Also, like Madame de Maintenon, she was very moral, and hounded low-class tarts from the streets and placed them in reformatory institutions. Yet she was a feminist through and through, and when it came to cases of unfaithfulness, she always took the side of the unfaithful wives against their husbands. In this I see an expression of her belief that women have more grit than men. And, as far as she was concerned, it was true.

She was about twenty years younger than Justinian and died young, probably of lung trouble.

Everything known about her is uncertain and the accounts of her contemporaries are contradictory: either she is whitewashed by those who were in court circles, or she is blackened by those who

had an axe to grind. Like everybody else, I have picked out what
suits me to make up my own opinion about her.

I must say that the mosaics in San Vitale are another illustration of
my theory that riches should be slapped on with a generous trowel.
Let us take a lesson from the grown-ups.

I emerge from the golden shower-bath and step into the garden
which lies at the back of the basilica.

According to my guide-book, I should find in the garden the
mausoleum of the Empress Galla Placidia. It is named thus for purely
negative reasons, because Galla Placidia was not buried here. Well,
there is something in the garden. A little house of grey brick, old
though certainly not ancient-looking. Judging by its style and size it
might be a public convenience.

There is only one entrance, though. The doorway is covered with
a yellow curtain. I step inside and remain standing in complete darkness. That's a damn silly way of showing a mausoleum, I must say.
But, good God, a fire must have broken out somewhere, outside. If
only the guard had a look what's burning, instead of lounging by
the door.

The fire is all around me, I can see it glowing behind the windows.
But, really, I say to myself, if there are windows, why is the place so
dark? It does not make sense. Actually, the place is not so very dark.
I can see quite well by now, my eyes have become used to the darkness. And the windows do not show a fire somewhere outside, it is
they themselves that are on fire. An instant later I see that they are
not windows the way we know them, but slabs of flame-coloured
translucent stone.

The burning windows stand as a reminder of the restless world
I have left behind me, while, by now, the room has risen to a life
which is not of this world, with every gilt star on the cross-vaulted
night-blue ceiling, with every leaf on the apple-boughs which frame
the panels, with every couple of doves feeding from a communal
bowl, with every couple of saints seated above the doves and
beneath the boughs.

All this is done in mosaics too, but a century earlier than those of San Vitale. In feeling it is as mystical as San Vitale is worldly.

In technique of presentation, in sheer showmanship, it is of a subtlety which is breath-taking.

The deliberate creation of darkness is calculated to fill the beholder at first with the feeling of being lost. Then, gradually, the stars appear on the sky, the leaves and apples grow out of the night, and the saints move forward like a revelation which appears only when one is ready for it, and one is seized with a foreshadowing of that remembrance which will come when the soul awakens from its sleep.

In the afternoon, while drinking coffee in the square, I find myself in the company of the Tired Ones. This is my own name for them.

Although I have been in Italy many times, I have never been part of Italian life. But there is a pimple on the face of Italian life which I know well. And this pimple is the company of the Tired Ones.

In every provincial town they form a group, and their headquarters are in the most elegant café, in the main square.

They are men of about thirty to forty years old and bachelors, all of them. They are wealthy. They own factories and big estates. Most of them hold a university degree and make no use of it. They do not work. They have no intention of getting married. They are tired of life.

When war broke out they joined up with pleasure, not because they were patriotic but because it was something new. Most of them fought well, often heroically. And as soon as the war was over they returned to their small towns and were tired once more. They own huge and powerful cars, often racing cars. If someone should ask them what sort of car they have, they will answer wearily: "Oh, I've got an Alfetto." 'Alfetto' is a contemptuous diminutive of 'Alfa Romeo'.

Although they have a good appreciation of art when it comes their way, they are too tired to look at it. Their one remaining pleasure is the chasing of women and, because they have already explored all the women which it is possible to explore, they turn to foreigners to relieve their boredom.

In their quest for foreign women they are different from the ordinary Italian. To him, the foreign woman is a make-do, time saving, and an easy way out. To the Tired Ones she is a necessity because she is to him the only source of excitement.

The Tired Ones have developed a fine technique for approaching the foreigner. First, they mark down the woman in the café, where she is bound to sit in the afternoons and evenings. They observe her for two days to make sure that she is really on her own.

Then their favourite waiter is dispatched to reconnoitre. He will come to the table with his most winning smile and say something like this: "Has madam everything to her liking? More Seltzer water? Another cube of ice? Is madam comfortable? Does she like Ravenna? Ah, yes, our town is unique – has madam yet seen San Vitale? And Sant' Apollinare? Not yet? But we have got such a nice brochure in our café, a local guide. We have got it in many languages. Which is madam's language?"

"English."

"We've got it in English, of course. I shall bring it at once." And he brings the leaflet, which has been written and produced by the local tourist association. While I look at the map and the photographs the waiter goes back to the Tired Ones and says: "English." This is enough.

In the evening, when I take my *apéritif*, the Tired Ones are assembled in full strength. One of them is picked for the job. He must be the one whose English is best and whose looks are the most engaging.

He approaches me with a nice show of hesitation, stops near my table, wavers, advances, is about to retreat, takes courage, smiles shyly, and says at last, in English: "I am so sorry to trouble you, madam. Would you be good enough to help me? You see, my friends and I – my friends over there – we have seen you during the last few days – we could not help noticing you – so charming, so attractive – and we have been wondering what nationality you are. My friends said French or American – but I said English. I was sure you were English – I have been to England several times, of course. Anyway, I must admit that we all made a bet. So will you please tell us what you are? Please do not let me down."

After this it is plain sailing. One would have to be very churlish indeed if one were to tell this respectful, shy young man to go to hell. He begs if he may sit down. He talks for a few minutes about his impressions of England. He talks well. Soon he asks your permission to introduce his friends, because they might not believe him if he told them himself that he has been right in his guess. You have been so kind already. Will you be kinder still and tell them yourself?

Before you can say San Vitale you are surrounded by about ten gentlemen, names are buzzing round you, chairs are scraped. The Tired Ones have made a new conquest.

Some of them talk English. They try your French, and as soon as they see that your French is tolerable every one joins in the conversation.

No matter that you speak Italian. This is not what they want. It is part of the game that a foreign language should be spoken. While all is smiles and liveliness a battle begins to rage within the group. They are all of them capable and willing. But who shall it be that will take me to dinner in the end?

I know full well that I have the choice and that, if I wish, I can run through the whole scale of Tired Ones as though I were playing the piano, with the next one taking over where the last one left off. And I also know that here my parable of the piano stops short. Once played, I cannot play the scale all over again.

We talk about food. They are amused when I tell them about the soapy dinner at the Regina. I am told that all restaurants in Ravenna are devoted to the feeding of tourists and serve 'polite food', beautifully presented and bad.

The Tired Ones eat in *trattorias*, where foreigners do not set foot because they cannot find them. Or, frequently, the Tired Ones drive to Bologna just for dinner. It is well known that the best food in Italy is to be found in Bologna. There is a third possibility. One can drive outside of Ravenna, where there are two restaurants by the sea-side which serve only sea-fruit. Do I like this sort of thing? Can they take me there?

I like it. And I want to go. They are excellent company. The Tired Ones always are. They are too cynical to take themselves seriously and therefore they have a light hand with conversation. Besides, they will tire of me soon enough.

We set off in two Alfa Romeos. I go with a lawyer and with the original young man, who is a student of mathematics. What will he do when he has taken his degree? He does not know.

A *marchese* follows us on his own. He has flashy black-and-white good looks. While talking he gesticulates violently. If one were to tie his hands one would render him speechless. The rest vanish into the night. We drive out of town at a most unpleasantly high speed, past a gloomy canal, till we get to the sea.

The restaurant is a wooden barn with a glazed verandah. The chairs and tables are rough, the lights glaring, the floor bare. There is no pretence of either elegance or sham rusticity. Despite it, it has the unmistakable air of an expensive place. First we eat a kind of shell-fish, larger than a shrimp and smaller than a crayfish. It has a pale, waxy meat. Then lovely small soles fried with sprigs of rose-mary. Then squids, grilled on wooden skewers over a charcoal fire, blackened by soot and sated with the deliciously bitter smoke. They have not been cut up into neat strips, but torn into irregular shreds, and their flesh, white inside, is rosy with crimson freckles on the out-side, like the lip of a pink orchid. We order one skewer after the other and eat it faster than the waiter can bring it. We finish with a green salad.

They assure me they will take me to Sant'Apollinare in Classe and to the pine-grove where Lord Byron took his daily rides, and to San Marino, and that they will introduce me to the man who sleeps in Lord Byron's bed every night.

They start making fun of the *marchese*, who lives in a palace in the town. The lawyer stayed with him once for a week and was given a room in one wing of the palace. It was a bedroom with seventeen chairs in it. Every time he wanted to go to the lavatory, he had to walk down a lengthy corridor, descend a flight of stairs, go out into the street, go to the main door, ring, be admitted by the butler, enter the hall, and ascend the main stairs before he could reach his destination.

At midnight they deliver me at my hotel. I am to meet the lawyer to-morrow afternoon in the square, and he will take me to Sant' Apollinare in Classe.

On the following afternoon the lawyer is not there. Instead there is the young man, and with him a man I do not remember, but he was probably one of the ten of the night before. The lawyer is ill and cannot keep his appointment and has sent his friend to take me along. The lawyer must be ill. Work could never have kept him away.

We set off in an Alfa Romeo larger and noisier than the one of the day before, and get to Classe after ten minutes.

Sant'Apollinare stands alone in wide, flat country. Once, in Roman times, Classe was the premier port of the Empire, military and commercial, and it was called Classis because this means 'fleet' in Latin. It was ideal for a port, not only because of its position on the Adriatic but also because it was surrounded by large woods of umbrella pines, which were used for the building of ships. It was connected by canals with Ravenna, and all along those canals lay the suburbs which stretched in an unbroken chain down to Ravenna. Ravenna was built on lagoons, just like Venice, and its main streets were canals. Classe lay right on the sea. Centuries later, the sea retreated and Classe was left, literally, high and dry and lost the purpose of its existence. And with it, Ravenna.

All that is left is the famous basilica and, to the east, the equally famous pine-grove, which is the last remnant of the former woods.

This is one of the occasions when it is fit to quote "*Sic transit gloria mundi*", and I am glad that the phrase is for ever graven in my heart. It was not always thus.

At school, in our first year of Latin, a boy in my form was requested to translate *Sic transit gloria mundi* and, although the request was repeated, he remained as mute as a flounder. M. Ruelle, our Latin teacher, was an unfrocked priest and had a fine knowledge of the world. First, he swore slowly, horribly, and sacrilegiously, but afterwards he calmed down and said: "Now look here, boy. One day you will be grown up and you will inherit your father's big estates. And you will be standing outside, in front of your gate, when the postman will arrive from the village. He will take you by the button-hole and he will say: 'Sir, you are a clever man, sir, you are a learned man, sir, you have been to school and you have studied Latin. Pray, sir, could you tell me the meaning of *Sic transit gloria mundi*?' And you will pick your nose and say: 'I have no idea.'" This is how we all knew it for life, ever after.

Sant'Apollinare was built about forty years later than San Vitale, and it is quite different and I do not like it so much. It is an exceedingly long stretched sausage of a basilica, made longer in appearance by two rows of pillars which divide the aisles from the nave; its length is still further underlined by two long, straight ribbons of mosaics which run along the nave and right up to the altar. There is none of the magic of San Vitale, because San Vitale is built in the round and has many curved surfaces, and a mosaic on a curved surface has much more life; it receives light from so many different angles.

Still, it is beautiful, and perhaps I should not have compared it with San Vitale at all.

The ribbon on the left has twenty-six virgins, and I quite believe it that they are because they look so bored. The ribbon on the right has twenty-six martyrs. In the choir, very large, Sant'Apollinare presides over the lot, with lambs at his feet, on a grass-green ground.

The virgins all have white robes with a sort of narrow apron down the middle, and their coloured cloaks are draped in such a manner that the ends fall slantwise over their skirts. Each virgin holds her head inclined to one side as though she felt like falling asleep, wears a halo, and carries her crown in one hand. They have ridiculously tiny feet, narrow and pointed like tulip leaves, and they remind me of the feet of ladies in Victorian fashion-prints.

The martyrs opposite are equipped in a similar manner, but they have no cloaks and their feet are large and natural and shod in sandals. Clearly they are less vain than the virgins.

The colour scheme is noble but insipid, white, fawn, pale green, and gold.

Both these compositions are very monotonous. The virgins and the martyrs are all turned the same way, in the same pose, with the same expression, like cows in a field, who also sometimes, for reasons unknown to me, are all facing the same way.

Yet, it would be much more boring to look at those cows than at the mosaics in Sant'Apollinare. The strange thing is that, though these mosaics should be boring, they are not. One can look at them for ever.

I admit they are not exciting. The deadly opposite of exciting is boring. But the praiseworthy opposite of exciting is soothing. The mosaics are soothing. If one looks at them long enough one sees that each figure, though essentially the same, is different from the others in a small way. The face is different. The folds of the drapery are different. The tilt of head and crown is different.

It occurs to me that it is this difference within the frame of sameness which does the trick.

Looking at those mosaics is like lying on the seashore and watching the waves break on the sand. Each wave rolls up in the same way, dissolves into foam, and vanishes, and each time this happens it imprints a slightly different pattern into the sand, and the tongues of spray mingling with the water are formed, each time, into slightly different arabesques.

It is also like being in church and listening to a litany of the Holy
Virgin. The Virgin is addressed by many names, all similar, yet each
different. The virgins and martyrs are really a litany represented in
mosaics.

During the drive back, past the *pineta*, I try to air my pleasure
about this discovery of mine.

"This is no art criticism," says the Tired One at the wheel. "This
is sheer irresponsible fantasy. But, of course, you are a woman."

We are not allowed to enter the *pineta*. From March to September
it is closed to the public because it is feared that fires might be
started by thrown-away cigarettes. We enter the *pineta*, and I do
not even experience the added joy of trespassing because I feel so
confident in the company of the Tired Ones. With them the world
is lined with cushions.

The umbrella pines are enchanting trees, as graceful and feminine
as ballerinas. They have not a shred of dramatic dignity, like, for
instance, English elms. No matter how old an umbrella pine be, one
could never talk about it as being "immemorial' like an oak or a
lime. They have no massed foliage which gives play for light and
shade. Their charm lies entirely in their outlines. They are the
embroiderers among trees. They transform the stretch of sky behind
them into a piece of Japanese needlework, black on a blue ground.

"To-morrow I shall introduce you to Professor Orselli," remarks
the Tired One at the wheel. "He is the greatest authority on mosaics
in the world. Don't let him hear that bit about the litany."

I promise to master myself.

But as soon as I get back to the hotel, I go up to my room, fish
out my copy-book and start making notes about the mosaics, breaking waves, cows, litany and – there is a knock at the door. It is the
padrona, a dark, serious woman of about forty, and she has a preoccupied air.

"There is a gentleman who wants to see you, madam."

"Who is he?" I ask. At first I can think of no one but the Pal. Did
I ever mention I was going to Ravenna? Perhaps I did. Or could it

be the national monument? Or the theory of relativity from the station in Mantua?

I know the Pal's name. "What is his name?" I ask, determined to be out if it should be he.

"I don't know his name. He is from the police."

"Tell him I'll be down in a minute."

I like that, I must say. What could be nicer? My conscience is clear. I have not engaged in any transactions with foreign currency. And there is no other crime that could be laid at a traveller's feet. That is to say, of course, at a non-criminal traveller's feet.

Downstairs I find a very young man with curly brown hair and round brown eyes, staring at me aggressively. He shows me a metal disk with the word 'police' and a number embossed on it. I have always wondered how detectives can prove that they are really detectives. Now I know.

"Can I see your passport?"

He studies it for a while and then informs me that I arrived in Italy by air in Rome on the twenty-first of April.

"No," I say; "that was last year."

I feel hurt. Couldn't they at least have sent someone who can read entry stamps correctly? I know that one cannot expect to get Scotland Yard in Ravenna, and besides, I am a woman of no importance. But it rankles.

"How long have you been staying in Ravenna?" he asks.

I have no idea. When I travel I never take notice of dates, Sundays, and public holidays.

I have to ask the *padrona* for the date of my arrival and she looks it up in her register. This, I feel, stamps me as reckless, ruthless, and hardened criminal straight away.

"Why have you come here?"

"Mainly to see the mosaics," I say; "in Sant'Apollinare, for instance, what I feel is – "

He is not interested. Will I never find anybody who will listen with kindness and understanding to my theory about the litany?

Now I am told the nature of my crime. It appears – and I cannot deny it – that I have been staying four days in Ravenna.

The policeman's eyes grow larger and rounder and it is clear that he expects me to burst into tears at his pronouncement. Hardened criminal that I am I stare back at him. We have reached an emotional deadlock.

The *padrona* makes it clear that she will not help, either, and bends over her ledger, to avoid looking at us.

He runs a finger through his curls. "There is a law in Italy that you cannot stay longer in one place than four days without obtaining a police permit. Surely, you must know this."

Surely, I do not. I say: "I have stayed in Rome much longer than four days, and in Florence and in Venice, and I stayed for months on end in Sicily and nobody ever asked me to report to the police."

"Is that really so?"

"Yes, that is really so."

He asks me, somewhat more peaceably, to come with him to the *prefettura*. Will I come now? Of course I won't. If they want me they can wait for me.

As his bluff of "come straight away" has not worked, he sighs and says I can come to the *prefettura* whenever I want – as long as I do come. I tell him I shall attend to-morrow morning. Good-bye.

After he has left, the *padrona* makes an apologetic gesture.

"What do you want, *signora*? Ravenna is a small town. They have nothing to do. They make themselves some work."

"Damn them," I say.

"The trouble with the police," she remarks, "is that they have no culture. Everybody who comes to Ravenna comes to see the mosaics. To see the mosaics the average tourist takes two days and the police know this. We have a saying that here in Ravenna we have got a mad-house and that every traveller who stays longer than two days is put inside."

At *apéritif* time I meet four of the Tired Ones in the café. The lawyer arrives for a moment, just when I am relating my encounter with the police. He is very ill, he tells me, but he does not know what ails him. He has had one injection already and in a few minutes' time he will have to go back to his doctor to have another. The doctor has no idea either what it could be, and he will try him with various drugs till he kills or cures. At least his doctor is sincere.

The lawyer listens to my story. "I don't like it," he says. "With the police you never know. Don't worry. If they have got something against you, tell me. I have got a friend in the *prefettura*. There is always something which can be done. And if the matter is serious and has gone as far as Rome, don't worry either. I have a friend in Rome."

I begin to feel like Mr. K., in Kafka's *Trial*, who was arrested, tried, and executed for a crime without ever being told what the crime was.

I feel it is useless to protest my innocence. "But what could be done?" I ask instead.

"If they have something against you," says the lawyer, "it will be written down in their files in the police archives. It is possible to make a file disappear. Good-bye, for now. I am due at the doctor's."

On the next morning I should very much like to go back to San Vitale and look at the Emperor and Empress, but I think it wiser to look at a new mosaic instead. What if the police ask me how many I have seen? I must go and look madly.

I choose the Baptistery of Neon which, on the map of my guidebook, is next door to the cathedral.

I get to the cathedral and find an old little round building, just the thing. I try the door. It is locked; a poster is stuck on it, printed in German, English, French, and Italian. It reads; "This is the church of St. Justina. It is not worth seeing inside. The Baptistery is at the back of the cathedral."

I am touched by this wonderful thoughtfulness of the town authorities, and go round to the other side of the cathedral, where I find the Baptistery. It looks equally old and small.

The mosaics are all round the walls and on the ceiling. Standing inside one feels like standing in the centre-piece of a round-about that has just stopped revolving. Instead of chariots, swans, and lions, there are saints, and the colours are just as lively, loud, and garish as those decorating a carousel.

The round-about mosaics are done in a style which I find surprising. They are saints, of course, but they are jolly, romping, athletic, soldierly saints. They are first cousins to the gladiators done in mosaic on the bathroom floors of Roman villas. Also, they are not as flat as the Byzantine-style mosaics which I have seen up till now. They are modelled with light and shade, and therefore they do not have to rely so much on outlines as the other ones.

The *prefettura* is situated in the main square. And, as I enter, I feel the eyes of all Ravenna upon me.

The police occupy only one floor of the palace, one flight up. In the corridor I meet a man, tall, energetic-looking, with thinning hair and a hatchet face. I ask him the way.

"Are you the *Signora* Templeton?" he says. "I have been expecting you."

This means that, either I must be a very promising criminal, or that the *padrona* was right and that the police are dying of boredom.

In the office there is the curly-headed young man, looking depressed and filing his nails. I think he is not a fully-fledged detective yet, only an apprentice detective. He gives me a half-hearted greeting.

The hatchet face is, on the contrary, very cheerful. He tells me once more about that blasted law for foreigners and I tell him once more that it is new to me.

"It is not my fault that the police are slack in other towns," he says gaily. "Here. Read it for yourself."

He puts in front of me a framed paper with a text printed in four languages. I read it in all those four languages. There are no grammatical mistakes in it, nor are there spelling mistakes. The paper itself is yellow with age.

"Well?" he says, "can you see?"

"I can," I say, "I can see that this law did exist once. What you have shown me is not valid any more."

"Why not?"

"Because of the wording," I say. "Italy is referred to as 'The Kingdom of Italy'. That was before the war. Now she is a republic."

"So she is, of course," he remarks, "but the law is still the same."

"How do I know?" I say.

"Because I tell you so."

I am not impressed. His verily, verily I say unto you and if it were not so I would not say so, is in its place in the Bible, but not in a police station.

I say: "You could tell me anything, just to be awkward. Show me the up-to-date text."

"I have not got it," he says.

"It is not my fault that the police are slack in this town," I say. He gets up, excuses himself, and leaves the room. I imagine he will return with handcuffs and a prison warder to prove to me that they are not as slack as all that.

He returns alone, unarmed, and quite cheerful.

"I will now give you the permit," he says; "please let me give you the permit. It will not cost you anything. It will be valid for two months. And then you can have it renewed. And it is valid for the whole of Italy. You will never have trouble again."

I feel like our cook when she went to hospital: "Not that they do me any good because they don't, madam, but I don't like to disappoint them."

I offer a cigarette to hatchet face and I also offer one to the detective apprentice, who is still dejected and filing his nails. I feel sorry for having been so bitchy to hatchet face, and in front of his apprentice, too.

He gets out a form, a fine large one, for the permit and stamps it with two different rubber stamps and begins to write.

He copies out a wealth of information from my passport. Then he asks for my mother's maiden name. I tell him, spell it, and he bears it with equanimity.

And now my father's name.

He cannot take it. "But, how, now, your father has a different name from yours. Are you – illegitimate?"

I explain to him that my different name is accounted for by the fact that it is my married name.

"But, surely, you do call yourself Miss Templeton, don't you?"

"No, I don't. Mrs. Templeton."

"Exactly. That's what I said. That's the way it is on your passport. Miss Templeton."

"No, Mrs."

"What's the difference? You say Miss and I say Miss?"

I spell it out to him and tell him that Mrs. derives from mistress. He does not know whether I make fun of him or not and decides to let it pass.

Now all is peace and he writes in silence. Even if I were illegitimate there is nothing he can do about it. I sign my name and he signs his. He stamps across his name but not across mine. I am certain that he does it out of spite, to show me that he is worthier than I am.

"When you leave Italy, will you please surrender this document at the frontier?"

Perhaps yes, perhaps no. I go back to my hotel. The *padrona* is waiting for me.

"For the love of God," she says, "what have you done to upset the police? Only ten minutes ago they sent a man round – another man this time."

"Too bad," I say, "I was out."

"I told him you were out. And he said he knew you were out. He wanted to speak to me. 'She says she is here to study the mosaics', he said, 'but what does she really do?'"

We look at each other. I realize now that it was hatchet face who sent out his emissary when I thought he was getting the shackles.

"What of it?" remarks the *padrona*. "I know that you are a good, brave lady and you have my sympathy."

In hotel-keepers' language this means that she is sure I will pay my bill. I thank her, go upstairs, tear up the permit and throw it into the waste-paper basket. Then I change my dress and go out to eat.

After lunch I go to the square, where a fleet of parked Alfa Romeos betrays the presence of the Tired Ones.

They are waiting to take me to San Marino. We first have a Campari. The lawyer looks in on us between two injections. He is yellow in the face, but there is no telling whether his colour is due to his illness or to the treatment.

"The worst of it is," he says, "that I am too weak to make love. Every day that I cannot make love is a day lost in my life." He must have been a boy scout in his youth.

He orders a champagne cocktail, livens up, and tells me:

"At exactly the spot where you are sitting now, and at this time of the day, twenty-six years ago, the famous fascist General M. happened to be passing.

"A political adversary of his was standing over there, between the two columns with the saints on them, and fired three shots at the general. In broad daylight, with the café full of people.

"One of the bullets passed through the general's body and, coming out, it hit this shop window here – you see – where the men's shirts are displayed – and the window was not mended till a year ago.

"Now, the general always walked about with two loaded pistols in his belt, but just on this day he had left them behind, in his car which was parked over there. So he was helpless.

"But he had a friend whom he was supposed to meet at this hour. This friend was the Olympic champion for pistol shooting, and he was walking on the other side of the square, towards the general. When he saw what was happening he got his own pistols out, took aim and shot the man who was still standing between the two columns – from all that distance – and killed him. I was a small boy at the time, and I watched it all from the corner over there."

"And the general?" I ask.

"He survived. He was in hospital for two months. It made such an impression on me that from that day on I learnt to shoot and as soon as I was old enough I took out a licence for fire-arms, and I never go out without a couple of pistols. My friends used to pull my leg about it, but then, one night, one of them was sitting in his car with a girl and he was shot at by a ruffian. He was not hurt, but he didn't feel like love-making any more. It really spoilt the evening for him. After this, he too carried arms."

The lawyer takes his leave and I go to San Marino with one of the others. He has a bad limp. He was a parachutist in the war and was shot to pieces, straight away, on his first jump.

"I was a soldier only for five hours," he says.

He was a fascist and still is, the Tired Ones nearly always are. He knew Mussolini quite well and was very fond of him. "They strung him up like a quarter of beef," he says. "What do you expect? When something goes wrong the people must find a scapegoat."

He tells me that Mussolini had beautiful and compelling eyes and knew how to make use of them. When he was receiving somebody in audience, he would sit in a long room behind a desk with his eyes cast down. He waited until the person had walked the whole length of the room and then, when he stood in front of the desk, Mussolini suddenly would raise his eyes and 'turn the power on'.

"I was present at the conference in Stresa," he says, "and I talked to Chamberlain several times. Chamberlain too was susceptible to Mussolini's spell. Do you know what he said to me when he left? He said, what a good thing Mussolini is not a woman. Because if he were, with those eyes of his, he would create havoc." The Tired One is clever by regaling me with that sort of rot. If he were to give me a lecture on Mussolini's achievements, political, economic, and so on, I would be bored. Rot always entertains. It is mostly by rot that people's hearts are gained.

We drive through a part of the Romagna which is tidier than the Po valley. It is flat, with the fields planted at regular intervals with mulberry-trees, which are very neat trees, with straight, rounded stems, and crowns from which the boughs radiate evenly in all directions, and large glossy leaves, which look as though they had just been washed and polished.

We reach the sea and take a road skirting it and pass through Rimini and other bathing-resorts, all still shuttered and empty. Here the promenades are lined with aloe and agave, which look ridiculously out of place, and there are a few palms which are equally unconvincing. One can almost breathe the smell of family *pensions*.

We leave the coast and come to a river. It is not really a river, but a trickle of water with a river bed which looks much too large and is filled more with stones than with water.

In Italy, water is treated with respect. At every bridge there is a post with the river's name and its title. They differentiate between river and torrent.

At the head of this little bridge which we are about to cross there is written "*Fiume* Rubicon".

"How ridiculous," I say; "look at that name. It is like a child wearing its father's top-hat."

The Tired One is amused. "This is the Rubicon," he says, "the Rubicon, which Cæsar crossed."

I find it hard to believe. I only know that the crossing of the Rubicon was such an outstandingly important step in Cæsar's career that it has become proverbial ever since. And now I behold the measly original of the saying. It is laughable. A child of ten could wade through the water. An athlete might be able to clear it in a jump. So could a horse. What a come-down. And yet, crossing it must have been an achievement, otherwise Cæsar would not have made such a fuss about it. "Perhaps the river was much larger in Roman days," I say.

"No, it wasn't," says the Tired One, "it was just as it is now. It marked the boundary where Cæsar's sphere of influence ended and where Pompey's territory began. By crossing the Rubicon Cæsar invaded Pompey's territory and declared war on him. Then Pompey retreated to Greece and Cæsar followed him there and beat him."

We cross the Rubicon and turn inland where hills begin to rise in the distance. Soon we begin to climb. We have left Italy and entered the Republic of San Marino. It is the smallest republic in the world, and when war broke out it remained neutral. It was bombed, however, by the Allies when they flew over Italy, and after the end of the war San Marino tried to sue the Allies for damages. But without success. I cannot see any sense in San Marino. It never pays to be as small as that, and whatever such a republic does is bound to look ridiculous in the eyes of the world.

It consists of the capital with a few miles around it. The town is built on cliffs which seem inaccessible because part of the road is hidden by the crags. I do not recommend this excursion to those who are given to car sickness.

The Tired One tells me that, before the war when Italy was still a kingdom, people used to drive to San Marino and send postcards to their friends with the words: "Long live the republic", which was a dig at the King of Italy but could not be stopped by the government because in that case the people would pretend that they had meant San Marino, while writing those words. The town when approached seems to be one vast fortress, bristling with turrets and towers and all that sort of thing. There is something not quite right about it. In my opinion, it looks more as though it had been designed by Walt Disney instead of by medieval knights.

Despite yesterday's flop in art criticism, I voice my opinion and this time I do not reap contempt. I have been right. Practically the whole town is a fake. The fortresses and keeps date from the nineteenth century.

We drive into the town on a terribly steep road and get out at a café which overlooks an open-air dance-floor. There should be something more medieval, but it seems that the imagination of San Marino came to a stop here.

The view is fine all round, with the chains of the Apennines on one side and the Romagna with the sea on the other. I don't really like it, though. The colours are too wishy-washy, too mild, the outlines too relaxed. I like a view to be a tiger, not a lamb.

The place is filled with day trippers who buy and write postcards. At first we make nasty remarks about these tourists with their deplorable touristy habits, and then the Tired One and I begin to buy postcards too and to write them. Then we buy some stamps. The San Marino stamps are really the purpose of these postcards. I imagine that the sale of the stamps is the staple industry of San Marino. I say so.

The Tired One replies: "Oh, no. How could they make a profit out of those stamps when you consider that they sell the fifty-lire stamps for exactly fifty lire and the eighty-lire stamps for exactly eighty?"

I write a card to my friends, saying that I have crossed the Rubicon. Months later, when I am back in London, my friends ask me what I really meant. Had I decided to run away to South America with a man, or what? I get cross. That comes from too much education.

On the way back the Tired One, who has a tenor voice of which he can be proud, sings for me all the songs I want to hear. He is very patient with me. He never says: "No, that one is too silly for words."

His way of singing reminds me of Heine's poems. A poem by Heine usually starts sweet and lovely and romantic, with the sun and roses and pearls and lilies. Before he gets to the end, however, his bitterness has come through the romantic stock-in-trade and he winds up with a parody of the poem he had started. The Tired One, too, begins his songs with a lilt and a tear in his voice, in the hackneyed Italian tradition, and he finishes with a parody of a popular tenor's rendering.

Returned to Ravenna we meet the lawyer on the square. He is still yellow in the face, and is with a friend whom I have not met before. He presents him to me and tells me that this is the Olympic champion for pistol-shooting. But not that one, of course. A new one. The champion is about thirty. He looks like an intelligent butcher and seems reassuringly stable.

They give no explanation why Ravenna breeds that type of man and tell me instead that in the 'eighties of the last century a man from Ravenna went to England to receive the V.C. from Queen Victoria's hand. But they don't know why. Then, as though life held not enough excitement for them, they talk of the stories by Edgar Allan Poe. They adore him. They say he is best read during a hang-over or if one is slightly feverish. I am not surprised. He seems to have written for the Tired Ones of the world.

They take me to dinner in a *trattoria*. I wish I knew where it was in order to benefit other travellers.

The *padrone*, who does all the serving, is a tree trunk of a man with a shrubbery of hair growing out of his ears and nostrils. A white apron draws the veil of decency over his open-necked shirt, behind which one guesses a chest with a jungle-like growth of hair. The Tired Ones address him as "*Signor Mezzo-Merlo*", which means "Mr. Half-Blackbird", with a good show of respect and innocence, and every time they address him thus he makes as though to hit them.

Mezzo-Merlo is not the *padrone's* name. The *padrone* is a keen shot and a bad one. Whenever he finds the time he goes out in the woods, in the company of a friend, to shoot pigeons. Most of the time they hit nothing at all. And when a bird drops at last, they both claim it for their own. And to make matters worse, by the time they approach their victim, they behold that they did not even kill the pigeon at which they both aimed, but hit a blackbird instead.

After the little pin-pricking interlude is over, we are served by the halved blackbird with a brick of rice, browned in the oven and gladdened by a ragoût of mushrooms and green peas. This dish provokes great merriment at our table, as on the menu card it is written down as "*gatto di riso*", which in Italian means "cat of rice". What was aimed at was, of course, *gâteau*.

We eat grilled *Fiorentina*, which is an *entre-côte de boeuf*, and with it a salad. Then the Italian asparagus, which is thin and green, as opposed to the fat, white French asparagus. The Italian asparagus has a charm of its own, though it lacks the majesty of the French one.

I think it has the shy and elusive waywardness which distinguishes wild plants from cultured ones, like the wild strawberry and the wild violet. It is done "*à la Bismarck*", with a fried egg on top. With this there is the San Giovannese, a fairly light but thoughtful red wine. A memorable meal, and very different from those I had in the Ravenna restaurants, where the food has been made 'polite' to such a degree that even the artichokes are served with the pointed top lopped off, to make them look prettier.

In the morning the young man who was the English *avant-garde* of the Tired Ones fetches me from my hotel and takes me to the Accademia del'Arte.

The Accademia is the Vatican of mosaic-makers and its head, Professor Orselli, is their Pope. While we are waiting for him, the young Tired One smiles ambiguously while telling me that now I shall be able to ask all the questions I want to about mosaics. He seems certain that I shall make an ass of myself. I am certain of it, too.

Also, just as one's tooth-ache vanishes as soon as one enters the dentist's waiting-room, all those lovely questions I had stored up are gone. I know the explanation of it. Fear drains the blood away from the brain and leaves one painless and questionless. Professor Orselli comes in. He is plump and heavy-boned, with a crafty, broad, fleshy peasant's face and the peasant's high colour. He looks very good-humoured, and in his speech there is an element of ribaldry. He wears a dark pullover which hides his linen. But whereas Professor Castellani of Parma looked like a poor down-and-out, who might have been glad of a penny, Professor Orselli seems to be a man who has deliberately chosen to be a vagabond because it suits him.

The English *avant-garde* leaves us and we mount the stairs and enter an oval library, where we sit down.

The professor talks excellent French. He has lived for twenty years in Paris and is a painter. Perhaps this is why he is so mercifully un-academic in his ways. He does not sell me his hobby-horse, and when he gives an opinion he does not care whether it is orthodox or not. It's his opinion, right or wrong. He is the strongest personality I have yet encountered on academic ground.

"What do you think of the Italians?" he asks.

"I cannot make them out," I say; "they seem to be so much happier than the other nations I know. And I think it is this happiness of theirs which has earned them the reputation of shallowness. But I don't think they are shallow, at all."

He laughs. "You know, we have not the slightest reason for being happy. We are happy in empty space. We are irresponsibly happy. When an Italian has a car, he will say, let's get in and go. And you will ask, yes, but where? And he will say, oh, anywhere. What does it matter? As long as we go? This is typically Italian. You know, or perhaps you don't, that our country is going to the dogs. And there is no chance to put it on its legs again. And it does not matter. A country can live for five hundred years on its resources, without producing anything worth while. We have only just started going down hill. So why should we worry?

"We had one world war, we had another world war. We lost both times. So what? Make us enter this union and sign that pact. We shall, we don't care. Tell us to be Fascist. We shall. Tell us to be Communist. We shall. Threaten us with another war. Threaten us with death. We don't mind. The idea of death just makes us laugh. We are happy for no reason at all and it is a very pleasant state to be in. Now, what is it you want to know?"

Before I start to say what I learnt from this conversation about the mosaics, I will say this much: I will not give any reproductions of them in this book. This is the greatest compliment I can pay them. And if anyone who reads my stuff becomes interested in the mosaics, let him go to Ravenna and look at them, on the spot. This would be the greatest compliment he could pay me.

And if he really does come to Ravenna, he will say, first of all, as I have said to myself: "Hang it all, I'm sure it is all very lovely, but why go in for mosaics at all? They are slow and tedious to make. Why not do it in paint?"

And the mosaics, come to life by the breath of Professor Orselli, will reply: "Of course, we could have done it in paint. But we didn't want to, see?"

At that the traveller will say: "Rot. People always come out with that sort of excuse when they cannot do a certain thing."

"Rot yourself," say the mosaics. "Because you are so stupid that you imagine that we made mosaics to imitate paintings."

"Well, didn't you?"

"No, you fool. Actually, we did want to imitate something. But not painting. We wanted to imitate carpets."

In those days, in the fifth and sixth centuries, Rome was played out. The Roman Empire was split into two, the West Roman and the East Roman, and the centre of good taste was in the capital of the East Roman Empire, in Byzantium.

Naturally enough, this taste was influenced by the culture of the surrounding population, which was Arab and nomadic. Now, the Arabs decorate the insides of their houses and tents with rugs, which they hang on the walls.

Ravenna was the capital of the Roman Empire of the West, but it took the lead in art from Byzantium. Therefore all that we see to-day in Ravenna is almost entirely Byzantine.

The Byzantine artists wanted to cover the walls, but they also wanted to make something more spectacular than carpets, and yet something in the same spirit as carpets, and so they decided to clothe the walls with mosaics. The little squares which make up a mosaic are really imitation gems and imitation gold, a cross between enamel and glass, and they are about the most splendid medium that art has ever devised.

The tradition of carpet patterns persisted and, just as there is no depth in a carpet, there is no depth in a mosaic either. It is this which makes so many people say that the mosaics are 'childish in conception.'

The Byzantines were not childish, of course. They wanted to represent their kings and saints magnificently, with beauty and dignity, and that was that. Let perspective go to the devil, they did not need it. This is how the Byzantine tradition began. This is why later on, when once more they took to painting, the Byzantines still painted flat and with all the drawbacks which had been imposed on them originally, by their choice. This is why the Byzantine tradition did not really change, and retarded the development of painting for centuries.

I ask: "Take all the people in San Vitale, the Emperor and Empress and their court. Why must they all have black-rimmed eyes and heavy black circles round their eyes?"

"They have to have it," says the professor. "If you don't put strong outlines into mosaics they just dissolve into a mass of meaningless little squares. You must be bold or nothing. You cannot fiddle about with delicate little effects of light, dot here and dot there, like the Impressionists could, for instance."

"Is this why they slash their mountains about?" I ask. "You know, those biblical gentlemen, Abraham and Moses, on a mountain with sheep, and the mountain is green and criss-crossed with thick black-and-white lines. Is this to show how craggy the mountains are?"

"Naturally," he says. "And this slashing is the seed of modern cubism. Only they did not choose cubism, they had no other choice. If they had shown the mountain as it was, they couldn't have shown Abraham and the sheep as well, because these figures would have looked like specks. They wanted to have their cake and eat it: they wanted to have a huge craggy mountain and they wanted a large Abraham and large sheep on it, too. So they solved it in this manner."

Another way of arriving at effect within their limited means is what the professor calls the 'hierarchy of colours'. The hierarchy of colours is the perfect expression of those days, when the feeling of hierarchy was very strong in everyday life, and the Emperor was still Emperor by the divine grace of God.

At this point I ask: "Did the Emperor in Ravenna really have absolute power?"

"He had power," says the professor, "over everything that fell into his hands. What he couldn't grab, was not affected by his power."

The hierarchy of colours is like this: the colour of greatest standing was, of course, the Imperial purple, which in those days was a darkish brown tinged with mauve. Therefore Christ gets this purple on his cloak, and so does the Emperor.

Then come the neutral colours, which are to the purple what the courtiers are to the Emperor. That is to say, they must be stately in their own right, in order to give dignity to their Lord, and at the same time they must be less striking than the purple, otherwise they would steal his thunder.

I have always thought that the neutral colours are those hateful biscuits and fawns of which furniture dealers are so fond.

Not so in Byzantine days: the neutral colours were gold – that is to say the metallic, glittering gold – black, white, light blue, and dark blue. Instead of white, sometimes silver. All I can say is, happy days, when gold and blue were considered neutral.

Therefore, to start with, all the backgrounds are gold. The robes of the courtiers and ladies are mainly black and white, to indicate that they are underlings.

And now comes a new problem.

The artists wanted to show the Emperor with his court and, naturally, they wanted to give him lashings of courtiers to prove what a big and important court it was and that he was a great and important Emperor. Yet they did not have enough space on the walls, because mosaics must be done large to make themselves felt. They could squeeze in only a handful of men.

What now?

I don't know the answer but, thank God, the professor does. The hierarchy of colours comes to the rescue. They worked on the principle: "We can't have lots of people, but, by God, we can make a lot of noise. There will be so much noise that you will think we are showing you a whole regiment."

So they dragged in the complementary colours. Splash in red, splash in green. Let one courtier hold a buckler of such a green against a sleeve of such a red that it will stun you. Red and green together make a lot of noise, like the rolling of drums. And now the other side, Empress and ladies, please. Give them a curtain of azure and orange, clash the one against the other. Let no one go to sleep here. This is a big show. Sit up, all you people, and take notice.

"Yes," I say, "but now, where is your precious tradition of the carpet, of which you are so proud? A carpet is flat on a flat wall. And you must keep this mosaic flat in effect. Let everybody keep well inside the picture. Is it fair that a courtier should stand out only because you have given him such a devilish green shield? If it goes on like this, he will squash the Emperor."

"Look again," say the mosaics.

And I look. True, there is the green and the red, the azure and the orange; but, as they are complementary colours, in the long run they cancel each other out.

And everybody is happy. A lot of noise has been made but, nevertheless, order has been kept throughout and the courtiers have kept to their lowly rank. The Emperor has remained in command and nobody in the audience has gone to sleep.

This was so then and it is still going strong now, fifteen hundred years later, when people come from all parts of the world to gaze at the mosaics. And they still say: "What an Emperor! What a show!"

I have said before that the Byzantines were wonderful stage managers.

As is well known, the stage manager's constant worry is the lighting of the stage. And I have said already that with their alabaster panes they got effects of such beauty that it made my breath stop and my heart jump.

But this was not enough for the artists. They had to deal with several panels in a church, and of these, two panels they wanted to have well lit and two panels dim. Yet, the light was the same all over the place.

So, when they wanted to tell the beholder: "This is bright" and "this is dim", they took one colour and made it the sheep-dog to keep all the other colours from straying. The sheep-dog chosen was green, and it was generally used for the ground. The figures are either in the open, in which case they stand on grass. Or they stand in the room of a palace, and in that case they stand on a green carpet. It is the key of this green ground which controls the tone and vivacity of the other colours.

In San Vitale, for instance, the Emperor Justinian panel is meant to be bright, and therefore the figures are placed on a bright green floor.

On the other hand, the lunettes in the Galla Placidia mausoleum have a green ground which is dusty and muddy, infused with grey and brown, because all other colours are meant to be sombre, too. Or there are the twenty-six virgins in Sant'Apollinare in Classe: there the green is pale and silvered and brocaded, to enhance the aimed-at monotony of design and colour.

All these tricks work on the beholder without his knowing it. All the time he is led up the garden path by the artist, and keeps on saying: "Extraordinarily simple, really, these mosaics. Ignorant lot, these Byzantines. No perspective, no modelling with light and shade, no feeling for substance, no feeling for masses. Could have been done by a child of five. Damned if I know why they are so marvellous. First I feel worldly, now I feel mystic. Damned if I know why."

I say to the professor: "But really, why didn't they do any modelling? It could be done, you know. In the Neonic Baptistery, where the saints are like gladiators, there is a trace of modelling with *chiaroscuro*. And that was made a hundred years before the main glory of San Vitale."

He is very amused. "Which mosaics do you like better?" he says.

"The San Vitale, of course," I say.

"Of course," he says, "but why?"

"I cannot explain," I say; "I just know."

This reminds me of our teacher of literature. She had a deceptive appearance. She was a thin, elegant blonde who would float into the classroom and take a seat like a lady dressed for a bridge party who, by mistake, had strayed into a school. She used to keep her hat on, but, to indicate that she was willing to stay with us for some time, she would peel off her long suède gloves and loosen the collar of her Persian-lamb coat.

Languidly she would ask us to get out the Ronsard. One of us read a sonnet aloud. Then, still with an expiring voice she would ask: "My dear children, do you like it?"

"Yes," we screamed, "it is beautiful."

She leaned forward, and now her voice was harsh: "Why?"

And there the dear children sat and were silent. It is the eternal beastly question. Is it beautiful? Yes. Why?

Thank God I am grown up. And I have full confidence that the professor will supply the answer.

"You like San Vitale better," he remarks, "because it is better. It is much more subtle that the Neonic mosaics. But you can only feel the subtlety, you do not consciously see it. Would it surprise you if I said that in the mosaics of San Vitale the modelling is there?"

"Where?" I ask.

"There," he says, and taps my cheek. "It is on the people's faces. The ordinary way of modelling is to put light and shade side by side. There is another and more sophisticated way of getting the effect, and this is obtained by placing complementary colours side by side. Thus, your cheek is not blue and orange by nature, but if, in a picture, you make it blue and orange, the surfaces will come out, curve and recede, just as they do on a real cheek. It is the method used by Modigliani. And it is the same on the mosaics."

A child of five indeed. The simplicity of the Byzantines is entirely in the eyes of the beholder.

"But, as they are so frightfully effective," I say, "why did the mosaics remain in fashion for only about a hundred years or so? If

Italy, I mean? I know they came back later in Sicily, but that was only through the Norman-Arab style when the Arabs conquered Sicily."

"There are two reasons for this," he says. "First, it takes a long time to make a mosaic. It needs an artist to create the design and a team of craftsmen to make the squares and stick them on the walls. It is much easier and quicker to cover the walls with paint.

"Secondly, the mosaics are very durable, and this very fact makes them annoying. You know how fashion changes. Imagine the son grew up and took over the basilica from his mosaic-loving father, the Emperor. He wrinkled his nose and said, Papa was sold on this but I don't like it myself. I want something else. I would like my Christ done in this way, not in the old-fashioned way. And I'm sick of San Vitale. I prefer another saint. And so on. And, of course, it is much less trouble to paint out a fresco and to paint a fresh one over it, than it is to tear out a mosaic."

By now it is half past one, and although the professor says he does not care and that he eats when it suits him, I feel that it may suit him to eat just now and that I must go.

He says I can come back to him as often as I like. He is really wonderful. If I were the greatest living authority on mosaics in the world I should be so snooty that I would not even speak to myself.

I go to a restaurant called Byron, a few houses off the Regina, because I cannot find the *trattoria* of the halved blackbird. The dining-room is full, and the waiter pays no attention to me. Not only this, but he takes orders from guests who have arrived after me. I grow bad-tempered. The longer I sit and wait the more I am certain that the Byron is named after the same principle as the mausoleum of Galla Placidia, because Lord Byron never ate here.

At the table next to mine I notice that the hog-faced, grey-haired Italian who used to dine alone during the last few days has got himself a woman, a girl of about twenty-two. She is quite pretty, slim, and pert and chatters in French.

I begin to ponder over this. For she does not look the sort of girl who will have lunch with fat, unlovely, elderly men. And on the other hand his taste in women would – I'm certain – run to blondes with frills and giggles.

I am still pondering when the door opens and –

I must tell this in the style of my Irish charwoman, who used to stay away for days on end and would say upon her return: "You'll never believe this if I tell you, madam, but the other night I was sitting quietly at home minding my own business, when the door opens and who should walk in, but you'll never guess who, but my sister from Cork whom I haven't set eyes on for twelve years." She was right. I never did believe her.

Well, the door opens and in walks – you'll never believe me when I tell you and you'll never guess who – but Josephine Baker. I know at once it is she, but it is only now I remember that there have been posters in the streets advertising her guest performance. There were variety artistes billed with her. This is a case like the one about the modelling with colours by Modigliani: one sees it without perceiving it. This is a surprise. I never thought I would set eyes on one of the idols of my mother's days.

She sits down at the table with the Italian and the French girl. Now I understand. He must be her manager for this tour through Italy, and the girl must be her secretary.

I think Josephine Baker must be at least fifty-five, taking my mother's generation as a yardstick. She does not look her age. She looks no more than thirty-five. She is hideously attractive. She looks sulky. I used to hear so much about that broad, inviting smile of hers but I am not to see it. She has a tall, sturdy body, with wide shoulders and wide hips.

She is dressed in a jersey of thick yellow wool and a grey flannel skirt, both quite baggy, and her frizzy hair is dragged back from the face and caught in a meshed net of coarse grey wool. The only exotic touches are a couple of leaf-shaped gold clips on the neck of her jersey, and her gold ear-rings, which are quite extraordinary. They form a double line of gold bars curving exactly to the outline of the ear and thus framing the ear. I cannot see how they stay on.

The girl does the ordering for her. Ham. Raw smoked ham is brought and sent back. She wants boiled ham. Then she wants an omelette, "with nothing in it". Then cold boiled potatoes, which she mashes up with the fork and eats with olive-oil.

She behaves exactly as I always imagined a star would behave: she eats a morsel or two, stabs the rest with a contemptuous fork and leaves it. Then she drinks lemon-tea and then they all tell each other that they have to leave by the three o'clock train and they get up and go. Clearly she has not been befriended by the Tired Ones. If she had, she would now be leaving in an Alfa Romeo.

After lunch I go once more to San Vitale to check up on Professor Orselli. Then I tear myself away from the mosaics to have my first good look at the basilica itself. I must say, even if there were no mosaics at all, San Vitale would still be one of the marvels of the world.

The plan of the church is maddeningly complicated, and I cannot understand it. I think it has ten sides but only eight niches. There are seven pillars which divide the rim from the centre, so that a sort of circular promenade is formed. The proper people call this an ambulatory but this does not make it any easier.

One of the troubles is, that the pillars seem to be six-sided, seen from one angle. But from another angle one finds that some of the corners are canted, so as to form yet more sides, and the longer I contemplate them the more muddled I get. It is all domes, arches, vaults, crossing and counter-crossing and one flowing into the other.

When one is dizzy looking at the ground plan, one looks up and sees galleries with the golden windows, and more pillars and arches growing out of those galleries, dividing and branching off into new ones, which one has not noticed before. It is so elusive that I could weep. The best way to describe the blueprint of San Vitale is to say it was kneaded of bread and that the bulges and niches and vaults were squeezed in by the architect's thumb.

I get into conversation with a young German woman. She is a student of the history of art. She thinks that San Vitale is the most complex basilica of its kind in the world.

I ask her about the ground plan.

"I cannot pin it down, either," she says, "and it drives me even crazier than it does you."

I return to the square and have coffee with the Tired Ones. And here is a story about Count Orsini which has nothing to do with early Christian basilicas, mosaics, and the West Roman Empire. I like it:

Count Orsini is a member of the famous Orsini family. He now lives in the Argentine. He had to flee Italy after the war because he was a Fascist. Before that he was a soldier.

Count Orsini had only the rank of a captain, but he was an important captain as captains go. He wore his hair long – down to his shoulders – and so did all the men who were under his command. This was an unheard-of eccentricity and quite against army regulations, but the military authorities let it pass because he was so well bred and such a good soldier.

He kept his men under iron discipline, and he had a pack of hounds, about a dozen couples of them, who also lived in barracks, and they too were trained in a very strict way as though they were animal soldiers. They were fed twice a day, and were allowed to start eating only when he gave a certain signal.

One day, in the morning, Count Orsini went into the regimental kitchen and asked the orderly for some raw meat. He cut several chunks of it with his own hands and carried it outside into the barrack yard. He put it on the ground and ordered the hounds to be brought out.

When they were assembled he stood near them without moving. Most of the animals kept quiet, but two of them ran up to the meat and ate it.

After this dreadful breach of discipline the Count ordered his men out and had them lined up to form a square, and all the hounds were lined up too and he made them a speech. He said he had made a test of their loyalty and that two of his creatures had betrayed him. Then he called for a firing squad, and the two offending hounds were executed according to the military procedure fit for traitors.

Then the Count gave the order to dismiss. He went upstairs to his quarters and wept for an hour.

One does not know how much the hounds understood about what had happened. For the next two days they showed signs of sadness and none of them touched any food even when the signal was given.

This story is told me by one of the Tired Ones who was a friend of Count Orsini, a colonel in the war and holder of the Gold Medal which is the highest military decoration in Italy, similar to the English Victoria Cross.

I say that I find it odd that the Count went upstairs and wept. The Tired One, colonel and great hero, looks at me with astonishment and says: "What is so odd about it? I myself go to my room nearly every day and weep."

I think of Bismarck, the man of 'blood and iron', who used to have weeping fits in the Emperor's ante-room while waiting for an audience.

It is not these men who are odd. It is our conception of them.

To-night I am very hungry and I order *capellini in brodo*. I find out too late that I have made a dreadful mistake. I imagined they would be like *vermicelli*, that is to say, worm-like, whereas, as the name indicates, they are like long hair. I stare at the whitish blond strands floating in the soup. It is impossible to see the end or the beginning of a single one of them. In feeling I should say they are pre-Raphael-ite, and belong to the period of water-lilies on tiles and sunflowers in poker work.

The waiter brings me a fork to break me in, as he says. He en-courages me to shovel up a mouthful on the spoon, stick the fork into it, and twist it round and round till I have gathered the lot on the fork. The real people need only the spoon for the winding up.

The waiter watches me as I toil and then says: "That's all right now. Now put it in your mouth."

It is hard work. I ask the question which a thousand travellers have asked before me: "Why can't you cut them up?"

"If the *capellini* were not an arm's length they would not be *capellini*."

"But," I say, "wouldn't it be easier if they were short?"

"Ah, yes, but then, if they were shorter, life would be too easy all together."

Italian waiters never stale in their infinite variety.

And here is what Monsieur Roche felt about them. On this occasion he had to give a geography lesson because the geography teacher was ill. We were supposed to learn about the Alps of Italy.

"I don't know anything about the Alps," remarked M. Roche, "but I will give you in a word the whole of Italy. When my wife and I went to Rome we went to a restaurant. And among other things we ordered a salad. When the salad came there was oil on it. I called the waiter and said, 'My dear friend, this salad is dressed with oil, and my wife, she cannot eat oil.' The waiter said he understood and he took the salad away. After a while he comes and brings a new salad. And when my wife starts to eat she finds that there is oil on it again. You see, there you have the whole of Italy."

During dinner one of the Tired Ones arrives and says he will take me to see the head of the modern library.

The street in which the library stands was once the main canal of Ravenna, and the library was built in 1920, on the ground of the hotel where Lord Byron stayed when he first came to Ravenna, and the head librarian is the man who sleeps in Lord Byron's bed.

When I ask him about the bed he gets very coy and says that they are only pulling his leg and that the bed could of course have been Lord Byron's bed in the Casa Ricetta – which was the name of the hotel – but that it is not at all certain.

Lord Byron came to Ravenna to be with Teresa Guiccioli, and after having lived for some time in the hotel he went to live with

Teresa and her husband in the Palazzo Guiccioli.

This arrangement was not as good as it sounds, because they had always to make love in the afternoon, after lunch, when the husband retired to rest, and even then they were always afraid that he or one of the servants might catch them at it. On top of it Byron did not stay there as their guest and had to pay for the floor he occupied.

I have seen the Palazzo Guiccioli and, really, it is not a palace at all. It is a tall house in a narrow, dingy street. But then, of course, I am terribly spoilt in the way of palaces.

I have also seen the Palazzo Gamba, which was Teresa's maiden home; she belonged to the Gamba family, who have a leg in their coat of arms. This palace is equally dim.

I have by now lived for ten days in Ravenna, and I must say I am very sorry for Lord Byron.

Ravenna to-day is a miserable, shoddy little place with narrow, mean, and decaying streets. The main square alone is enjoyable and there are two smaller squares, also neat and pretty, at either end of it.

The celebrated baptisteries and basilicas look from the outside like something the cat has brought in – not even ancient, only tatty, and they are strewn all over the place like so many rotten apples. And, if I come across a rotten apple, how can I guess that it has a core of gold? There is practically nothing left in the place to remind one that one is in Ravenna, which was once one of the two capitals of the world.

I am certain that it was not much different, either, in Lord Byron's time. What was there for him, apart from the love-making? There were his daily rides in the *pineta*. And then? Perhaps writing a new stanza of his *Don Juan*, which he called the "Donny Johnny". Card parties. Dreary small-town social evenings. And then? Nothing, of course. And to think that this was for a year or two the life of the man who was the most discussed figure of his time and who, to-gether with Goethe, was judged the greatest poet of his day.

Even in those days the police of Ravenna were very interested in foreigners. It seems to be a Ravenna tradition. They were the

Vatican police, because the Romagna was part of the Papal estates, and apart from reporting to Rome, they were also in touch with Austria, with Metternich's police, and I should like to think that they were more intelligent than the creatures of to-day. They must have been – with brains like Metternich's and those of the Vatican behind them.

So they got on to Lord Byron and plagued him. They hoped he might be a spy. I imagine that even then any foreigner who stayed longer than two days became suspect.

I think he welcomed their attentions because of their nuisance value. It made a change for him. In the end he got so desperately bored in Ravenna that he decided to give the police something to worry about and he got himself involved in a political plot; I have never quite understood what it was.

There was a secret society called the *carbonari*, although they were not charcoal burners at all. They were plotting to bring about the usual things – freedom and universal peace – and they wanted to overthrow the existing government. Freedom and the existing government never seem to go together. In the north of Italy there were the Austrians, and in the middle was the Pope, and in the south were the Spanish Bourbons, and what with these three governments to overthrow, the *carbonari* had quite a big programme.

Lord Byron got in with them through young Gamba, Teresa's brother, and, I am afraid, he was one of the chief plotters. He was English, in any case, so he could not say that he was being suppressed, but I think that all liberty stunts appealed to him because he was an exile from his own country and therefore enjoyed kicking against any authority.

The whole affair was piffle, and a romantic schoolboy gesture. In the end, when the uprising in the north should have tied up with a revolution in Naples, after several false alarms, the plot folded up completely.

I don't see how it ever could have worked considering that it was in the hands of amateurs. To mean well is not enough. If I ever planned the overthrow of a government I would hire experts for it.

I must say that this sort of thing would have never happened to Goethe. Goethe was in the government himself, he was a professional, he was Minister of State in Weimar, and on the right side of the fence. Goethe was born a top-dog, he admired power in all forms, whether old established or new gained, and he had no romantic illusions about the fatherland and that sort of thing. He admired Napoleon, even while Napoleon conquered Germany, and the Germans hated Goethe for it. Goethe once said: "The down-fall of the fatherland is not a disaster. But when a farmstead burns down, that is a disaster."

Talking of two poets brings me to the third one.

During the last years of his life Dante lived in Ravenna at the court of the Polenta family. After his death the city of Florence wanted his bones back but the Ravenna people would not let go of them. Quite right, too. It is a bit thick, first to kick out a poet – they did not kick him out, they condemned him to be burned alive in his absence while he was on a diplomatic mission to the Pope – and then, when he has made good and is famous and safely dead and no more a fire-brand, to turn round and want him back.

Dante's tomb lies in a colonnaded square called the *Zona Dantesca*. Above the tomb there is a low-relief portrait of Dante, done a hundred years after his death by Lombardo. Lombardo was not a bad artist, but in this case he made a hash of it.

You see Dante in profile, wearing a laurel wreath and a veil, with an open book in front of him and turned to a lectern by his side. He looks as though he would like to pick his teeth and it is painfully obvious that he has got no teeth and so he is staring and wondering if he should pick his nose instead.

In the house close by they have installed a Dante museum, and there is a belfry where the Angelus is rung every evening in memory of a stanza from the *Purgatorio*. Isn't this just like people? Why could they not have chosen a verse from the *Paradiso* instead? I should have thought it would have been more pleasant.

The museum contains barely anything belonging to Dante. It is full of solemn and tasteless mementoes from the various Italian towns, to honour the poet, and they all date roughly from the beginning of this century. Mostly bronze wreaths.

The largest and lushest tribute comes, oddly enough, from Palermo, through which Dante never passed. It is done in sickly white marble and gilt, and shows a beautiful naked woman with two beautiful naked men at her feet, musing. The woman is meant to be Sicily and the men are the Past and the Present.

Most un-Sicilian, this. I will refrain from making personal remarks about Sicily's past, "seeing that I've never known it" as our cook would have said, but I will guarantee that no Sicilian man of the present could be found sitting at a naked woman's feet, musing.

There is Dante's death-mask. He looks a nasty piece of work. Dante was most unpleasant company; he was very impatient and got in a temper straight away when people did not agree with him. Then there is the effigy of one of Dante's sons, who was a notary by profession and lived in Ravenna. He lies on the lid of his sarcophagus, and they did not portray him as a lawyer but as a knight in armour, with the visor drawn up above his brow, his hands folded on the breastplate, and his head turned to one side. He looks ravishing. He did not take after his father.

It must have been hell to be married to Dante. Nobody ever says much about his wife except that she came from a good Florentine family. When Dante got married Beatrice was already dead, but he never snapped out of his love for her. People always talk about his love for Beatrice, and nobody ever thinks what Mrs. Dante must have felt about it.

Dante's first work about Beatrice is the *Vita Nuova*. If I had been married to Dante I would have let this pass as I should have thought that he must work it off and get it out of his system. But then, his much greater work is the *Commedia*, where Beatrice is raised to a guiding angel, and very sickening she is, too. Never a word about his wife. If I had been in her shoes I should have had something to say about this.

Dante took some of his children with him into exile and his wife remained in Florence. I am sure she was glad to be rid of him.

While Dante was in Verona, at the court of Can Grande della Scala, who was his best patron, the city of Florence said that they would let him come back if he would pay a heavy fine and simmer down and mind his own business. Dante refused. He wanted to make a come-back in glory or not at all. He wrote back that there was no need for him to be in Florence and that he could contemplate the stars in Heaven in any part of the world.

It was a good thing he refused because, shortly after this offer, the government of Florence turned once more from Ghibelline to Guelf, and Dante was again condemned to death in his absence.

In the morning I go to the *Bibliotheca Classense*, which is the historical library in Ravenna. I have an appointment with the librarian.

Before I get in I am pestered by the porter, who tells me that his daughter is married in England and that last year there came such a wonderfully kind English lady to Ravenna, to the *Classense*, and he gave her a parcel for his daughter and she took it with her in her luggage and delivered it. Now, wasn't that sweet of her?

I listen stony-faced. *Je vous entends venir avec vos gros sabots.* I am determined not to be wonderfully kind. There are people who have not yet awoken to the fact that there exists an efficient postal service in most parts of the world.

Once at Christmas-time I was going to Paris to stay for a few months with my aunt Cecile. On the eve of my departure one of my grandmother's friends appeared – she had heard I was going to Paris – wasn't that nice? and would I take a little parcel with me and deliver it to her niece in Paris?

I was only nineteen years old at the time and still had good manners. I said, yes, with pleasure, and she sent the parcel to our house. It was one of those Bohemian Christmas cakes made of yeast dough with almonds and raisins and baked in the shape of layers of plaits, piled on top of each other, starting at the base with a five-stranded plait and tapering towards the top. The cake was as large and heavy as a six-months-old baby.

I put it in the bottom of my trunk. When I got to the French frontier the custom official dug it out at once, which was not astonishing considering its size. After a few minutes I had all the custom officers on duty in my compartment, gazing and tight-lipped, in the way French people can be tight-lipped.

I explained that it was a traditional Bohemian Christmas cake and they neither believed me nor disbelieved me but, in their turn, suggested that it would be very easy to hide something inside the cake. I agreed. They were glad that I agreed. I was glad that they were glad. And still they stood and gazed. At last I offered to cut the thing open for their benefit and as soon as I had made this proposal they lost interest and withdrew.

After my arrival in Paris I lugged the cake to the niece's flat. Although I had made an appointment beforehand on the telephone the niece received me in the bathroom clad only in curlers and surrounded by three cats.

She was not pleased to see the cake. Why had not her aunt sent a Prague ham instead? The cats were fond of Prague ham. They were not fond of Bohemian Christmas cake.

I imagine she gave the cake to the *concierge*. Of course, the *concierge* might also have had something to say – perhaps she, too, kept cats.

I get past the porter, after having been shown his daughter's address in Suffolk and am received by the librarian, who is a minor owl. He begs me to excuse the state of the building; it is closed to the public because the builders are at work on the first floor. I say that I am sure it will be much nicer when it is finished and find that he is in the same state – made up of exhilaration and despondency – as housewives engaged on spring cleaning.

We walk through a number of libraries, some round, some oval, in the Baroque manner, with swags of carved fruit growing between the book cases and wooden galleries encircling the low walls. The last room is shuttered and dark.

He opens a safe and takes out some cases.

First there is a plain mahogany box which Lord Byron used as a desk while travelling. Then there are souvenirs kept by Teresa Guiccioli after his death. The usual conventional keepsakes. A medallion with Lord Byron's miniature strung on a cord of Teresa's hair, which is of a golden reddish brown. Several other glass-backed medallions containing Lord Byron's and Teresa's hair – very scruffy looking, untidy wisps, swept up and bunched together. The colour is the same in both cases.

In an envelope one of Lord Byron's handkerchiefs, white lawn yellowed by age and as unappetising as all soiled handkerchiefs are.

Then a piece of a twig taken from an oak-tree where he and she used to meet. Bits of satin and tapestry from a room in the Gamba Palace, where she sometimes received him. A handful of chestnuts and an acorn, gathered by him in Newstead Abbey, and treasured by her.

Of course, these objects appear terribly meagre and insipid and trivial to the cold eye of the observer, because we cannot know what words, what incidents, they recalled to Teresa. They are the hieroglyphs of a language of passion which we cannot decipher. A great disappointment seizes me.

Some years ago I read volumes and volumes of Lord Byron's letters till I had to stop. While reading, his seductive personality came through so strongly that I could not bear to think that he was dead and that I would never be able to see him.

These relics in the library were my last hope. Am I to be excluded thus for ever? Is there nothing, not a scrap, which will yield the spark of the lost fire?

By now we have come almost to the end of the collection. There is the casket in which Teresa kept Lord Byron's letters. Quite ugly, woven of raffia, with a lid inlaid with ivory, ebony, and mother-of-pearl. Anything else? Oh, yes. Her favourite book.

I take it in my hand. It is a small, fat book bound in mauve velvet. It is a copy of Madame de Stael's *Corinne*, in the Italian translation. On the last leaf, on two blank pages, Lord Byron has written a letter to Teresa. There is only part of it, he must have started on another leaf which is missing.

It is surprisingly easy to read his hand. He has written untidily in black ink grown rusty by age, sometimes he has crossed out a word, sometimes he has underlined one, and as I read, the tears come to my eyes and by the time I have finished I am weeping bitterly.

He has not written anything special – at least I do not think so – and there is nothing poetical in his words either. There is nothing but the full heat of·his love and it goes straight to the heart's core. Perhaps it is so moving because the language is so plain. Here he stopped being a poet, here he was only a lover.

All very well, one might say, but why dissolve in tears about it? What else can I do but weep? This is love. And as I read I know what up till now I have felt only dimly: very few people in the world have ever known love.

Here are the words as I have copied them:
"but you will recognize the handwriting ot him who has passionately loved you—you will divine that near a book which was yours he cared only for love. In *that* word, beautiful in all languages –but most beautiful in yours – amore mio – is comprised my existence here and hereafter. I feel that I exist here and I fear that I shall exist hereafter – to what purpose – you will decide my destiny – with you – and you are a woman of 17 years of age – and two out of the convent – I wish you had stayed there with all my heart – or at least that I had never met you in your married state – but all this is too late – I love you – and you love me – at least you say so – and act as if you did so – which last is a great consolation in all events. – But I more than love you and cannot cease to love you. Think of

me sometimes when the Alps and the Ocean divide us – but they never will – unless you wish it.

"Byron. August 29th.

"Bologna."

Beneath the figures 17 there is a word crossed out. I think he had first written 'seventeen' in letters.

I do not think seventeen is correct. I think she was eighteen when he first met her and by then had been two years out of the convent where she had gone to school.

This letter was written after Lord Byron had already been in Ravenna for some time. Count Guiccioli took her to Bologna with him, where he had some business matters to attend to, and Lord Byron followed her to Bologna and lodged even in the same house as they did.

One day, while she was in the country, Lord Byron went into Teresa's rooms, found her book there, and wrote the letter inside it. He always refused to translate it for her. They left Bologna for Venice together, while her husband stayed behind.

The treasures are tidied away, the safe locked, the shutters closed.

In the adjoining room there is Teresa's bust. I cannot say to what degree it is flattered. A young woman with a broad, well-shaped forehead, a broad-boned, oval face, regular, small features, a pretty, short nose – an unexciting beauty. Even if I had not known that she was a blonde I would have felt it now, just by looking at the bust. She seems placid and obstinate and, though by no means stupid, without any real intelligence.

Many people believe that Teresa was Lord Byron's greatest love. I don't.

From his letters it is obvious that his greatest love was his sister Augusta. It is equally obvious that he had been, at one time, his sister's lover.

All that is certain about Teresa is, that she was his last passion, and lasted longer than those who went before her. I know exactly how Lord Byron felt in his love for Teresa. His love was never an harmonious stream, but was made up of two river arms, one clear and fast coursing, the other slow and troubled with mud.

In one way, that is to say, as a woman, Teresa was all that he wanted a woman to be. In the other way, as a human being, she was inadequate. With her he never reached that complete understanding which I believe he reached with his sister.

He could never forget that Teresa was, to him, a foreigner, that she was un-English. English society was the only society for Lord Byron, and because he had made himself impossible in England and was forced to live abroad, English society was all that he craved for.

His love for Teresa was essentially a torture. It was not so wonderful when he was with her, but it was unbearable when he was away from her. Human suffering is deeper and more varied than human happiness. It is not an accident that in Dante's *Commedia*, the *Inferno* and the *Purgatorio* take up more space than the *Paradiso*, that the *Inferno* makes much better reading than the *Paradiso* and that Dante's imagination is ever new and fresh when he describes the sufferings of the souls; whereas, in the *Paradiso* he dries up, his wonderfully precise gift for description fails him, and he is forced to use expressions like "indescribable" and "such as I cannot put into words" and so on.

Considering all this it would be surprising if love, which is one of the strongest human emotions, did not, usually, hold more sorrow than joy.

Most of the time, when they did not actually make love, Lord Byron was bored with Teresa. He knew it, and yet he could not tear himself away from her.

The only lasting love, the love that never fails and never disappoints, is found by those who are able to love God. Here again one can go to Dante or to Goethe for an illustration. In the *Commedia*, Beatrice is raised to a minor divinity who will intercede in heaven on Dante's behalf. That she is cold and unattractive, in my opinion, in this role, is beside the point. Dante liked her that way.

In *Faust*, too, Gretchen in the end is transfigured in heaven and is part of the blessed, and she, too, will see to it that her lover can follow her.

Dante and Goethe were among the few fortunate ones who, at least for short times and at odd moments, could embrace the heavenly love. Lord Byron, like most of us, could not. And so he remained for ever tied to this mixture of delight, obsession, boredom, misery, disgust, and despair which we call love, and which, imperfect as it is, is rare in the world.

The librarian cannot understand my tears. No one has ever wept over the letter in *Corinne*, as far as he knows. He is not interested in Lord Byron.

He cares only for the social history of the West Roman Empire. He takes me to his study and wants to inundate me with books I should read, including a work on the inland water-ways of tenth-century Romagna.

Contrary to common belief the early Middle Ages were not a picnic for the Church. The Church, in order to become popular, created lots of public holidays connected with religious festivals, and produced plays which enacted the life of the Virgin, the Passion, and so on. Despite all this, the pagan festivals persisted in the country, with horse-shows and fairs and circuses and puppet-shows, and these attractions were a great competition for the Church. Just now the librarian is reading an eleventh-century chronicle written by a local bishop. In it is the following story:

A man used to go to Mass at five o'clock every day. One morning in winter he rose when it was still dark, said good-bye to his wife, and left. Another man, who had observed his habits, entered the house shortly afterwards, undressed in the dark, and went to bed. The wife said: "You are back, already?" and he said: "Yes, it is so nasty and cold outside that I thought I'd not go to church." Then he made love to her, got up, dressed, and went out. Later on the husband returned, the wife remarked on it, there were exclamations and explanations, and the wife realized what had happened. She went to church to do penance and found that her wickedness was so great that no penance could absolve her. In her misery she allowed a demon to enter inside her and, under his influence, she dashed her head against the wall till she dropped dead.

"What do you think of this story?" asks the librarian.

"I think it's damn silly," I say; "crude and utterly unconvincing. I don't expect them to have had a Somerset Maugham in the eleventh century, but really, this story is embarrassingly bad."

"But don't you think it is curious?" says the librarian.

"It is as curious as a freakishly grown vegetable," I say. "In that way it is curious. Do you think the bishop believed it?"

"Oh, no, he made it up. It is a moral tale. We can learn from it a good deal."

"What?" I ask.

"We can see from it that people were immoral and that the Church had to fight hard to make them mend their ways and to put the fear of God into them."

I must say this had not occurred to me. Still, I have learnt something from the tale. In the eleventh century, at least in Ravenna, people did not lock their houses.

Downstairs I am once more waylaid by the porter. Curse his daughter in Suffolk. Curse all the little parcels in the world.

I go to see more mosaics in Sant'Apollinare Nuovo. There, again, the mosaics are in two long ribbons, with twenty-six martyrs to one side, and anybody who has thought that there are twenty-six virgins on the other side will now write a hundred times "I should not jump to conclusions". There are only twenty-two virgins on the other side. They had to keep the virgins short because they had to get the Madonna in, with angels and the three Magi as well.

It is most lavish and nothing has been spared. A picture of Theodoric's palace has also been thrown in, and a picture of the port of Classis with ships in the harbour. It would have been too much to expect Theodoric to build a basilica and not leave a reminder of himself behind.

Theodoric's palace is no more, but there still exists the façade of the palace lodge, in the same street as the basilica. It has arches and pillars of beautiful proportions and great simplicity. It is quite modern in feeling. I cannot help thinking that the modernity of the lodge derives from the lingering influence of the Roman Empire. We are much nearer to antique Rome to-day than we are to the Gothic of the Middle Ages.

Also, in Theodoric's time, people still took baths, hot baths and steam baths; this too, was a trace of the old Roman way of life. It was only in the eighth century that the bath habit disappeared and saintliness went hand in hand with dirt, and lice were called the 'pearls of God'. It is no good telling me about the bright lights which lit up the darkness of the Middle Ages. I would much rather have a hot bath a day than read a story from an illuminated manuscript. As far as I am concerned, civilization stopped in the eighth century.

I have now seen yards of mosaics and it is very easy to observe that they are all quite different in style and execution. In San Vitale alone there are three different schools.

Yet the mosaics of Ravenna were all done roughly at the same time, with intervals of twenty or thirty years between them. One cannot speak of a development of art in this case. In the heyday of Ravenna there existed different currents of art – just as to-day. This is all the more understandable as the age was full of wars, threats of wars, threats of invasion, and persecutions – just as to-day.

These various co-existing currents of art in Ravenna can still be found to-day among the bakers. In the aesthetics of rolls three schools are discernible:

1. The modern neo-classic.

2. A certain debased Rococo trend, which I would like to call utility Rococo.

3. Romantic symbolism.

The first needs no explanation. The second adopts the shape of scallop shells, one slid inside the other, which create the impression that they have been baked for the mistress of an eighteenth-century monarch. The third type incorporates elements like cannons, antennae, and indented foliage into an abstract design. Here, most significantly, there are signs of strain and stress. If one breaks off one corner the rest will crumble to pieces.

While I am pursuing these studies to-night at the restaurant I meet the German girl student to whom I spoke in San Vitale. The waiter is delighted that we should sit together, because it clears one table for him.

She is very pretty, with a narrow Botticelli face, dark blonde curling hair, and a long, graceful neck. She is dead tired after having sketched architectural features all day long.

Needless to say we do not talk about art but about Italian men. She, too, has come across the Tired Ones, though not in Ravenna. She refers to them as "the Brethren", but thinks that my name is better and adopts it at once.

"If it has to be a man – *if*, I say – give me a Tired One every time," she says.

"Why?" I ask. "This is interesting."

"Because they are so easy to get rid of. And they are so easy to get rid of because they are so tired. In most cases they drop you before you drop them. The ordinary Italian can make life hard for you if you have been fool enough to go out with him once, in the most harmless way, and refuse to see him again. He is quite capable of coming to the restaurant where you are having dinner and of making a ghastly scene in public, calling you the greatest tart that ever lived, and so on."

"What do you do in such a case?" I ask.

"Just go on eating," she remarks, adding: "They can be very fluent on such occasions. But it does not really mean anything because they call the Holy Virgin a tart too, if she does not grant them their prayers."

She has finished a dry omelette and I have finished a dry cutlet. We ask for cheese. It is brought on a salver covered with a napkin. After the unveiling we behold a lack-lustre piece of Gruyère and a slice of *peccorino*, which is its Italian imitation. It also has holes, but on a more modest scale than the Gruyère. It too looks stale.

With sorrow I recall the glistening creamy cheeses of sweet Mantua. Good food, that is to say, fresh and original food, can be found only in prosperous little country towns free from tourists. As soon as a place trades in travellers, like Ravenna for instance, up come the insipid dishes of cosmopolitan repute.

But if one goes to the other extreme, and goes to places used to travellers of sophistication – like Venice or Taormina – one gets the juicy regional dishes once more. One should always spurn the golden middle way and go to extremes.

We decline the cheese and have fruit instead. Here, too, the pernicious tourist influence has been at work: the apples are small and mealy, but they have been rubbed with lard and polished. And, eating food fit for tourists we revert to talk fit for tourists, about the marvels of Ravenna.

There is the mausoleum of Theodoric, which lies a mile outside the town. It is small and round, like a baptistery, and has a roof made of a monolith. Nobody understands how it was possible to transport this stone and put it in its place. We agree that there is nothing like slave labour to produce architectural feats which puzzle posterity.

Then we talk of the inevitable mosaics.

"Didn't you get a shock," says the German girl, "when you came across Christ without a beard?"

"Yes," I say, "and it makes him all wrong and too gentlemanly and man-about-town for words. And Sant'Apollinare in his meadow with his sheep, he too is beardless, and he is really a Christ figure too. Why did they go in for it, do you think?"

"They couldn't help it," she says; "they had the new religion round their necks, with Christ as the new God, and they could not yet cope with him. They were much more familiar with the old Greek gods, and there they had two types of male beauty to choose from: either Jupiter who is a mature man, powerful and with a beard, or the youthful, dazzlingly lovely Apollo. So, one lot of gods were made like Jupiter, Vulcan, Neptune and so on, and the other lot were made like Apollo, Mercury, Bacchus, and Orpheus. For Christ they took the Apollo type because they knew he had died young.

"In one case we can even prove it. The Sant'Apollinare in Classe did not see the light of day as Sant'Apollinare at all. He was an Orpheus surrounded by beasts and holding a lyre. A Greek monk in Byzantium copied the design and passed it on to the artist who came to Ravenna to do the mosaics, and he just replaced the lyre with the shepherd's staff and left the rest. If you look carefully you can see that the sheep's head nearest to the staff does not balance the pattern properly, and that there is a break in the flow of the lines."

This is an example to show that artists do not care what they do as long as they can do their stuff, just as soldiers do not care who the enemy is as long as they can fight.

After dinner she goes to her room to do her packing, and I go to have coffee in the square.

The only Tired One in the place is the young student. I imagine the others have got sick of me already and have gone to Bologna to eat.

He talks about England, and then he puts a question which none of the others would have put. He says: "What is an English gentleman? Surely, a gentleman is a gentleman as long as he behaves like a gentleman?"

"Nonsense," I say, "a gentleman is born and bred. Once a gentleman always a gentleman. If a gentleman turns criminal he is still a gentleman. Just a gentleman gone wrong."

He finds it difficult to believe. And to make him understand I tell him the story about Dick's flat.

Dick is a friend of mine. He lives in Campden Hill in his own house, in which he lets a small flat on the ground floor. Last year this flat was empty and Dick advertised it. After a few days an elderly, upright, pompous gentleman presented himself – let us call him Carstairs – and he was shown over the flat and said he would like to take it.

He wanted to move in straight away. He carried an umbrella and had no luggage. He told Dick that his luggage was with his friend General Ponsonby-Brown, who lived in the country and with whom he had been staying for some time. The General would send his things to London on the following day.

He told Dick that he had been in the Foreign Office for thirty years and was now retired. He moved in, saying that he was going to buy pyjamas and a tooth-brush for the night.

On the following morning Dick met him on the stairs. Mr. Carstairs said that he was going to his club.

"To which club do you belong?" asked Dick.

"To the Junior Carlton Club."

"But surely," said Dick, "you belong to the St. James's as well? As far as I know all diplomats are members of the St. James's."

"Yes, quite so," said Mr. Carstairs, "only I had not mentioned it because it is a matter of course," and he left.

Half an hour later there was a call on the telephone for the new tenant. Dick took the call and said that Mr. Carstairs was out. The voice on the telephone said that this was General Ponsonby-Brown speaking, and that he had called up only to say that Mr. Carstairs' luggage had been sent off and would arrive in London in due course.

There was something in this conversation which struck Dick as wrong, although at the time he could not define it. He was still standing by the telephone and, as he intended to go out for the day, he thought it a good idea to ring up the Junior Carlton Club to let Mr. Carstairs know about the luggage. He rang up and asked for Mr. Carstairs.

"There is no Mr. Carstairs here, sir."

"I understand that Mr. Carstairs is a member."

"No, sir. Not to my knowledge. But if you'll wait a minute I'll look it up and make sure."

Dick waited and received the assurance that there was no Mr. Carstairs on the members' list of the club.

Upon this Dick wrote a letter, saying something like this: "I have ascertained that no person of your name belongs to the Junior Carlton Club. Unless you can furnish me with a satisfactory explanation I must ask you to pay me a night's rent, put the keys on the hall table, and leave the flat at once," and he placed the letter in the tenant's sitting-room.

In the evening, when Dick returned, he found that Mr. Carstairs had gone. He had left the keys but not the rent money. Later on in the evening there was a telephone call for Dick, from an unknown man who said he was Mr. Carstairs' lawyer and his intimate friend. He wanted to say that he thought it disgraceful that Dick had forced Mr. Carstairs to leave. Actually, Mr. Carstairs belonged to the nobility and did not want to use his illustrious name for reasons of his own – but that, at his club, he was of course known by his real name. This explained why Dick had drawn a blank with his inquiry. Also, Mr. Carstairs would send a cheque on the following day to settle his debt.

By the time the lawyer rang off, Dick understood. The General had been Mr. Carstairs. The lawyer, too, had spoken with Mr. Carstairs' voice badly disguised.

Dick did not expect the cheque to arrive and it did not arrive. Mr. Carstairs must have been down and out, trying to get a roof over his head by telling lies. His lack of luggage made one suppose that he already owed money in one house and that his belongings had been seized in lieu of payment.

All this is neither here nor there. But now the interesting point arises: Was Mr. Carstairs a gentleman?

He looked like one, he spoke like one, and he carried himself like one. Dick was sure he was not. He thought he must have been a butler or valet and acquired a gentlemanly bearing. But this is only supposition. Up to this stage one may say: Mr. Carstairs may have been a gentleman or he may not. The odds are even.

Yet, considering the story once more, it becomes clear that Mr. Carstairs was not a gentleman. Why?

Because after he had been found out and knew he had lost the flat anyhow, after being forced to leave, he still rang up disguised as a lawyer, to clear his name.

A gentleman, too, might have tried to get a roof over his head by dishonest means. But once the game was up he would not have cared a rap what people thought of him. He would not have worried whether, in their eyes, he was a cheat or not. Being a gentleman he would have had no need to bolster up his own self-esteem.

URBINO

On my last morning in Ravenna I run into the lawyer. He is less yellow in the face. He has recovered from his illness, whatever it was.

"But I must be careful with my diet," he says; "my doctor tells me I must not drink any champagne for some time."

It is cheering to know that such doctors and such patients still exist.

"It won't be so bad," he remarks. "In any case, I drink champagne only in the morning. If I get up every day at noon I shall not miss it. It is a good idea, don't you think?"

He is well enough, however, to take up his amorous boy-scout activities. "There is nothing doing in Ravenna at the moment, in the way of women. I want to go away for a time. But it is so difficult. The prettiest women in Italy are the women of Trieste. But Trieste is not comfortable just now. The women who are the best lovers are those of Ferrara. But they are not well groomed, they are not really what I like. The greatest beauties, strictly speaking, are the Roman women, but they are all much of a muchness. They are too classically beautiful to be interesting. And the women in Perugia are lovely, quite lovely, with a sweetness as though done by Raphael. That is to say, they are sweet as they go, only they do not go very far. Of course, I can always go to Florence or Venice and see what the tourist season has to offer. Here in Ravenna it has not yet started."

He ponders. "The main thing is," he says, "never to waste one's time. One must be able to judge at once. Women are like teeth. Some tremble and never fall and some fall and never tremble."

I express my hope that he will come to a happy decision, and say good-bye.

The square is empty of Alfa Romeos. Truly, my days in Ravenna have come to a close. Will anyone miss me? No one except the police.

In order to get to Urbino I have to take a train to Rimini and change to a train going to Pesaro. In Pesaro change again. The ticket collector at the station assures me that I will not have to wait long at Rimini, because there will be a good *coincidenza*. This is the Italian word for connection. It is a well-chosen word. Usually in Italy it is a happy coincidence if the train one is waiting for arrives on time.

As soon as I am in the train for Pesaro the conductor tells me that there is no train at all to Urbino. There has not been one for the last eight years. My travel agency in London, with the golden insouciance of travel agencies, gave me a rail ticket for Urbino and made me pay for it. But this is another matter.

In Pesaro my porter tells me that there is a private car going to Urbino with two passengers and that there will be room for me. The driver charges three hundred lire, which is ridiculously little. I am very glad and accept.

The man sitting next to me in the car is large and greasy, with the baggy, tired profile of an Emperor of the late Roman period. The other man, who sits in front with the driver, looks devilish and shifty. He has a goatee and a number of black moles on his face.

As soon as we are on our way the late Roman Emperor starts an activity which in Italian is called, strangely enough, *manu morte*. I shift as far away from him as possible. I place my coat between us. It is no use. The dead hand follows.

I tell myself that this is the way the Italians are and that it would be silly of me to get worked up over it. I tell myself that it is just this overflowing sensuality which gave rise to the masterpieces of the Italian Renaissance. And that, like all else, sensuality has its drawbacks. I tell myself that surely, somehow, it is my own fault, and that this would not have happened to an Italian woman. But by now I am too annoyed to reflect on national differences. Besides, I am not living in Renaissance days. I decide I must speak up. But how? What does one say on such occasions?

My guide-book features only phrases like: "Please show me the short-cut to . . .", which is the opposite from what I am aiming at.

I say: "This displeases me."

The man in front turns round, radiant. He does not ask me what it is that displeases me. He seems to have his own ideas.

He says, happily: "Perhaps we will ask the *signor* to move away from the lady so as to allow her more room."

How wonderfully tactful they are.

The offending *signor* jerks himself into his corner without a word and a glance and, to show that he has understood, he places his brief-case between himself and me. This is a fine gesture. It reminds me of old tales of a hero who had to share a bed with a princess and who placed a sword between himself and her as a token of his good behaviour.

Now I can enjoy the ride. We drive through a lovely stretch of country, with wild acacias in bloom pouring down gorges like white-foamed waterfalls, with poppies flooding the green fields like scarlet rivers, with green hills all around us, with higher hills girdling them, and the whole wreathed round by far-away blue mountains, while sometimes a row of cypresses or a single umbrella pine embroiders the horizon.

We skirt the sloping wall of a fortress and enter a street and stop in front of arcaded houses.

The two men get out.

"Will you please take me to the Albergo Luna?" I say to the driver.

"This is the Albergo Luna."

I follow the two men through a door beneath the arcade. The driver tells me that the man with the goatee and the black moles is the owner of the hotel, and a swine. The other man he does not know, he is probably a commercial traveller. The driver and I agree that he too is a swine.

The Albergo Luna is, I think, the only hotel in Urbino. In the guide-book it is not labelled with any category at all, which in guide-book language means that it is beneath contempt. Therefore I do not expect much. But I get much more than I expected.

I am met by the manager, who stands in the dim, chill entrance hall on a floor of cracked flags. He is grey, lean, and elderly, and compresses his lips like the French custom officers when they looked at my Bohemian Christmas cake.

We cross the hall, walk past three wicker-work settees grey with dust, and climb up a flight of dark, dank, slippery, slimy stone stairs. The manager says I am to have room number one, and opens a door which bears a white enamel shield with the words: *Sala di Lettura*.

For a bedroom it is excessively large, though for a reading-room it may be just right. It is gloomy, with high walls. In the middle is an early Victorian dining-table with bulbous legs, and there are eight dining-chairs.

There is no wardrobe, but instead of it there is an upright piano. There is no chest of drawers, but instead there is a what-not, a nostalgic piece of drawing-room furniture with an arrangement of shelves and little columns carved to resemble bamboo reeds. Of course, this is what I always demand in a bedroom – an upright piano and a what-not. This is one of the reasons why I never take rooms at Claridges, because they would not provide me with an upright piano and a what-not. I have never asked them, but I know.

A lamp is suspended from the middle of the ceiling. It is a bouquet of glass flowers which shelter light-bulbs in their chalices, and they dangle a flex with a switch. It does not work the light. It works the bell.

At home in our dining-room we also had a flex growing out of the lamp and it also worked the bell. Only, instead of a plain switch, it had a bronze in the shape of a young girl wearing a crinoline, and the bell button was hidden under her skirt.

During meals I used to sit at the foot of the table, nearest to the bell, and every time my grandmother wanted to ring for the next course she said to me: "Edith, press on the virgin." I never found out whether she referred to the parlour-maid or to the bronze.

There is a key stuck into the door, and, though it is as good as a crossword puzzle it is provided by the management free of charge. First one tries to turn the key in the lock in the ordinary way. Then one discovers that the keyhole is a long and crooked tunnel, and the key is tried in various stages of its labyrinthine depths. If one feels that the entertainment is too good to be savoured alone, one can call somebody from the staff – maid, scullion, or cook – and they will come upstairs and have a go at key-turning for their own delectation.

Further, there is a mahogany sideboard and four-branched cande-labra set with wax tapers. This pleases me, because they are genuine. I would have expected the Albergo Luna to provide no candles at all, or imitation candles of wood. Between these candelabra there is a bronze clock crowned with the figure of a Neapolitan fisherman hoisting sail.

This figure, too, reminds me of my grandmother's dining-room. There we had in one corner a life-size bronze of a young Savoyard in national costume, holding a marmoset under his arm. Apparently young Savoyards always go round with marmosets under their arms. To judge by the modelling of the bronze and the expression on the face, so typical of Victorian times – the joy of being content with one's lot – these two *objets d'art* are closely related.

We all loathed the Savoyard, even my grandmother, but she did not want to throw him away because in those days it was sinful to throw away anything which was in good condition.

When we left the house and moved to another place my aunt Alice bribed the furniture removers and the Savoyard got 'lost'.

There is one good piece of furniture in the room. I would gladly buy it and live with it. It is the bed, of fine-grained mahogany, late Napoleonic. The ends are carved out of a single slab, curved and rolled back like the seat of a gondola or the seat of a sleigh or a tulip when it gets overblown or a swan's breast or the profile of a lyre; the bed conjures up one image after another. It is luxurious. When I say luxurious I do not mean 'luxury', but I mean the Roman word '*luxuria*', which I cannot translate.

I unpack a few things and put them on top of the sideboard and the piano.

After I have done this the manager comes and says that to-morrow I can have the room opposite mine, which is ordinary as rooms go and even has a number on the door. He shows it to me. It has a brass bed and a wardrobe and a chest of drawers and I say no, I will stay where I am.

He is speechless. Have I not, half an hour ago, kicked up a fuss because in my room there was no chest and no wardrobe? Still, I am a foreigner. More than that, I am a woman. Foreigners are mad and women are capricious, and the combination of the two, there is no telling, by the love of God.

I could explain to the manager and I could tell him about the force of association of ideas. But let it be. He did not have my grandmother.

He promises to have a can of hot water sent up and assures me that, apart from not running hot water, the wash-basin is in perfect order. That is to say, the cold water runs when it runs, that is to say, that at times the water does not run at all. It is good to hear this. Because the sight of the basin is such that it should be called a non-wash-basin and, if there is no water one does not have to use it.

I inquire about the price of the room. It costs as much as the clean, good hotels in Parma and Cremona. I express my astonishment.

"But of course," says the manager, "we are an hotel of the second class."

I can see nothing 'of course' about it. The only 'of course' I am certain of is that if the author of the guide-book came here and had the same conversation, he would faint. He does not know San Sigismondo, but he is good on categories.

I do not wait for the hot water and go out to have a drink. The arcades lead into the main square, which is a small triangle filled with parked buses and parked cars and paper-sellers and all the inhabitants of Urbino with their children and their dogs.

As Urbino has no railway, this main square has not the chance to be the leisurely drawing-room it should be but has acquired the unpleasant restlessness of a station instead.

To make matters worse, the coming elections can be overlooked no longer. As far as the eye can see the walls are covered with posters. Even the sky has been obliterated by election banners which stretch across the streets overhead.

The posters are of two kinds. One kind is serious and shows the emblem of a party and no effort on the part of the copy-writers. "Vote for the so and so's." That is all.

The other kind is much more rewarding. It is not an advertisement for one party but a jeering at another rival party. A parrot says: "I always vote for the Democratic Christians." Leaders of the Government party are drawn in caricature and hold huge spoons, knives, and forks instead of banners. They say: "*You* vote for us and *we* shall do the eating for you."

A space reserved for the parking of cars in the square is guarded by a board with the words: "Car park for bloated plutocrats only." On one poster, Christ is crucified by the Communists.

There are several versions of miserable groups of half-starved families, trudging down a road in ruins, and their miseries are variously ascribed to the Democrats, to the Church party, and to the Communists.

There are about seventy different political parties in Italy. My favourite party is the 'Beefsteak Party'. This is not a funny name; it is really called this. The founder of the party promises a daily beefsteak to every inhabitant of Italy. He is a professor of economics in Rome. "May beefsteak be your daily bread" is the most intelligent slogan I have heard for years. I am therefore sorry to learn that the party is small and is not likely to have any success.

I return to the hotel for dinner. The dining-room is dismal, with dusty water carafes on the tables and vases with dusty snowball flowers. The food is bad and expensive, which is just what I expected. Considering that this is the only restaurant in Urbino worthy of the name it does not have to be good.

In the morning I do not feel like sitting down in the square, which stinks from the exhaust of the cross-country buses. I find a café in the vegetable market, which has a border of lime trees and is more dead than alive. Youngsters sit on piled crates and stare into space and women stand about clutching their shopping-baskets and meditate.

I begin to meditate too. I am waked up by a blast of music and find the market crammed with people.

The music comes from somewhere behind a stand and on the platform on the top there are two middle-aged men looking embarrassed and a young man who looks cocky.

I realize that it is Saturday morning, and that we are going to be treated to an election speech.

The young man adjusts the microphone, jumps down from the platform, and stops the music. I think everybody is sorry that the music has stopped. The Italians are such a music-loving people that all political pronouncements have to be introduced by music to be palatable.

On the last day before the elections, when it is forbidden to make any more speeches, the government party usually hires the most famous singers from the Scala and from Rome and sends them into important provincial towns, where they sing arias till midnight on the main square. The only advertisement provided is a banner, saying: "By the courtesy and with the compliments of the government party." This eloquence often works better than any speeches.

By now I have had time to study the two speechmongers and I find that one of them looks pale and sickly and emaciated. The other looks unhealthy in a bluff, blustering way, with a short neck and a purple face. I imagine one has a kidney and the other a heart.

The kidney now straightens up and speaks into the microphone. He says he is introducing to all of us Mr. X, the famous lawyer, and that of course, Mr. X, being so famous, does not need any introductions. He goes on for a long time introducing him. After this the kidney says that Mr. X's deeds are so well known that they need no telling and tells them at length.

During this, lawyer X stands to one side and hangs his head.

At last he is allowed to have his say.

That he makes his speech in the face of utter silence of the crowd does not mean that the crowd is respectful and enraptured. In Italy there is a law which forbids heckling and interruptions during election speeches. Anyone airing his opinion is seized at once and gets two days in prison.

That lawyer X speaks for some political party is obvious, but I cannot tell which it is because he speaks for peace, liberty, and prosperity.

At the end of forty minutes, I am glad to say, his face is redder than before and he looks nearer to a heart attack than he did at the beginning.

I decide to take a walk through the town.

Urbino is called a town, but I would never call it a town. If one judges by its flesh then one must say that Urbino is a village, because its people are peasants. And if one judges by its bones, that is to say, by the streets, then one must call it a fortress. Urbino is a fortress turned village.

Urbino is built on twin hills, and where they join there is the bus-ridden main square which is the only level surface to be found in Urbino. From there one street shoots up to the left and the other to the right, and to such heights and at such steep angles that it makes one sick to look. These two streets are Urbino, and this simple two-sided plan of the town is already laid down in its name, which derives from the Latin *urbs bina*, the two-fold city.

There are alleys branching off these two streets like the small ribs in a leaf running away from the central rib, and they are so narrow that two people leaning out of opposite windows could shake hands, and they are so short that, looking down each of them, one finds that it opens on to the wonderful panorama of green hills and blue ridges.

This is moving; those dark alleys, which seem like the beginning of a labyrinth full of poison cups and daggers, breaking off almost as soon as they have started, and forming windows for the blue-green loveliness of the Marches. Walking past those alleys is like turning the leaves of a medieval illuminated manuscript whose black capital letters at the opening of a chapter are made into frames to hold gilt scrolls and rose bowers. This is not all. The two streets and the alleys would, in other places of this size, be composed of hovels. Here they are formed by buildings which are smaller than palaces but much nobler than ordinary houses. If one can speak of a hierarchy of dwelling-places I would say that the Urbino buildings are patricians. They mostly date from the fifteenth century and are pink and pinky-grey brick. They are all of menacing height, with small windows and projecting eaves, and they have not straight walls but slant away from the pavement in the forbidding touch-me-not manner of fortress walls.

Also, very often, they do not turn a corner in a sharp way but bulge round the corner in a curve, which is the way a fortress would behave and not a house.

Each house in Urbino is a fortress. Or, perhaps I should say that as the squares of a mosaic form a picture, so the houses of Urbino form a single fortification.

The alleys are paved with the same brick of which the houses are built. The whole makes a substantial and satisfying *ensemble*, like a woman who has her top-coat made of the same tweed as her tailor-made. At intervals the pavement is raised into ridges, which afford a foothold on the sheer slopes.

In the afternoon I watch two motor-coaches filled with school-children climb up one of the streets. It is a breath-taking sight. To start with, it seems miraculous that the coaches stand upright at all, and remain so. I should have thought they would topple over. There is less room than a foot for them clear on either side. Everybody in the street has to stop and make way. No accident happens, though I cannot think why. A coach has no more business to drive through Urbino than a fly to climb up a skyscraper.

In the evening there are more speeches. We get more liberty,

peace, and the fatherland. The only statement by a politician which
I ever heard and which seemed true to me, is Danilo's song in the
Merry Widow. Danilo is something in the Foreign Office of his
country. He sings:

> "*Then I go to Maxims,*
> *Where all the girls are dreams;*
> *Dodo, Lolo, Frou-Frou,*
> *Margot, Suzette, Loulou.*
> *With sweet Claudette*
> *And Melisande,*
> *At last I can forget*
> *The beloved fatherland.*"

In the morning I climb up the street where the coaches went on
the day before. I get to the cathedral, which is large and pompous
Baroque. Next door to it is the Ducal Palace, which must be enormous and built on different levels: the fortress walls which I passed
when entering Urbino already belonged to it, and yet, half the town
lies between them and the main entrance of the palace.

It is considered a masterpiece of the fifteenth century. I do not
care for it. It has towers on four corners like a fortress, and with them
large Renaissance windows, which make nonsense of the towers.
Fortress windows should be kept small. They do not serve for ad-
mitting light and air but for pouring boiling pitch on the heads of
the besieging enemy. Apparently the Duke of Montefeltro, who
had it built believed in the principle of: if sour herrings are good and
whipped cream is good, how supremely good will be sour herrings
with whipped cream.

Opposite is the church of San Domenico, small, old, and slovenly.
The façade is so uneven that it looks pimply. Also, it has lost an eye,
that is to say, the wheel window has gone. Yet it is beautiful. My
mother would have said: "Quite simple, you see. Nothing to it," in

that voice of subdued pride she used on those occasions when she showed a model dress from Paris to one of her friends.

The only thing which spoils it, as a good dress is spoilt by a vulgar brooch, is a relief lunette above the portal by one of the della Robbias, Madonna and angels, the usual della Robbia stuff, white figures rising from a blue ground. The della Robbia reliefs are cheap eye-catchers and tourists' delight, but because they are fifteenth century nobody dares to say a word against them. Take, for instance, the famous medallions of babies in swaddling clothes, white on blue, on the foundling home in Florence. They are best sellers.

They are sweet. They are cute. The very fact that people can call them 'sweet' is a give-away. One calls something sweet with which one is on familiar terms. True art commands awe and respect. Who would dare to call the Apollo of Delphi 'sweet'? But people do not really like great art because it makes them feel uncomfortable. And if they have to look at it they try to drag it down and make it cosy.

I get a fine example of this when, later on, I enter the Ducal Palace to look at the gallery of the Marches.

I happen to stand in front of two Madonnas, one by Timoteo Viti, who was Raphael's teacher, and the other by Giovanni Santi, who was Raphael's father. Two middle-aged English women come in and begin to dither. Which Madonna is the better picture? At last one of them decides: "I think this one is better. Because the baby is bonnier."

Although I have hardly entered I walk out again.

To-day is Sunday and the place is full of students. They fill the alleys and the squares and they pop their heads out of the tall, menacing houses and scream at each other across the streets. There is a great deal of horse-play among them, bordering on hooliganism, mainly between the lads and lasses.

I disapprove of it very much. If they want a cuddle let them put their heart and soul into it and do it seriously. *On ne badine pas avec l'amour.*

Urbino is not a proper university town. It has only two faculties, law and pharmacy. The students seem very third-rate, too. But then, who in their senses would study in Urbino?

The students wear a headgear of felt, shaped like a boat with an inordinately long prow. It is rimmed with feathers and gold fringe and spangled with medals and various atrocities, such as bunches of pompons, miniature bottles, skis, celluloid ducks, dolls, and dachshunds.

I am told that all Italian students wear these hats. The colour varies according to what they study, and the objects are also varied, and individual, and are meant to represent important incidents in the students' lives. It is a horrifying idea to carry one's life-history on one's hat. As though one's face were not enough.

On the next day I go to the gallery again. I have an introduction to the head owl but find that he has gone to Venice. For this I cannot blame him. Probably the only way to bear Urbino is to live in Venice.

I am escorted through the rooms by the assistant owl. Nobody is a prophet in his own country, and as Urbino is Raphael's birthplace, the custodians of art in Urbino are very strict with him. The assistant owl makes it clear at once that he is not willing to let Raphael get away with anything.

I am told that Raphael is not as wonderful as I believe him to be and as so many people before me have believed. Raphael did not invent anything new in painting. He was not obsessed with any problem, like Uccello who was crazy on perspective, or Piero della Francesca who was keen on making everything look heavy, or Giorgione who wanted to create moments of stillness, or Bonnard who used his men and women as part of the furniture.

Raphael just painted, it seems. And so marvellously, too. It is unforgivable.

Raphael's father was court painter to the Dukes of Montefeltro in Urbino. In his youth he had worked in Ghent and got influenced by the angularity of Flemish art. They lived in one of those fortressy pink houses in one of the two streets and after his father's death Raphael went to Perugia and continued painting in Perugino's workshop. He got introductions to patrons of the arts in Florence and after this he never looked back. In the end, when he lived in Rome in all his glory, surrounded by a court of fifty young men, he employed his old teacher Timoteo Viti in his workshop.

Raphael was always successful and fashionable and he is not only the prince among painters, but he was treated like a prince during his lifetime.

He was the favourite painter of Pope Julius II and that was something, considering that the competition was stiff in those days, with people like Michelangelo and Leonardo still about and doing.

It was lucky for him that the Pope was more interested in life and art than in religion. So was the following Pope, Leo X, who also became his patron. It is said that when he was elected to the Chair, he exclaimed: "Now that God has granted me this office, let us enjoy it." This Pope believed in the antique Olympian gods but was doubtful about Christ. He thought, for instance, that the immortality of the soul was uncertain – a moot point. He spent all his money on art and even pawned the jewels of his tiara. Alexander Borgia, one of the following Popes, was also shaky on Christian dogma and ritual so that, while celebrating Mass for a king, he had to be prompted.

Raphael got all the big commissions without having to apply for them, whereas Michelangelo had to intrigue and to scratch and bite.

The trouble is that Raphael had too much on his hands. He was commissioned to design St. Peter's. He became superintendent of all the works in the Vatican, and had to conduct the archaeological diggings in Rome. He had to do frescoes of private palaces and private portraits as well.

He died young, at thirty-seven, after a fortnight's illness. He was born on a Good Friday and died on a Good Friday. It is thought that he died from nervous exhaustion – too much work and too much love. The women ran after him, and he was not the man to turn them away.

About this Vasari tells the following story: Raphael was commissioned by Agostino Chigi, the banker, to paint frescoes in the Chigi Palace. After he had started on the rooms on the first floor he fell in love with a woman and was so obsessed by his passion that he abandoned the work. Chigi tried all persuasions he could think of to make him return. It was no use. At last, through friends and relatives of the lady, Chigi persuaded her to come and live in the palace for the time being and installed her in apartments close to those which Raphael was supposed to decorate. It was only then that Raphael resumed work.

Vasari also relates that Raphael was a close friend of the Cardinal of Bibbiena, who nagged him for years that he should get married. Raphael, who was obliging to a fault, gave in and became engaged to the Cardinal's niece, who did not attract him. He kept putting off the marriage, saying that he was not ready for it yet, and that he would get married a few years later. After this time had passed the Cardinal reminded him of his promise and Raphael felt that he had to come up to scratch. But he still put it off by saying that he had heard a rumour that the Pope would award him with a dignity in gratitude for his work in the Vatican and that for the sake of the Cardinal's niece it would be better to wait for the wedding till then. Shortly after this, after returning from a secret assignation with the woman he loved at the time, he caught a chill, fell ill with a fever, and died.

I believe that one of the qualities which are unique in Raphael is his apparent serenity. I say apparent, because if it were real serenity his pictures would be dead. Life is a struggle, and the only serenity is to be found in the boneyard. Raphael's serenity is deceptive, like taking a walk in the country. The sky is blue, the flowers are in bloom. "What peace, what tranquillity," we say. This peace surrounding us is a battle-field. Unseen animals are chasing and devouring each other. The plants struggle with their roots in the soil. The blue sky itself can remain blue only as long as one current of air can maintain itself against the pressure of another. And so on. Raphael is the life itself, he is at once in the battle and above it.

I keep most of my thoughts to myself, but when the assistant owl has finished running down Raphael I murmur something about his serenity.

"Oh, that," he says; "of course you realize that Raphael was so serene because he was influenced by the landscape of Urbino"; and he takes me to one of the towers in the palace to look at the panorama. "Look at the serenity of this," he tells me.

What rot. The landscape is not serene. The longer one looks at it the more one becomes aware of its movement. It is a swirl of green hills and blue mountains. It dances round and round, it streams round, it spills round.

The assistant owl is just another of those booksy boys who repeat what their predecessors have written down.

One is always told that the great Snookello learnt from Snooketto and was influenced by Snookaggio. And so he did. And so he was. But the greatness of the great Snookello was acquired by himself. Raphael did not learn his serenity from Urbino. Raphael learnt it from Raphael.

Sometimes, when I am in a gallery, I look at a picture by an Italian master and say to myself: "Really, this is every bit as good as Raphael."

And then, perhaps, there is a Raphael there as well, and I perceive that, after all, Raphael is the one and only one. If I had to turn out copy for an advertisement for Raphael I would write: "Rely on Raphael. He's always got that something extra." This sounds frivolous, but it is not meant to be. Examine all the learned stuff that has been written about Raphael through the ages. In the last resort nobody can explain him, even Berenson falls as flat as a flounder, and I come to the conclusion that my guesses are as meaningless as anyone else's.

If I were a prisoner in the dock accused of idolatry of Raphael, and the Counsel for the Defence said to me: "Now, Mrs. Templeton, will you please tell the Court in your own words what you claim to feel about Raphael?", I should fold up and be led away.

And yet, when people do not feel about him what I feel I get furious.

A little while ago there was an exhibition in London of pictures from the Royal Collection. It was mainly Flemish stuff. In one of the rooms there was a small pencil drawing by Raphael, a Leda with the swan. Next to it was a minor Flemish master of the seventeenth century, I believe, a tavern filled with sprawling, drunken burghers.

I went to the exhibition with an acquaintance of mine. He gave the Raphael a passing glance and stopped in front of the tavern. I stopped in front of the Leda.

"Come and look at this," he said.

"Come and look at this," I said.

"Ah, I've seen yours," he said.

"And I've seen yours," I said.

"But look," he exclaimed, "this is life. This is the truth. This is the way people really are. Every face – do you see? is here with every wrinkle and every wart."

What could I say for Leda? She was only an outline. She had no warts and wrinkles, and no intention of acquiring them either. And then I understood that for most people nowadays truth is only truth when it has warts and wrinkles. If you distil truth, goodness, and beauty, and present only its quintessence, you are a slick, superficial bore to them.

And the booksy boys do not like you either, because, pray, sir, where is your problem?

And if you can persuade somebody to come and look at a Raphael he will not let it go without saying something like: "Well, you know, this Madonna you are admiring so much was in reality a Florentine tart."

We leave the tower and go back to the gallery.

First there is a Piero which, according to the assistant owl, is the best piece in the collection.

It is the mortification of Christ, and Christ is mortified indoors while a few Roman soldiers are standing outside. Neither Christ nor the others seem to care about what is happening. Piero has carved the picture into two halves by means of a pillared hall. This two-halves effect is very unpleasing. It makes the thing look unfinished and undigested, and one cannot help asking why Piero did not paint two separate pictures instead?

I am expected to like it and I do not like it, and say so. I will not be bullied into seeing things I do not see and feeling things I do not feel.

I know perfectly well that at the moment Piero is considered to be one of the greatest painters, because he struggled with problems and painted them. For instance, he was obsessed with the stoniness of stone, and this is why he puts masonry into so many of his paintings. I can say no fairer than my charwoman who, when I asked her opinion of my portrait, said: "I call it interesting, madam."

There is another Piero, a Madonna with angels. All the angels have lantern jaws. I am told that one of Piero's aims was to achieve a static effect. He certainly did. With their thick necks and nut-cracker faces and their robes of cast iron and their wide, open mouths, the Madonna and angels look like a group of cannon barrels to me.

"But don't you think he is great?" urges the assistant owl. I cannot tell. If he is not fair to me what care I how fair he be?

Now Uccello. He has painted a long, narrow strip of a picture called the "Profanation of the Host", in which he tells a story in six phases on the same principle as a modern strip cartoon, and the story itself could have been invented by that eleventh-century bishop of Ravenna.

1. A woman carries the Host and puts it in a cupboard in the

church. A Jew breaks in by night and steals it. 2. The Jew is in his kitchen. He puts the Host into a frying-pan above a tripod, but the Host refuses to be burnt and sheds a stream of blood which runs down the kitchen floor and seeps through the door. 3. Soldiers who have seen the blood enter the Jew's kitchen and put him in shackles. 4. The Jew is tortured to death while the bishop celebrates Mass with the retrieved Host. 5. The woman is hauled up the gallows because she was so careless and an angel appears to comfort her. [Here Uccello is downright mean; if the angel could be bothered at all to make an appearance he might just as well have saved her from the gallows while he was at it.] 6. The woman is dead on a trestle table somewhere in Purgatory, and angels and devils contest for her soul.

The whole is cramped, crude, and with little merit, and I am exhorted by the assistant owl to look how hard Uccello tried to get his perspective right.

I have read my Roger Fry as attentively as the assistant owl, and I, too, know that Uccello was a pioneer among painters. Despite it he painted some splendid pictures, but this one is not among his happiest efforts and is only grist to the mill of the booksy boys.

At last we come to a Raphael. It is a recent acquisition. It used to be in the Uffizi in Florence, and Urbino made a row because it was Raphael's birthplace and did not own a single one of his paintings. The Uffizi had to disgorge, much against their will. When we come to it, my companion leaves me and looks out of the window. A picture which is not only good but pleasant is more than he can bear.

It is one of Raphael's best-known portraits; an unknown lady, head, shoulders, and hands. Critics say that he copied the pose from Leonardo's Mona Lisa. Raphael copied anything he liked from anybody.

Apart from the resemblance in pose one could also say that the lady is the same type of woman as the Mona Lisa; she is a bitch, and knows she is a bitch and enjoys being a bitch.

Raphael has treated her quite differently, though. For one thing, the painting is perfectly straightforward. There are no tricks of dreamy, hilly backgrounds, which add mystery to the sitter. The background is plain and dark. There is no rising and sinking into light and shadow, which might render her more intriguing than she really is. He has painted her as a not very lovable, quite attractive, and ordinary woman, and was not willing to lend her some of his own glory.

Raphael is as shatteringly realistic in his portraits as he is transcendental in his Madonnas. He always goes with the subject, whereas many other artists will force their own particular conceit upon it.

Although he is not adored in the sacred arty halls of Urbino, the people still cherish him.

Wherever one goes, whether it is to buy safety-pins or cigarettes or to inquire about the time-table of the buses, one finds his self-portrait on the wall in the place of honour.

He is a young man wearing the floppy fashionable cap of that time, with a peaked corner to one side. His hair is straight and falls to his shoulders. He has a long, pale, oval face, dark, seraphic eyes, and a long, white throat. He seems neither happy nor unhappy, neither kind nor cruel. He has an ethereal, swan-like beauty and looks modest and inquisitive.

AREZZO

I have now stayed for some time in Urbino, and I have seen that the horse-play between boy and girl students is not confined to the sexes. It seems universal also among the men of the town. I cannot go into a tobacconist's shop without having to dodge mock fisticuffs between customer and shopkeeper. I cannot have coffee at a table without having to watch one of the louts advancing towards the waiter with a raised chair, threatening playfully to push him over and upset his tray. I cannot buy a book without having to take cover behind the shelves in order to escape being hit during a matey scuffle between the salesman and a client.

This detestable mock-fighting habit is a part of the place and as jarring as an ingrown nail in a human foot.

Now, this habit has not descended on Urbino from the sky, overnight. It has nothing to do with our modern age and our living conditions. It must be very ancient. These things always are.

It is, for instance, not an accident that the highly organized students' rags are more cruel in Florence than in other Italian towns; Florence has the tradition of most unpleasant practical jokes, which were already in full swing in Boccaccio's day.

Nor is it an accident that the people of Taormina have the mastery of flattery and pleasure-giving at their finger-tips; Taormina was already the playground of millionaires and exquisites two thousand years ago, in the antique world.

I do not know what gave rise to the universal horse-play in Urbino, but I am certain that it was widespread already in Raphael's time. And I cannot see Raphael having the time of his life when, say, grinding colours, he was threatened by one of his cronies with the mortar, while another pretended to break the table over his head.

No and a hundred times no. I cannot see him in Urbino. He was born there but it did not nurture him. He cleared out at thirteen, and returned there only once in later life when he had to unwind some affairs connected with his parents' property.

I once asked a friend of mine about his youth. He told me: "You see, I was born in Bradford. All my youth was taken up with the single thought of how to get out of Bradford."

I have given Urbino a great deal of thought and this is what would do with it if I were the tyrant I should like to be: The Minis try of Health would issue a manifesto saying that, owing to an out break of bubonic plague the university would be closed forthwith and that the student population would be well advised to leave ti further notice.

I have chosen bubonic plague because as far as I know it is viru lent, incurable, and cannot be held in check with inoculation.

After having cleared out the students I would stage another S Bartholomew's night, but I would not wait till St. Bartholomew day. Any odd saint would do for my purpose. The banquet woul take place in the Albergo Luna, and to give it unprecedented spler dour the water-jugs would be washed and polished.

In order to save unnecessary expense I would cook only the fir course. I have always wondered if Catherine de Medici, when sh staged her banquet, went to the trouble of preparing the who menu. During the eating of the *pasta*, the backbone, the salt, an the cream of Urbino would be murdered, which would do awa with all the louts and yokels.

After this I would get hotel managers from Venice to lick th place into shape, install an open-air theatre on the Piazza Raffael which jags so magnificently above the panorama of the Marche and import the strong and gentle men and women of Umbria, pre ferably from the neighbourhood of Perugia.

I am certain that within a year Urbino would be a going concer and that from every window of every fortress house, rich, elderl heads would pop out and admire the view in American accents.

The only original inhabitants remaining in the neighbourhoo would be the oxen.

The ox is my favourite Italian animal. His skin is of subtle, smooth, gleaming white akin to the white of pearl and oyster. The folds of skin hang from his shoulders like drapery. His horns are broad, tawny, and smoked pale grey at the ends; they curve away from the sides of his head or twist back in a graceful S. His aspect is of medieval nobility. When he stands among the furrows of a field in his white dignity I see the crenellations of towers behind him, and narrow, striped pennants unfurled among the glittering criss-cross of lances and halberds.

Now that I have settled Urbino's fate I must go elsewhere. I book a seat in the bus going to Arezzo, pay my bill, and am on the square at eight in the morning.

I wait there for three hours and then I am told that the bus has broken down on the way from Fano and will not run to-day at all. I return to the Albergo Luna, where the manager says how lucky that the sheets have not yet been stripped from my bed.

The bus journey to Arezzo takes three hours, and it is beautiful in the full sun of May which holds the promise of ripening cherries and berries. The fields are encarnadined with flowering clover, and a fodder plant which looks like crimson pipe-cleaners. We leave the valley and climb up the mountains, which are bare and yellow and twisted into whirling folds like hard, unbleached linen.

The Albergo Continentale in Arezzo is situated on the perfectly round Piazza Guido Monaco which, seen from a distance, looks like the full moon on a slightly cloudy night; the shrubs and flower-beds in the piazza are the spots in the moon, and the ring round the moon is formed by the circle of houses around it.

My room has a telephone by the bedside, and curtains, and a quilt of egg-yolk yellow satin, and an oval basin with white tiles behind it, and light switches which can be worked from the bed. The price is lower than at the Albergo Luna. My guide-book places the Continentale in the third category. I was willing to forgive him San Sigismondo, but this is the end of the relations between us.

I take lunch in a *trattoria*, where the *padrone* receives me seething with indignation, clearly fresh from a row. I add to his temper by refusing *pasta* in any shape. He is stubborn.

"Have it in soup," he says. "To-day we have *tortellini*."

I know them. They are shaped like little hats with the crown filled with herbs and mincemeat. I refuse.

"Have them in the red," he says, meaning tomato sauce. I refuse.

"Have them in the white," he says, meaning butter and grated cheese. I refuse.

He throws up his arms. "If you will not have *pasta* why come to eat at all?"

He turns to the kitchen and yells: "Quiet, there," although there has been no sound from that quarter. He comes back to me. "There is no beef to-day," he says, "but we could make you a beef-steak of veal. Would you like that?"

I would. I ask for my usual quarter of wine and once more he is exasperated: "I cannot be bothered measuring out the wine. Here is the bottle: here, drink."

I spend the afternoon at the hairdresser's, who wants to know what irresponsible swine has been entrusted with the care of my head up till now. He praises God on my behalf and assures me that it was divine providence which guided my steps to his establishment. My previous hairdresser must have been a *mortadella* and a *salame*. It is odd that the Italians use the names of their good sausages as insults.

He shapes my hair beautifully, and when I say so he becomes dispirited and remarks, really, what is the good of dressing my hair when he knows full well that I am going to comb it the wrong way round.

He orders me to come to him every day to have my hair combed by him, not because he cares for me but because he cares for his reputation. Yet, what is the good of giving me such orders, when he knows that I will not comply?

"You are too selfwilled," he remarks, "that's what's the trouble with you. The only easy-going thing about you is your hair, which is so obedient that it does not need setting lotion. Ah, life is a misery."

I am glad to get out and, to console myself for my character, I buy a bagful of the first medlars and eat them in the street.

I will say this about Arezzo; it is dull as long as one walks through level streets and it is pretty as soon as one starts to climb into the hilly parts.

There is a church of the twelfth century, the Pieve di Santa Maria, which has a front entirely made up of colonnades rising above each other in three tiers, and each column is shaped in a different pattern. Behind the church is the Piazza Brandi, built on a slope. It is a charming architectural salad, with houses of different periods, a sampler in stone and brick. There is even a bay-fronted house of the Regency style which might have come from Park Lane in London.

In a street further uphill I pass Petrarch's house, reconstructed, looking as brand-new as it is. The street leads up to a garden set on a platform.

The garden is dull and the view is beautiful. In the valley beneath me the vines are set in crooked rows, stretching scrolled and curling garlands from tree to tree. In the distance, where the low hills are rising, the vine-leaves and soil draw green and ochre stripes over the swelling slopes, and the twisted stems stand out in black as though scrawled in with ink with a thick pen.

I go to dinner in the Bocca di S. Francesco, which is near the church of that saint. It is a vaulted cellar of dubious age, probably quite new.

The walls are stencilled with heraldic animals. The water-jugs, salt-cellars, pepper-pots, lamp-stands and ash-trays are made of majolica. Even the tooth-picks are bunched together in majolica containers. The food is not made of majolica but it is not good.

I order a dish which is excellent to eat in hot weather when the appetite needs whipping up. It is called *vitello tonnato*, and is composed of slices of marinaded cold roast veal covered with a sauce of shredded tunny-fish and capers.

Three French women take the table next to mine. They are women of that age and type which the Italians describe as "having a few cartridges left in her belt", and they remind me of a remark which an English sergeant made to me. He was describing his leave in Paris just before the end of the war, when the French who had fought on the side of the Allies were called the Free French. He said: "The best thing was, that every morning I had breakfast served to me in bed by a young Free French woman – more French than young – more free than French – and above all – a woman."

The three women are dressed in what I call the Capri style, and are in what I call the Capri mood. They are fluffy in hair and skirt and behaviour. They giggle their way through the menu, shout for "*musica Italiana*", and tell me that they have just come from Capri.

I grow dispirited. It is really as easy as that to diagnose people? And whose fault is it, mine or theirs? This is not life, the way I know it.

They eat wild strawberries and they eat them in the way I thought they would, with sugar and marsala. In Italy there are three ways of eating strawberries: with marsala, with white wine, or with lemon.

I do not approve of the marsala way. Strawberries and marsala are a flashy, swanky dish, somewhat obvious and vulgar. I think the marsala is wrong because it is too sweet and has too much personality of its own – selfwilled, as the hairdresser would say – and in this instance it is meant to play second fiddle to the strawberries and is not willing to do so.

The charm of wild strawberries lies in their fragrant bitterness, and this must be brought out, not suppressed.

This can be done with white wine, but I think a drenching of red wine is still better; red wine has a tang of its own which is in sympathy with that of the fruit. It should be a modest, local red wine, simple and robust, and one should be chary with it.

In the morning I go to San Francesco. It is a little grey mouse of a church, old, and with no pretensions.

Once it must have been covered with frescoes inside because there are still shreds of them to be seen, like old posters on a wall in a slummy street, where they have been left to rot away throughout the years.

The famous Piero frescoes are in the choir. There are people who consider them among the greatest paintings in the world. There are people who say that Piero's fame has never spread as widely as, say, Raphael's, because Piero happened to paint his best pictures in obscure little towns like Arezzo and San Sepolcro, off the ordinary travellers' route. Now I want to see for myself.

Piero has spread himself on each side of the choir, in three instalments, so to speak. The first, which is at eye-level, is a battle-scene. Above is something less hectic and more holy, and above this is yet another lot, still quieter and with a touch of the idyllic.

On the bands of wall which frame the windows of the choir, there are driblets of saints and angels, well adapted for the narrow space, the sort of thing one slaps on when one is under contract to decorate a whole choir.

The battle-scenes are the core of the frescoes. My first impression is: "Yes, yes, yes and no, no, no." With this I mean something like: "Yes, I understand why a certain type of person will call this one of the greatest pictures in the world. And no, it will not do for me."

Once in Paris I went to an exhibition of French colonial art, and in the carpet pavilion there was a hand-woven rug from French Morocco. I gave it one look and wanted to move on. Before I moved, my eye caught a label under the rug and I read something like "Snow White and the seven dwarfs". I stopped and read the whole text. It said that the rug above had been woven by natives and was meant to tell in its own ruggy way the story of Snow White and the seven dwarfs.

"Fiddlesticks," I said to myself, "how can you weave a story in pictures when you have got nothing but geometrical designs at hand?" And to prove to myself how right I was and how wrong the rug was, I gave the rug a long stare. It began to speak. The first border round the edge was the conflict between Snow White and the stepmother, I could see it quite clearly. The second border with the leafy pattern was, of course, the wood where she had been sent with the gamekeeper, who was supposed to kill her. And so on. I could follow the whole tale with ease guided by the symbolism of the abstract squiggles and the clash and harmony of the colours.

That the natives of Morocco had rendered it so well is not as surprising as I thought at the time; I found out later that Snow White is an African Negro tale which was brought to Europe by prisoners returning from Portuguese Africa and it was introduced to Germany as late as the seventeenth century.

I imagine that the princess in the story was then given the name of Snow White because the Germans wanted to forget as quickly as possible that the girl who represents the quintessence of Teutonic folk-lore was, originally, black.

To return to the rug story. What does it prove? It does not prove that the rug really did represent the tale of Snow White and the seven dwarfs. It proves that one can tell me almost anything and that I will not only believe it, but 'see' it.

So, really, when it comes to the Piero frescoes, no one can say that I had not been sold Piero in advance. And although I did not like his stuff in Urbino, I was quite ready to believe that those were minor works, as in the case of Uccello, and that all those people who have exalted him had something better to go on with.

To start with, the battle-scenes. The paint is flat and neat and set against the cold, bleak, barren light of a wintry sky. There is a carefully ordered disorder of men and horses. Above the struggling bodies there grows a forest of spears and lances and flags. Now, each leg or arm below is balanced above by a spear or flag. There is not one movement in the whole of the picture which has not got its 'opposite number' in another part.

The longer one looks at it the more it is clear that the scene is nothing more than illustrated algebra – the painted rendering of a mathematical equation. If I had a trained eye I could explore it more thoroughly and I could sketch diagrams and take them back to London and bore my friends to tears by demonstrating that the horse's behind plus one arm plus two legs crossed by the spear yonder is done on the principle of the plane of intersection of two cones.

Brains – that is what is wanted to look at Piero's pictures.

Brains. The emphasis is on brains. It is a purely cerebral business, exceedingly clever and – and what? Well, just that. I give the battle-scene a rest and let my eyes wander from the ground floor to the floor above. I see several cones and cylinders – badly disguised as men and women – walking towards a house. They are clad in greyish garments so as not to distract the eye from their geometrical servitude. Piero, who loved stone, has succeeded so well in imparting stoniness to his figures that it would need ten wild Rolls-Royces to uproot them from the spot.

Goethe said: "One grows aware of the intention and it irritates."

But then, why should it irritate me to this degree? I can see Piero in his studio saying to his model: "Miss Cylinder, will you kindly shift to the left?" It is a degradation of human dignity to paint human beings like geometrical bodies in space.

But then, why shouldn't he use them this way if he feels like it? If one dissects the composition of most great pictures one finds that they fall into geometrical patterns.

Besides, what I feel about human dignity is rot. Many masters have used human bodies for their own purposes. Veronese strings his people along a balustrade like a garland of flowers, and uses their foreshortened limbs like waving flags and masses their upturned faces like baskets filled with fruit. I have noticed all this and yet I adore Veronese.

What is it, then, which is to me so utterly repellent in these frescoes? I perceive that the soldiers' faces are painted in a nasty, loveless way, like caricatures.

'Loveless' is the clue. Piero has no love. His painting reveals a bankruptcy of love. If you have no love and no warmth and no passion, all your cleverness comes to nothing.

And now I understand why Piero can appeal only to those who themselves are lacking in love, to clever, dried-up old maids of both sexes, to the owls of the world.

To them he is a tremendous relief. I can hear them say: "Thank God, just for once a painter who makes no demand on my heart and soul. He does not bother me like that bore Raphael, for instance, who is so overflowing with love that I feel like suffocating."

The rest of the world does not feel that way. Love is something which you cannot fake, and when one looks at Raphael one does not concern oneself with his composition but only feels the fullness of his love, which embraces earth and heaven alike.

You can use your human bodies in any way you like if you have the sensuality of Veronese or the heat of Rubens or the tenderness of Matisse. But you cannot feed people on cones and ellipses only.

"I cannot offer you my heart, darling, but please take this mathematical formula instead."

Will that do? No, that will not do.

When I return to the hotel I am told to go to the offices of the local tourist association; there is a message waiting for me there. I cannot think who sent it.

On my way I buy a bag of cherries and eat them in the street, spitting the stones carefully into the gutter and thinking of Piero.

The tourist association is run by a man with a goatee, rather like the owner of the Albergo Luna, but without the black moles, and less satanic.

He says he had a terrible time tracing me and that he inquired in all hotels in Arezzo till he found me.

The message is from my Aunt Alice, who, too, had a terrible time tracing me. Before we get any further he wants to know who Aunt Alice really is, and warns me of the fickleness of men in general and Italian men in particular.

"Aunt Alice is herself," I say.

He is not convinced.

"I have not seen her for sixteen years," I say, "and she was supposed to come ashore in Genoa and meet me somewhere. Only she could not make up her mind where we should meet and I did not know how long I would stay in the various places and so we left it open."

"Never," he says; "you can't tell me that Aunt Alice is as vague as that. I bet you anything, Aunt Alice had it all planned in advance, months ahead. And you gave her the slip."

"You don't know what you are talking about," I say; "Aunt Alice is vague and she always was vague because she is so brainy. One day at lunch when my dog Lumpi got left in the dining-room and was yearning to get into the kitchen, my Aunt Alice addressed him in a perfect distichon, made up on the spot, you know, an hexameter followed by a pentameter.

" '*Had you only followed the steps of the maid to the kitchen;*
    Now bewildered you stand, broken and wretched at heart.'
She had even got the break in the middle of the pentameter, just as it should be. But who got up and opened the door for Lumpi? Me, of course. Because I'm practical. I could tell you twenty stories like this."

"Well," he says, "if you are so practical, why didn't you leave your Arezzo address in Urbino, before you left? Aunt Alice had your address in Ravenna and wired to Ravenna when you had already gone to Urbino, and when she 'phoned to Urbino you had already gone to Arezzo and nobody knew where you would be. Is it practical to let Aunt Alice chase you over half of Italy?"

"I did not know where I would stay in Arezzo," I say; "I wanted to have a look at the hotel first."

We reach a compromise. He comes to the conclusion that I, though less vague than Aunt Alice and more practical than Aunt Alice, am not as practical as I think I am.

Aunt Alice is going to meet me in Tremezzo in two days' time, in the Hotel Tremezzo. Will I please wire to her that I shall meet her there?

That he still has a bad opinion of me is clear by the fact that he does not trust me with the wire. He offers to send it himself, here and now, by telephone.

"Very well," I say. "But why Tremezzo? Where is Tremezzo? I have never heard of it. Have you?"

"Madam, I am the head of the tourist association and not an office-boy. But even my office-boy would know about Tremezzo."

"I don't believe it," I say, and why should I? He did not believe me about Aunt Alice either. "Call him in and ask him."

He says: "I have not got an office-boy. But if I had one he would know it."

He informs me that Tremezzo is a famous beauty spot on the Riviera Tremezzina on lake Como. He approves of Aunt Alice's taste.

"I thought she wanted to go to Lugano," I say.

"The lake of Lugano," he remarks, "is for the rich. But the lake Como is for the great of the world, for its princes and its ambassadors."

I say good-bye to him respectfully. He is a good salesman.

And so I go to Tremezzo. After I have changed trains in Milan the conductor informs me that part of my ticket is not valid for the last stretch and that I shall have to pay six hundred and thirty-eight lire in addition. But he cannot make out the ticket just now, he has more tickets to inspect. He will come back to me later.

I recline in my seat, pondering over Aunt Alice. I feel jittery now that Aunt Alice is drawing near.

What will she look like? Last year she wrote me a letter, saying: "I am old, grey, and fat. How are you?" The question is, how old, how grey, how fat will she turn out to be? Will she look majestic or ruined? Sixteen years is a long time.

What will she say? What am I going to say? What does one say when one has not met for sixteen years?

It would make a good opening for a play. The station would be no good, though. It would have to be set in a drawing-room. The butler is adjusting a lampshade when the curtain rises. He goes on adjusting the lampshade till all the late-comers have found their seats. Then I come in, adjusting my pearls.

This would betray my restlessness. I ask the butler if Aunt Alice's room has been got ready – the room which has been closed for sixteen years. This will tell the audience that I have not seen Aunt Alice for sixteen years. And that I have got the sort of house which is so large that it can afford closed rooms. The housekeeper enters and adjusts her apron. This will tell the audience –

Here is the conductor again, crossing the corridor. He gives me a smiling salute and passes by.

The housekeeper says that everything looks in good order, and I am about to dismiss her when she crosses herself and exclaims: "I knew something was wrong."

Here is the conductor again, passing the corridor, without even giving me a glance. I go out of the compartment and run after him.

"What about my ticket?" I ask. "We'll get to Como in a few minutes and there I am getting out."

"Oh, I can't be bothered," he replies. "Let it be. Give me a kiss next time you come to Italy."

It is the last I see of him.

The train is drawing into Como. Aunt Alice will be waiting for me on the platform. Shall I say "You haven't changed at all, I hardly recognized you"? No, that's rot, it must be either one way or the other. Shall I say: "Together at last"? That would sound affected. Or she might think it flippant.

If I said – oh, God, the train has stopped.

Here is Aunt Alice.

I rush up to her.

"No, leave it," she says.

"Not at all, I'll take it," I say.

"No, don't, it's much too heavy, he'll take it," she says, and we follow the porter down the platform.